Handbook of
Mammals
of the
South-Central States

Handbook of
Mammals
of the
South-Central States

Jerry R. Choate,
J. Knox Jones, Jr., and
Clyde Jones

Louisiana State University Press
Baton Rouge and London

Designer: Bob Nance
Typeface: ITC New Baskerville
Typesetter: G&S Typesetters, Inc.
Printer and binder: Thomson-Shore, Inc.

Library of Congress Cataloging-in-Publication Data

Choate, Jerry R.
    Handbook of mammals of the south-central states / Jerry R. Choate,
J. Knox Jones, Jr., and Clyde Jones.
        p.   cm.
    Includes bibliographical references (p.   ) and index.
    ISBN 0-8071-1819-2 (cl)
        1. Mammals—Southern States—Handbooks, manuals, etc.   I. Jones,
J. Knox. II. Jones, Clyde. III. Title.
QL719.S83C48   1994
599.0976—dc20   94-7369
                                                        CIP

The paper in this book meets the guidelines for permanence and durability of the Committee
on Production Guidelines for Book Longevity of the Council on Library Resources. ∞

Dedication photograph courtesy of the American Society of Mammalogists.

In Memory of
J. Knox Jones, Jr.
1929–1992

*a professional colleague, mentor, and close friend
who influenced the lives and careers
of countless mammalogists
and whose contributions to the science of
mammalogy will forever endure*

Contents

Acknowledgments

W E ARE GRATEFUL to the many scientists who, over the years, have contributed to the considerable data base that was the source for the information presented in this book. We are also in debt to a number of colleagues for providing us with photographs of living mammals, especially to Roger W. Barbour. A credit line accompanies each photograph.

Many persons assisted us in one way or another as work on this book was in progress, and we thank them collectively here. Additionally, we thank our two institutions for their support. At Texas Tech University, Shirley Burgeson provided clerical assistance, Marijane R. Davis and Richard W. Manning helped us editorially, and Nicky L. Olson served as a consultant on photography. At Fort Hays State University, Deb Geier helped prepare the maps and Lesley Morissee provided clerical assistance.

Handbook of
Mammals
of the
South-Central
States

Introduction

THE SOUTH-CENTRAL region of the United States as here conceived represents the heartland of the South minus the Carolinas, Virginia, and Florida, for which colleagues are preparing separate books. In area, the coverage extends from the Atlantic Coast in Georgia westward across the Mississippi River to the western borders of Arkansas and Louisiana, and from the Gulf of Mexico northward to the Ohio River. The region comprises some 342,000 square miles of territory, broken down by state as follows (largest in extent to smallest): Georgia, 58,910; Arkansas, 53,187; Alabama, 51,705; Louisiana, 47,752; Mississippi, 47,689; Tennessee, 42,244; Kentucky, 40,409. The total human population of the seven states is about 30 million.

The geographic parameters of this book were chosen with several considerations in mind. First, the seven states covered make up a relatively good natural unit for land mammals, even though, for example, a few southwestern species barely penetrate the western boundary of the region, and some species with northern affinities are limited to the Appalachian Mountains of the northeast portion. Second, relatively recent accounts of mammalian faunas are available for regions to the north and west. And third, there is no modern treatment of mammals of three states at the core of the south-central part of the country—Alabama, Mississippi, and Tennessee.

Despite the relatively long-term effect of human activities on the environment of these seven south-central states, some pristine and considerable second-growth forest occurs in the region, as do other important natural habitats for mammals. In this book, we describe both the environmental setting and the biogeographic affinities of the mammalian fauna of the region.

The main purpose of this guidebook is to provide information on the distribution, ecology, and current status of wild mammals that live in the seven-state region today or that lived there when European man first arrived. In addition to a summary for each kind of mammal, a distribution map and a photograph are included. Keys to aid in identification are provided for all taxa covered, including eight species introduced to the region from outside North America. Three introduced rodents, the house mouse and two species of Old World rats, now have a broad distribution over the entire south-central region, usually in close association with humans.

We planned from the outset to provide a guidebook small enough to be carried into the field in a backpack or large coat pocket, yet inclusive enough to provide the student of mammals with a summary of natural history for each included species and a means by which each could be identified. A great variety of literature was checked in preparation of the book, much of which is listed in the References section. Fortunately, good summaries of the mammals of neighboring states and regions were available to us. We consulted these regularly, but they rarely are cited in the accounts of individual species. Of special note is the book by Webster *et al.* (1985) on mammals of the Eastern Seaboard states from Maryland to South Carolina, the guide to mammals of the north-central region of the country (Jones and Birney, 1988), and the handbook devoted to Plains States mammals by Jones *et al.* (1985). Also, important works on the mammalian faunas of the adjacent states of Illinois (Hoffmeister, 1989), Indiana (Mumford and Whitaker, 1982), Missouri (Schwartz and Schwartz, 1981), Ohio (Gottschang, 1981), Oklahoma (Caire *et al.,* 1990), and Texas (Schmidly, 1983) proved useful, as did the book by Hamilton and Whitaker (1979) on the eastern United States and the two-volume set by Hall (1981) on North America as a whole.

Many cogent details were found in treatises dealing with several of the south-central states—Arkansas (Sealander and Heidt, 1990), Georgia (Golley, 1962), Kentucky (Barbour and Davis, 1974), and Louisiana (Lowery, 1974). As noted previously, there are no up-to-date summaries of the distribution and natural history of mammals in Alabama, Mississippi, or Tennessee. For Alabama, we consulted the early work by Howell (1921) and more recent papers on local faunas. For Mississippi, we used primarily the annotated checklist by Jones and Carter (1989), the list by Kennedy *et al.* (1974), and the information summarized by Wolfe (1971). For Tennessee, we found the work by Kellogg (1939) to be helpful, as well as material by Kennedy and Harvey (1979) on 24 selected species that occur in that state, and the book by Linzey and Linzey (1971) on mammals of Great Smoky Mountains National Park. Additional, more specialized publications are cited in the individual accounts of species.

For detailed descriptions of the orders and families of modern mammals, we recommend the book on that subject by Anderson and Jones (1984). For data on mammalian genera, the two-volume summary by Nowak and Paradiso (1983) is useful. A good text in mammalogy was authored by Vaughan (1986), and the laboratory manual by DeBlase and Martin (1980) also contains considerable pertinent information.

ORGANIZATION OF THE BOOK

As noted, our goal in preparation of this guide to mammals of the south-central states was to provide a concise yet authoritative account for all species of nondomesticated mammals that live in the region or lived there within historic time. With few exceptions, individual accounts of species are limited to a single page, with a photograph of the animal and a distribution map on the facing text page for easy reference. Thus, because of space restrictions, it was necessary to select carefully the information to be included for each taxon. For this reason, information (for example, on molt, parasites, or predators) applicable to two or more related species may be given in only one species account. We hope readers will understand how difficult we found the task of selecting the information to include for each of the mammalian species treated.

Following this introduction are a description of environments of the south-central states and a review of the zoogeography of mammals in this region. These precede a checklist, arranged in traditional phylogenetic sequence by order, family, and genus, of the 95 native land mammals (excluding man) and 8 free-living taxa introduced into the region. Species within each genus are entered alphabetically (specific and vernacular names follow Jones *et al.*, 1992). Entries in the accounts, which are grouped in chapters by mammalian order, follow the same sequence except for introduced taxa, which are treated in a section separate from native mammals. The chapter heading for each order contains brief introductory remarks, including mention of families; thus, there are no familial accounts.

Keys are provided to assist in identifying each species occurring in the south-central states. A key to orders follows the checklist. If more than one species in an order is known from the seven-state region, a key to species is placed in that chapter. In two instances (Rodentia and Carnivora), keys are subdivided by family because of the large number of included species.

The keys are intended to provide users with a ready method of identification of mammals covered in this book. Whenever possible, both external and cranial (or dental) characters are described. These pertain to adult mammals, but many apply to immature specimens as well. In using keys, readers also should consult descriptions, photographs, and distribution maps of individual species, all of which frequently provide additional information useful in identifying a specimen in hand. Each key consists of pairs of contrasting statements, referred to as couplets; each couplet is numbered on the left-hand margin with the same arabic numeral, one having a prime sign. Beginning at the top of each key, characteristics of a specimen under study should better fit one or the other of the two units in each couplet. At the right-hand margin of each unit is the number of the key couplet to which the user is directed next or the name of the species or group to which the specimen belongs. By careful selection of characters used in progressive couplets of each key, it is possible to provide means of identifying specimens of mammals from the south-central states, often with relative ease.

Technical terms used in the keys and the text are defined in the Glossary. Nonspecialists should consult the Glossary for precise information as to use and meaning of terms unfamiliar to them. Even then, some features will be difficult to comprehend without a hand lens or low-power binocular microscope. A millimeter rule or calipers calibrated in millimeters also may be needed to appreciate mensural characters. Dental formulae are used in keys and occasionally elsewhere. The expression "premolars 3/2," for example, simply means there are three premolars in each half of the upper jaw and two in each half of the lower jaw, as explained in the Glossary.

In the account of each native mammalian species, information is provided under the scientific and vernacular name in four categories: Distribution, Description, Natural History, and Selected References.

Distribution. This is a statement of the general distribution of the species along with an indication of its range in the seven states covered. Unless otherwise indicated, the statement refers to the historically documented distribution of the taxon, which is shown (except for introduced mammals) on an accompanying distribution map. Where former and present ranges of a species differ, the former, broader range is shown on the map unless indicated otherwise in the text. References cited in this Introduction, especially Hall (1981), as well as relevant subsequent publications were used to prepare distribution maps. In consulting these, the reader should remember that mammals, like other animals as well as plants, never occur everywhere throughout the general distribution of the taxon. Rather, they are found only in suitable habitats within the general geographic parameters. For example, the beaver and the muskrat live only in preferred aquatic environments within their otherwise broad area of overall occurrence.

Description. In telegraphic style, the general characters, such as size and color pattern, are given for each species, with special reference to features that distinguish it from closely related taxa. Ranges of measurements are those of typical adults from the seven states covered, rather than the absolute extremes that might be encountered. Measurements are in millimeters and, with few exceptions, include the four standard external dimensions, always in the following order: total length, length of tail, length of hind foot, length of ear. No ear measurement is included for insectivores or pocket-gophers because their ears are so small. A fifth measurement, length of forearm, is given for bats. Weights are in grams for small mammals and in kilograms for larger species.

Natural History. This section, which represents the bulk of each species account, reveals information on habitats preferred or tolerated, food habits, patterns of activity, population densities, resting or nesting sites, reproduction, and other biological features. Because of space limitations, some aspects of the natural history may be given for only one of several related species, as noted above. English (rather than metric) units of measure are used in this section because most readers are more familiar with the English system. Commonly used metric units are defined in the Glossary.

Selected References. One to five citations of important publications on each species are listed in this section. Ordinarily, general works cited in the introductory parts of this book, such as George Lowery's *The Mammals of Louisiana and Its Adjacent Waters* (1974), are not referenced here. Also, if a relatively recent account in the Mammalian Species series (published by the American Society of Mammalogists and intended as a concise but thorough summary of the biology of an individual species, complete with relevant literature citations) has been issued, it may be the only reference cited. Whatever the case, the references listed in this section will guide the interested reader to other pertinent literature on the species in question, particularly in the south-central states. In preparing this guidebook, we tried to consult all works published through 1990, and a few published in 1991 also are cited.

Following the accounts of native mammals, there is a short section on nondomesticated introduced taxa and another that lists species that may occur in the seven-state region but have not been documented there. Next are the Glossary, a list of bibliographic entries to literature cited in the text, and an index to scientific and vernacular names of land mammals of the south-central states.

Environments
of the South-Central States

THE ENVIRONMENT of an organism is the sum of all the physical (nonliving) and biological (living) attributes of the place where the organism lives. From the standpoint of a typical terrestrial mammal, three of the most important physical attributes of an area are its physiography, climate, and soils, and the most obvious biological attribute is its vegetation. The latter is a function of the former in that the interaction of physiography, climate, and soils dictates which plants may occur in different areas. The history of an area and the availability of seeds determine which plants actually become established there. Competition and other biological and physical phenomena influence the success of plants in particular areas. The resulting patterns of vegetation may exist over long periods of time unless one or more of the physical or biological attributes of the environment change. Together, the physical attributes of the environment and the resulting vegetation constitute what often is loosely described as the habitat of an animal.

Mammalian habitats in the south-central states are both diverse and complex. With respect to diversity, they range from below sea level to above tree line, from swamps to sand dunes, and from forest to grassland. With respect to complexity, there are more species of trees and shrubs (197) in Georgia than in any other eastern state except Florida, and the south-central states in general have an exceptionally rich flora (Watts, 1983). For these and other reasons, the habitats of mammals in the south-central states are not well known, and the effects of changing environments on mammalian species in the region are poorly understood.

Since settlement of the south-central states, most environmental changes have resulted from the activities of man. Agricultural development resulted in removal of much of the native forest of the seven-state area. Slow-growing trees were harvested and replaced with fast-growing species to serve as a cash crop on otherwise relatively unproductive land. Removal of natural vegetation caused siltation of streams and rivers. Reservoirs constructed for a variety of purposes changed stream flow and modified environments both at reservoir sites and downstream. Various chemicals were applied to the land to promote the growth of some species and to kill others. Pollution contaminated certain environments. In these and many other ways, man has modified the natural environments of the south-central states.

Nevertheless, natural environments persist, at least in fragments, and the natural beauty of much of the south-central region remains. Let us briefly examine the physical environment and the vegetation of the south-central states. Selected biological attributes of the environments in which specific mammals live are given in the individual accounts that make up the remainder of the book.

PHYSIOGRAPHY

Much of the ecological diversity of the south-central states is attributable to the physiography of the region, a vast lowland bordered on the northwest and northeast by highlands. These topographically distinctive areas represent four physiographic divisions: the Interior Highlands (including the Ozark Plateau and Ouachita Mountains), the Coastal Plain, the Interior Low Plateaus, and the Appalachian Highlands (including the Cumberland Plateau, Appalachian Ridges and Valleys, Blue Ridge, and Piedmont). Distribution of these physiographic units within the south-central states is illustrated in Map 1. Some of the major topographic features mentioned in this book are shown in Map 2.

The vast lowland area that includes all of Louisiana and Mississippi, western Kentucky and Tennessee, eastern and southern Arkansas, southern and western Alabama, and southern Georgia is the Coastal Plain. Included within this physiographic division is the Mississippi Alluvial Plain, known locally as "the Delta," which extends southward from the mouth of the Ohio River to the location of the actual delta of the Mississippi River in the Gulf of Mexico. The Mississippi Alluvial Plain encompasses a series of basins (the Atchafalaya and Tensas in Louisiana, the Yazoo in Mississippi, and the St. Francis in Arkansas) and is nearly featureless, with levees (both natural and man-made) and terraces (representing past or present riverbanks or coastlines, such as Crowley's Ridge in Arkansas) providing the only topographic relief. Both east and west of the Mississippi Alluvial Plain the Coastal Plain is marked by low hills, some of which have been dissected by streams.

East of the Mississippi River, the northern border of the Coastal Plain is marked by the Fall Line. This line, or zone, is characterized in many areas by an abrupt change in topography, from flat plains to rolling hills, and by

Map 1. *Approximate boundaries of physiographic regions of the south-central states (modified from Fenneman, 1939, and subsequent sources). A, Interior Highlands (A1, Ozark Plateau; A2, Ouachita Mountains); B, Coastal Plain; C, Interior Low Plateaus; D, Appalachian Highlands (D1, Cumberland Plateau; D2, Appalachian Ridges and Valleys; D3, Blue Ridge; D4, Piedmont).*

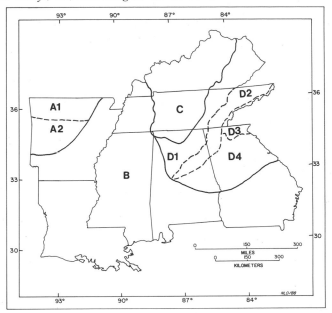

equally abrupt changes in soils and their parent rocks. Waterfalls or rapids occur along some streams in this zone of transition, and sandhills are a common topographic feature. West of the Mississippi River, the northern margin of the Coastal Plain is less well defined (Murray, 1961).

In northwestern Arkansas, the Coastal Plain gives way to the Interior Highlands. These highlands consist of the Ozark Plateau and the Ouachita Mountains, separated by the Arkansas River valley. The Ozarks feature a deeply dissected plateau with rolling ridgetops separated by steep slopes and narrow valleys. Near the south margin of the Ozarks, the Boston Mountains, with deeply dissected ridgetops rising to 2,500 feet, overlook valleys at elevations as low as 500 feet. The topography of the Ouachita Mountains is similar to that of the Boston Mountains, with elevations ranging from 300 to more than 2,700 feet.

East of the Mississippi River, in western Kentucky and Tennessee, the Coastal Plain abuts with the Interior Low Plateaus. These consist of numerous dissected plateaus (for example, the Eastern and Western Highland

Map 2. *Major topographic features of the south-central states.*

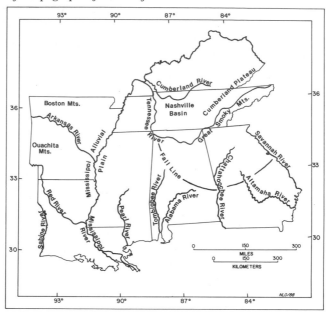

Rims and the Pennyroyal), relatively level plateaus (such as the Bluegrass Region), and basins (for example, the Nashville Basin). Elevations in the Interior Low Plateaus range from 350 to about 1,000 feet.

East and south of the Interior Low Plateaus are the Appalachian Highlands, the westernmost subdivision of which is the Cumberland Plateau. The Cumberland Plateau extends from northern Alabama across east-central Tennessee and eastern Kentucky. Elevation averages 1,000 feet at the base of the western escarpment of the plateau and 2,000 feet on the plateau itself. The topography consists of steep slopes and narrow valleys.

East of the Cumberland Plateau, in east-central Alabama, northwestern Georgia, and eastern Tennessee, are the Appalachian Ridges and Valleys, a series of northeast- to southwest-trending valleys separated by steep ridges. In valleys, elevations range from 600 feet in the southwest to more than 1,000 feet in the north. The highest ridges reach elevations of from 2,000 to 3,000 feet, rising gradually from southwest to northeast.

The next subdivision of the Appalachian Highlands is the Blue Ridge, a rugged mountainous region that extends into the south-central states in easternmost Tennessee and northeasternmost Georgia. Elevations on the Blue Ridge reach more than 6,500 feet on peaks of the Great Smoky Mountains in Tennessee and decrease gradually both northeastward and southwestward.

Beyond the Blue Ridge is the Piedmont, a dissected plateau with gently rolling to hilly topography. Elevations range from 300 feet in the south to 1,000 feet nearer the mountains. The Piedmont is clearly delimited from the Coastal Plain by the Fall Line.

Drainage Patterns

The south-central states generally are well watered. The abundant water has profound effects on soils and vegetation, and thus on both ecological diversity and complexity. Excess water collects in bayous, or backwaters, or is drained coastward by broad, sluggish rivers.

The predominant river in the south-central states, and for that matter in North America, is the Mississippi. The Mississippi drainage basin extends from the continental divide to the crest of the Appalachians and from the Great Lakes to the Mississippi Delta. In the south-central states, this includes all of Arkansas, Tennessee, and Kentucky plus western Mississippi, northern Alabama and Georgia, and all but southwestern Louisiana (Baker, 1983). The Mississippi River carries runoff water from this vast region to the Gulf of Mexico, where its silt is deposited in an ever-growing delta. En route, the river forms parts of the borders of Kentucky, Tennessee, Arkansas, Mississippi, and Louisiana.

The largest tributaries of the Mississippi in the south-central states are the Ohio and Arkansas rivers. The Ohio is formed by the confluence of the Allegheny and the Monongahela rivers at Pittsburgh. It flows southwestward, forming most of the northern border of Kentucky, and receiving numerous tributaries. The largest of these is the Tennessee River, which heads in the Appalachians and flows southwestward across eastern Tennessee, westward across northern Alabama, and northward across western Tennessee and Kentucky before emptying into the Ohio River near the mouth of another important tributary, the Cumberland River.

The Arkansas River heads in the Rocky Mountains of Colorado. It flows southeastward and enters the south-central states between the Ozark Plateau and the Ouachita Mountains in Arkansas. After meandering across Arkansas, it drains into the Mississippi River without receiving any major tributaries.

Another eastward-flowing drainage, the Red River, heads on the Llano Estacado in northwestern Texas and enters the south-central states in southwestern Arkansas. In Louisiana, it receives discharge from the Ouachita River and other tributaries to form the Atchafalaya River. The latter is connected with the Mississippi by a short channel known as the Old River, in which the direction of flow formerly depended on the relative water levels in the Mississippi and the Atchafalaya. Channelization of a short portion of the Mississippi in 1831 caused more water to flow down the Atchafalaya, which thus threatened to "capture" the Mississippi and leave New Orleans with insufficient water to serve as a port city. A complex of dams, gates, and channels now ensures that no more than 30 percent of the combined flow of the Red and Mississippi rivers passes down the Atchafalaya River into Atchafalaya Bay.

At times of high water in the Mississippi River, the Atchafalaya and other basins become large backwater storage areas. Conversely, low water levels trap water in oxbows. Such backwaters, or bayous, are characteristic of areas of low elevation and flat topography in the south-central states.

West of the Mississippi drainage basin, the Sabine River forms much of the western border of Louisiana. It heads in the hills of eastern Texas and empties into the Gulf of Mexico. Important rivers east of the Mississippi drainage basin include, first, the Pearl River, which drains much of southern Mississippi and forms part of the border of Louisiana and Mississippi before emptying into the Gulf of Mexico. Next are the Tombigbee and Alabama rivers, which drain runoff from northern Mississippi and Alabama into Mobile Bay. The Chattahoochee River heads in the Blue Ridge and, after forming part of the border between Alabama and Georgia and receiving several tributaries, flows across the Florida Panhandle into the Gulf. The Altamaha and its tributaries head on the Piedmont in northern Georgia and empty into the Atlantic Ocean. Finally, the Savannah River heads on the Blue Ridge and forms the border between Georgia and South Carolina before emptying into the Atlantic Ocean.

CLIMATE

Climate may have greater effects, both direct and indirect, on the species of plants and animals that occur in an area than any other environmental component. Certainly, climatic extremes exclude poorly adapted species and favor better-adapted species. The climate of the south-central states is relatively mild yet stressful to mammals in some respects.

The climate of the region ranges from humid subtropical to humid temperate, and it is influenced appreciably by latitude, elevation, and proximity to the Gulf of Mexico. In North America, the relationship of latitude to climate is expressed in the interaction of cool, dry, northern air masses with warm, moist, southern air masses. These air masses abut at fronts, the passage of which causes changes in weather. At high latitudes, cool weather predominates because fronts between cool and warm air masses often are located farther south. At low latitudes, warm weather predominates because fronts typically are located farther north. The south-central states (at latitudes ranging from 29° to approximately 39° N) thus are warmer, on average, than states at more northerly latitudes. Within the states covered, latitude is partly responsible for the average daily temperatures in January of only 42° F in Memphis (latitude 35° N) but 55° F at New Orleans (30° N).

Elevation also has an important effect on temperature. In general, the temperature of air decreases 3.5° F for every 1,000-foot increase in elevation. Within the south-central states, elevation ranges from a few feet below sea level in New Orleans to 6,642 feet on Clingmans Dome in eastern Tennessee. If all other things were equal, this would account for a difference in temperature between these sites of more than 20° F. Ranges of elevations in the south-central states are as follows: Alabama, from sea level to 2,407 feet; Arkansas, from 55 to 2,753 feet; Georgia, from sea level to 4,784 feet; Kentucky, from 257 to 4,145 feet; Louisiana, from minus 5 to 535 feet; Mississippi, from sea level to 806 feet; Tennessee, from 182 to 6,642 feet.

The proximity of the south-central states to the Gulf of Mexico has profound effects on the climate of the region. The prevailing southerly breezes are laden with moisture that evaporates from the Gulf, causing the relative humidity to be high. Moist air gives up and accepts heat less readily than dry air; therefore, humidity serves to moderate temperature fluctuations (both daily and seasonal). In winter, this humidity is partly responsible for relatively pleasant weather conditions near the Gulf while much of the remainder of the country experiences bitter cold. In summer, it results in hot, hazy afternoons followed by warm, sticky evenings. As moisture-laden air from the Gulf passes over land, it rises and cools. Cool air has less capacity to carry moisture than warm air, and the excess moisture in cool air condenses in the form of clouds. Therefore, areas nearest the Gulf and on the windward sides of mountain ranges receive more rainfall than other areas.

Proximity to the Gulf of Mexico also contributes to the frequency of tropical storms. The highest incidence of severe tropical storms (about one every three years) is in coastal areas of Alabama, Mississippi, and Louisiana. At the other extreme, tropical storms seldom affect northern Arkansas or western areas of Tennessee and Kentucky. Rainfall from tropical storms may exceed 10 inches in a 24-hour period, causing severe flooding in low-lying areas.

Average annual precipitation in the south-central states ranges from fewer than 45 inches in parts of Arkansas and Kentucky to more than 60 inches along the Gulf Coast and more than 75 inches on the Blue Ridge in northeastern Georgia. Most precipitation is in the form of rain, occurring as a consequence of frontal cyclonic storms in winter and convectional thunderstorms in summer (Christensen, 1988). Average annual snowfall ranges from more than 12 inches in Kentucky to less than one inch in coastal areas; in the latter, snow does not remain on the ground long and thus has little effect on wildlife. Glaze storms, however, may stress wildlife

Map 3. *Frost-free period (length in days of growing season) in the south-central states.*

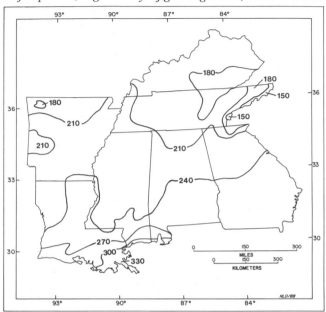

and cause starvation. They occur in almost all areas of the south-central states but increase in frequency from south to north, being most often encountered in northern Arkansas and Kentucky.

Maximum daily temperatures in winter average more than 60° F near the Gulf Coast and more than 50° F as far north as Kentucky. In summer, maximum daily temperatures exceed 90° F throughout the region except in Kentucky and on mountains. Temperatures in excess of 110° F are exceptional; record high temperatures for the south-central states are 112° F in Alabama and Georgia, 113° F in Tennessee, 114° F in Kentucky and Louisiana, 115° F in Mississippi, and 120° F in Arkansas.

Minimum daily temperatures in winter average more than 40° F near the Gulf Coast and above freezing elsewhere except in Kentucky and mountainous areas. In summer, minimum daily temperatures exceed 70° F throughout the region except on highlands. The frost-free period ranges from less than 150 days on peaks in the Great Smoky Mountains to more than 300 days along the Gulf Coast (Map 3). Temperatures below 0° F occur infrequently in most areas, and never along the coast. Record low temperatures are − 16° F in Louisiana and Mississippi, − 17° F in Georgia, − 18° F in Alabama, − 29° F in Arkansas, − 30° F in Kentucky, and − 32° F in Tennessee.

Soils

The most widespread soils in the south-central states are lateritic and thus appear yellowish or reddish in color. This is related to the fact that the ground in much of the region does not freeze in winter and thus leaching can occur throughout the year, causing oxides of iron and aluminum to accumulate. Also, the relatively warm climate facilitates rapid chemical decomposition of organic materials in the soil. Lateritic and other soils are discussed below using terminology from the new comprehensive soil classification (Brady, 1984). The geographic distribution of soils in the south-central states (Map 4) influences the distribution of plants, and vegetation, in turn, influences the distribution of mammals.

Alfisols are widespread in areas bordering the Mississippi Alluvial Plain as well as in the Nashville Basin of Tennessee and the Bluegrass Region of Kentucky. They were formed in humid areas, usually under deciduous forest but sometimes under grassland. They have a gray-to-brown surface horizon with clay in the subsurface horizons. Areas having one subtype, the Aqualfs, are saturated during at least part of the year and typically are used

Map 4. *Approximate geographic distributions of orders of soils in the south-central states (after Brady, 1984). A, Alfisols; E, Entisols; H, Histisols; I, Inceptisols; M, Mollisols; S, Spodosols; U, Ultisols; V, Vertisols.*

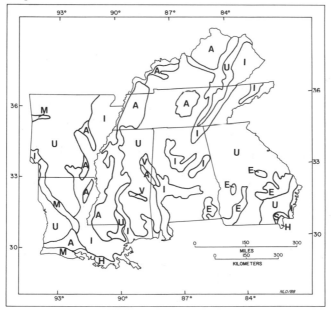

for pasture or woodland unless drained. Areas having the other subtype in this region, the more widespread Udalfs, are drier and thus are suitable for row crops, small grain, and pastures.

Entisols are recently formed mineral soils with no horizons below the plow layer. In the south-central states, they are most common in the sandhills of Georgia and other areas along the Fall Line. The subtype that occurs there, the Psamments, is a loamy sand that retains little water but is useful for production of crops and timber.

Histisols are organic soils (such as peat and "muck") consisting of partly or completely decomposed plant residues. They were formed in swamps and marshes and are saturated during at least part of the year. In the region covered, they occur only in the Okefenokee Swamp of southeastern Georgia and the coastal marshes of Louisiana.

Inceptisols have weakly differentiated horizons. The subtype known as Aquepts occurs throughout the Mississippi Alluvial Plain—which is the largest continuous area of alluvial soil in the United States (Brady, 1984)—as well as along the Pearl and Pascagoula rivers in Mississippi and in the Mobile River drainage in Alabama. It also occurs in coastal areas of Mississippi, Alabama, and Georgia. Aquepts normally are seasonally or permanently saturated, but most have been drained for production of row crops. Another subtype, the Ochrepts, occurs on moderate to relatively steep slopes in central Alabama, on the Cumberland Plateau, and in other areas of the Appalachian Highlands. This is a moist, shallow soil with low organic content, which formed beneath deciduous forest.

Mollisols are among the most important of soils for agricultural purposes. They formed under prairie vegetation, and they have thick, dark, friable surface horizons containing abundant organic matter. In the south-central states, a subtype termed Aquolls occurs along the coast of southwestern Louisiana and is used, in part, for growing rice and sugarcane. Another subtype, the Udolls, can be found along the Arkansas River in western Arkansas and on the floodplain of the Red River in Louisiana.

Spodosols develop from coarse-textured, acidic parent materials subject to leaching. They typically contain organic matter plus compounds of aluminum and especially iron. They often form beneath coniferous forest and are relatively infertile. In the region covered, the subtype known as Aquods is found around the perimeter of the Okefenokee Swamp in southeastern Georgia.

Ultisols are the predominant soils of the south-central states. They typically are moist soils that developed under forest vegetation in warm climates. They tend to be weathered and acidic, though less acidic than Spodosols. The Udults, the more widespread of the two subtypes that occur in the region, usually are not saturated and are suitable for production of crops. The Aquults, on the other hand, are saturated for part of the year and must be drained to grow crops; they occur only in southwestern Louisiana and southeastern Georgia.

Vertisols are clayey soils that form wide, deep cracks when dry. They are found in areas that have pronounced wet and dry periods during the year. In the south-central states, they are limited primarily to the Jackson Prairie of Mississippi and the Black Belt of Mississippi and Alabama.

VEGETATION

The species of plants that occur in an ecologically mature, or "climax," community are those that are well suited for the environmental conditions existing at that location. Such communities, or associations, are characterized by their predominant plants, and their distributions thus can be mapped. The distribution of mammals frequently corresponds to the distribution of vegetative associations that satisfy their biological needs.

The vegetation of eastern North America was mapped and described in considerable detail by Braun (1950) and Küchler (1964) and more recently by Christensen (1988) and Greller (1988). Braun's vegetation map was updated and simplified by Watts (1983). Map 5, modified from these

Map 5. *Vegetation of the south-central states (modified from Braun, 1950; Küchler, 1964; Christensen, 1988; Greller, 1988; Watts, 1983). A, Southeastern Evergreen Forest; B, Southern Floodplain Forest; C, Oak-Pine Forest; D, Oak-Hickory Forest; E, Mixed Mesophytic Forest; F, Oak-Chestnut Forest; G, Coastal Prairie.*

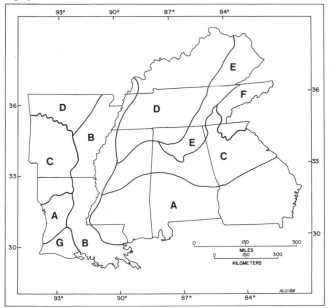

sources, shows the approximate distribution of the most important vegetative associations in the south-central states before the region was settled by European man.

The vegetation of most of the Coastal Plain is categorized as Southeastern Evergreen Forest. This association originally consisted primarily of pines and oaks, with longleaf pine (*Pinus palustris*) the predominant species. Today, forests of southern areas of the Coastal Plain consist mostly of this species plus slash pine (*Pinus elliottii*) and lesser amounts of loblolly pine (*Pinus taeda*), shortleaf pine (*Pinus echinata*), oaks (*Quercus*), and sweetgum (*Liquidambar styraciflua*). Forests of northern areas of the Coastal Plain contain more loblolly and shortleaf pines, oaks, and hickory (*Carya*), and fewer longleaf and slash pines. The term *flatwood* applies to any pine forest on the Coastal Plain having a well-developed woody understory (Christensen, 1988).

On the Mississippi Alluvial Plain and in other swampy areas (including most river floodplains on the Coastal Plain), Southeastern Evergreen Forest is replaced by Southern Floodplain Forest. Predominant species in this vegetative association are oaks, tupelos (*Nyssa*), and cypress (*Taxodium*). Additional species present include sweetgum, magnolias (*Magnolia*), red maple (*Acer rubrum*), American elm (*Ulmus americana*), and red ash (*Fraxinus pennsylvanicus*). "Cypress domes," forests of cypress in poorly drained depressions on the Mississippi Alluvial Plain and other regions of the Coastal Plain, are noteworthy for their abundant Spanish moss (*Tillandsia usneoides*). The Mississippi Alluvial Plain "was to the Temperate Zone of North America what the Amazon is to the Tropical Zone of South America" (C. Baxter, U.S. Fish and Wildlife Service, pers. comm.). Most land on the Mississippi Alluvial Plain has been cleared of natural vegetation and drained for production of agricultural crops.

A zone of Oak-Pine Forest stretches from the Piedmont to the Ouachitas, with a gap across the Mississippi Alluvial Plain. In this area, oaks and other hardwoods, especially hickory but also red cedar (*Juniperus virginiana*) and tupelos, gradually replace the loblolly and shortleaf pines of more southerly forests. This can be regarded as a zone of transition between the Southeastern Evergreen Forest and other forests located farther north. Less than half of the Oak-Pine Forest has been cleared for agricultural purposes.

The Ozarks of Arkansas and the Interior Low Plateaus of Kentucky and Tennessee are characterized by Oak-Hickory Forest interspersed with southern pines and red cedar. Common associates include tupelos, tuliptree (*Liriodendron*), elm, and maples. Braun (1950) and Watts (1983) used the term *Western Mesophytic Forest* for the vegetative association on the Interior Low Plateaus, Braun explaining that the region represents a zone of transition from relatively dry Oak-Hickory Forest in the west to other forest types farther east. Although included within the Oak-Hickory association, the Nashville Basin in central Tennessee is noteworthy for its glades of red cedar. The Bluegrass Region of Kentucky originally contained forest of this association, but most of the timber was cleared and the region now has the appearance of a prairie. In most other areas, less than half of the natural vegetation of the Oak-Hickory Forest zone has been cleared for agricultural purposes.

Mixed Mesophytic Forest, located primarily on the Cumberland Plateau of eastern Tennessee and Kentucky and northern Alabama, is rich in species of broad-leaved deciduous trees. Included are American beech (*Fagus grandifolia*), cucumber tree (*Magnolia acuminata*), basswood (*Tilia americana*), maples, chestnut (*Castanea dentata*), buckeye (*Aesculus octandra*), oaks, and birches (*Betula*). The most abundant conifer is hemlock (*Tsuga canadensis*). Ash, silver bells (*Halesia*), tupelo, black walnut (*Juglans nigra*), and hickory also are present. Less than a quarter of the Mixed Mesophytic Forest has been cleared for agricultural purposes.

Oak-Chestnut Forest originally dominated both the Appalachian Ridges and Valleys and the Blue Ridge. Oaks and chestnut occurred together on slopes, and oaks occurred alone in level areas, sometimes interspersed with tuliptree. Today, most of the chestnut trees are gone, a victim of chestnut blight during the first half of the twentieth century. Presumably for this reason, Küchler (1964) used the term *Appalachian Oak Forest* for this association. Within the Oak-Chestnut Forest association are "balds," naturally occurring, treeless areas on well-drained sites below the climatic treeline (which usually is located between 5,000 and 6,000 feet). The predominant vegetation of balds may be either grasses or shrubs. In most other areas, more than half of the land remains forested.

The Coastal Prairie of southwestern Louisiana warrants recognition as the only extensive nonforested vegetative association in the south-central states. The native vegetation of this region consisted largely of bushy bluestem (*Andropogon glomeratus*) and coastal sacahuiste (*Spartina*), but most has been turned under for production of agricultural crops. Additionally, the Black Belt of Mississippi and Alabama, so-named because of the nearly black soil there, originally was a prairie (Braun, 1950) but contained groves of sweetgum, oaks, and red cedar (Küchler, 1964). The Black Belt is not depicted as a separate vegetative association in Map 5.

We would be remiss if we failed to include agricultural cropland in this list of the most important vegetative associations in the south-central states. Fields cultivated for the production of cotton, soybeans and other legumes, corn, rice, and other agricultural crops presently constitute much of the land area in the region. Such fields lack the ecological diversity, complexity, and stability necessary for habitation by most species of mammals. However, even in predominantly agricultural regions, small areas suitable for habitation by mammals remain. These include fencerows, woodlots, roadside ditches, railroad rights-of-way, drainage ditches, swampy areas, brushpiles, and other places regarded by farmers as "waste areas." These serve as important refugia for small mammals when fields are bare, allowing certain species to move into cropland at more opportune times. Most such species cause little damage to crops and, in fact, may help farmers by increasing the friability of soil and by feeding on weed seeds and insect pests. In many instances, it would be good farming practice to encourage mammalian inhabitants by maintaining or developing suitable habitats around cropland (Fleharty and Navo, 1983).

Zoogeography

As already noted, distributions of mammalian species are influenced by the physical and biological attributes of the environments in which the animals live. Actually, this is an oversimplification; a mammal well adapted for survival in a particular environment cannot live in areas characterized by that environment unless it can colonize those areas. The nutria, for example, is well suited for survival in marshy areas of the Coastal Plain (and, in fact, its distribution in the south-central states almost coincides with the distribution of that physiographic region); however, it was unable to colonize the Coastal Plain until introduced from South America by man. If a species succeeds in colonizing an area, it becomes part of the biological component of the environment of the area. The presence of the colonizer then may affect other species within the area. Introduction of the nutria, for example, may have caused a decline in numbers of the muskrat (summarized by Lowery, 1974) and undoubtedly affected other mammals as well. Thus introductions of non-native species often have unanticipated and undesirable results.

Introduction of a species by man is just one example of how environments change. Fluctuations in climate (for example, periodic droughts) or even short-term weather phenomena (such as ice storms or hurricanes) can have long-term effects on environmental components—vegetation and the availability of standing water, to name just two—and these environmental components in turn may influence substantial expansions or contractions of the ranges of mammals. Even more important are environmental changes resulting from man's activities, such as clearing forests and draining swamps for agricultural purposes or residential development. For these and other reasons, local distributions of mammals are dynamic—they are constantly changing, even if imperceptibly. Nevertheless, distributions exhibit patterns that can be analyzed. The branch of science that seeks to interpret geographic distributions of animals is Zoogeography.

To search for patterns in the distributions of mammals, the overall geographic ranges of the 95 native mammals listed in this book were superim-

Map 6. *Superimposed distributions of the 95 native species of mammals in the south-central states.*

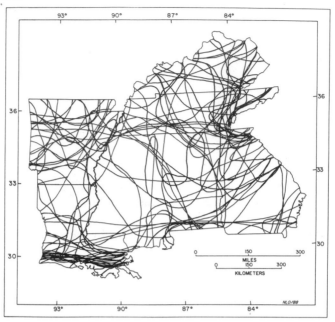

posed on one map of the south-central states. The resulting "spaghetti diagram" (Map 6) appears superficially to show nothing but clutter. Closer examination, however, reveals distinct patterns. For example, the ranges of many species reach limits in southern Louisiana, northwestern Arkansas, southern Alabama, northern Georgia, and eastern Tennessee and Kentucky. These distributional limits may correspond to zones of environmental transition, as illustrated in Maps 1–5, or they may be the result of other, as yet unexplained, phenomena. To understand the significance of these patterns, it is helpful to look separately at groups of mammals that have similar geographic distributions. The term *faunal element* has been applied to such groups (Udvardy, 1969), which may have evolved in the same region, may have followed similar routes of dispersal, or may have similar ecological requirements (Armstrong *et al.,* 1986).

All but 29 of the 95 native species of mammals in the south-central states can be assigned to recognizable faunal elements. The Appalachian faunal element consists of species with distributions that are restricted to the Appalachian Mountains and adjacent regions of eastern North America. These taxa do not occur in the boreal forests of Canada. The Austral faunal element includes species that have zoogeographic affinities with the south-central and southeastern United States. The Boreal faunal element is made up of species that occur primarily in the boreal forests of northern North America and do not range far to the south in boreal habitats on mountain ranges. The Boreomontane faunal element consists of species that are characteristic of the boreal forests of northern North America but that also are distributed far to the south in boreal habitats on mountain ranges. The Campestrian faunal element is made up of species that occur primarily on the prairies of central North America. The Chihuahuan faunal element includes taxa that have zoogeographic affinities with the deserts of the southwestern United States and northern Mexico. The Eastern faunal element is made up of species that are characteristic of eastern deciduous forests and are not restricted to the southeastern United States. Finally, the Neotropical faunal element consists of species that have dispersed northward from tropical Latin America. Three species cannot be assigned to any of these faunal elements because they have small, restricted distributions, and these are categorized herein as "locally distributed." The remaining 26 species occupy large geographic ranges in temperate North America and are categorized as "widespread."

The Appalachian faunal element consists of seven species:

Long-tailed or rock shrew, *Sorex dispar*
Smoky shrew, *Sorex fumeus*
Hairy-tailed mole, *Parascalops breweri*
Star-nosed mole, *Condylura cristata*
New England cottontail, *Sylvilagus transitionalis*
Rock vole, *Microtus chrotorrhinus*
Woodland jumping mouse, *Napaeozapus insignis*

These species range southward on the Appalachian Highlands and reach the south-central states primarily in the eastern parts of Tennessee and Kentucky and in northern Georgia (Map 7). Two exceptions are the New England cottontail, the distribution of which extends into Alabama, and the star-nosed mole, which occurs along the Atlantic Coast as well as on the Appalachian Highlands. The distribution of the rock shrew and rock vole, as their names imply, may be a function of suitable rocky habitats. Likewise, the distribution of the two moles may be restricted more by substrate and water than by other environmental components. Other species in the Appalachian faunal element apparently are associated with mesic forest and forest-edge habitats. Jones and Birney (1988) used the term *New England faunal element* for mammals associated primarily with the Appalachian Highlands.

The Austral faunal element, as might be expected, is the largest (other than widespread species) in the south-central states. It consists of 17 taxa:

Map 7. *Superimposed distributions of seven Appalachian species of mammals in the south-central states.*

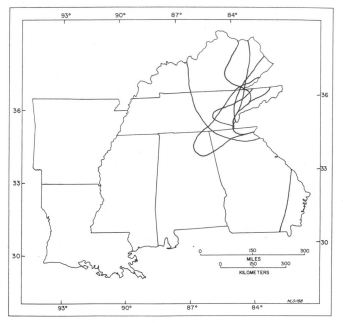

Southeastern shrew, *Sorex longirostris*
Southern short-tailed shrew, *Blarina carolinensis*
Southeastern myotis, *Myotis austroriparius*
Gray myotis, *Myotis grisescens*
Seminole bat, *Lasiurus seminolus*
Rafinesque's big-eared bat, *Plecotus rafinesquii*
Swamp rabbit, *Sylvilagus aquaticus*
Marsh rabbit, *Sylvilagus palustris*
Southeastern pocket gopher, *Geomys pinetis*
Eastern harvest mouse, *Reithrodontomys humulis*
Cotton mouse, *Peromyscus gossypinus*
Oldfield mouse, *Peromyscus polionotus*
Golden mouse, *Ochrotomys nuttalli*
Eastern woodrat, *Neotoma floridana*
Round-tailed muskrat, *Neofiber alleni*
Red wolf, *Canis rufus*
Eastern spotted skunk, *Spilogale putorius*

These mammals are characteristic of the south-central region and its various mesic environments, with the exception that only two of the 17 species occur in the coastal marshes of southern Louisiana (Map 8). The distributions of three of the bats (the southeastern myotis, the endangered gray myotis, and, to a lesser degree, Rafinesque's big-eared bat) are restricted in part by the availability of caves and mines in which they roost. The two rabbits are associated with standing water; that their distributions are mutually exclusive implies that they compete for limited resources. The distribution of another species associated with standing water, the round-tailed muskrat, also is restricted by competition, in this instance with the muskrat, *Ondatra zibethicus*. Two other species confined to the southeastern part of the south-central states, the southeastern pocket gopher and the old field mouse, probably evolved there after displacement of their parental stock by continental glaciation. The endangered red wolf once lived throughout the region but became nearly extinct. It now exists only where reintroduced by man.

The Boreal faunal element comprises only four species:

Woodchuck, *Marmota monax*
Meadow jumping mouse, *Zapus hudsonius*
Fisher, *Martes pennanti*
Least weasel, *Mustela nivalis*

Map 8. *Superimposed distributions of 17 Austral species of mammals in the south-central states.*

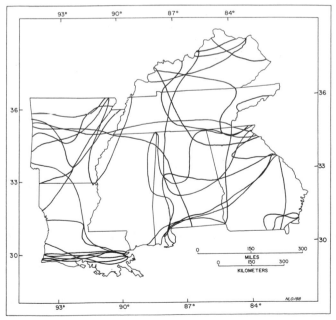

These northern species range southward into the south-central states, but their distributions (shown on pages 145, 209, 235, and 239) reveal that none occurs appreciably south of the Fall Line. The woodchuck, meadow jumping mouse, and least weasel prefer grassy or weedy woodland-edge habitats, whereas the extirpated fisher was a denizen of mixed deciduous and coniferous forests.

The Boreomontane faunal element comprises eight species:

Masked shrew, *Sorex cinereus*
Pygmy shrew, *Sorex hoyi*
Water shrew, *Sorex palustris*
Snowshoe hare, *Lepus americanus*
Red squirrel, *Tamiasciurus hudsonicus*
Northern flying squirrel, *Glaucomys sabrinus*
Southern red-backed vole, *Clethrionomys gapperi*
Meadow vole, *Microtus pennsylvanicus*

The distributional pattern of these species (Map 9) within the south-central region resembles that of species constituting the Appalachian faunal ele-

Map 9. *Superimposed distributions of eight Boreomontane species of mammals in the south-central states.*

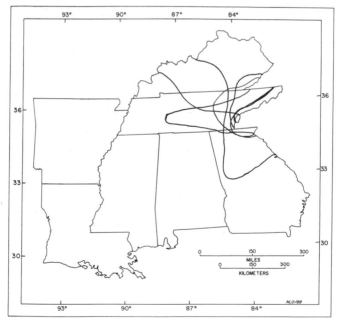

ment (Map 7). However, the geographic ranges of mammals in these two faunal elements differ appreciably in other regions of North America. The current distributions of the water shrew, red squirrel, and northern flying squirrel and the historic distribution of the snowshoe hare correspond closely to the area of the Great Smoky Mountains. The other species in this faunal element, especially the meadow vole, have broader limits of ecological tolerance. However, none occurs south of the Fall Line.

The Campestrian faunal element consists of only three species, which have distributions that extend into the south-central states from the West:

Hispid pocket mouse, *Chaetodipus hispidus*
Plains harvest mouse, *Reithrodontomys montanus*
Prairie vole, *Microtus ochrogaster*

The ranges of these taxa in the south-central states (shown on pages 161, 173, and 197) are dissimilar for historical reasons. The hispid pocket mouse extends into western Louisiana from eastern Texas in grassy old fields and stands of broomsedge (*Andropogon virginicus*). The plains harvest mouse barely reaches the northwestern corner of Arkansas in remnants of tallgrass prairie in the Ozarks. The prairie vole also inhabits remnants of tallgrass prairie in northern Arkansas, but its distribution extends farther eastward—into Kentucky, Tennessee, and northern Alabama. This probably is the result of a major, eastward extension of prairie that occurred during a warm, dry period 6,000–7,000 years ago (Purdue and Styles, 1987; Wendland *et al.,* 1987), forming what is known as the "prairie peninsula." The distribution of the prairie vole once extended south to the Gulf of Mexico and eastward into the Coastal Prairie of southwestern Louisiana, where it remained until extirpated by agricultural activities during historic time.

The Chihuahuan faunal element is made up of only four species:

Desert shrew, *Notiosorex crawfordi*
Black-tailed jackrabbit, *Lepus californicus*
Western harvest mouse, *Reithrodontomys megalotis*
Ringtail, *Bassariscus astutus*

In the region covered, these species occur only west of the Mississippi River (see maps on pages 67, 133, 171, and 231). The desert shrew and black-tailed jackrabbit barely reach Arkansas from more arid regions to the west. The ringtail ranges into Arkansas and Louisiana from forested areas of eastern Texas. The distribution of the western harvest mouse was extended by the formation of the prairie peninsula just discussed.

The Eastern faunal element, with 16 species, is the second largest in the south-central region:

Northern short-tailed shrew, *Blarina brevicauda*
Least shrew, *Cryptotis parva*
Eastern mole, *Scalopus aquaticus*
Eastern small-footed myotis, *Myotis leibii*
Northern myotis, *Myotis septentrionalis*
Social myotis, *Myotis sodalis*
Eastern pipistrelle, *Pipistrellus subflavus*
Evening bat, *Nycticeius humeralis*
Eastern cottontail, *Sylvilagus floridanus*
Eastern chipmunk, *Tamias striatus*
Eastern gray squirrel, *Sciurus carolinensis*
Fox squirrel, *Sciurus niger*
Southern flying squirrel, *Glaucomys volans*
White-footed mouse, *Peromyscus leucopus*
Woodland vole, *Microtus pinetorum*
Southern bog lemming, *Synaptomys cooperi*

The superimposed distributions of these species (Map 10) show that all
range southward into the south-central states but none is found throughout
the region (none exists, for example, in the coastal marshes of Louisiana).

Map 10. *Superimposed distributions of 16 Eastern species of mammals in the south-central states.*

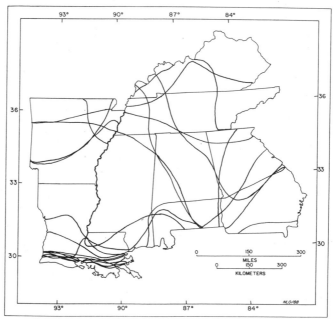

As is the case in other faunal elements, the ranges of most bats may be determined more by potential roost sites than by other environmental components. The terrestrial species dwell primarily in deciduous forests or forest-edge habitats that are mesic but generally lack standing water. The distribution of the white-footed mouse apparently is limited by competition with a closely related member of the Austral faunal element, the cotton mouse.

The Neotropical faunal element consists of seven species:

Virginia opossum, *Didelphis virginiana*
Northern yellow bat, *Lasiurus intermedius*
Brazilian free-tailed bat, *Tadarida brasiliensis*
Nine-banded armadillo, *Dasypus novemcinctus*
Marsh rice rat, *Oryzomys palustris*
Fulvous harvest mouse, *Reithrodontomys fulvescens*
Hispid cotton rat, *Sigmodon hispidus*

All species in the Neotropical faunal element evolved in Latin America and, at various times in the past, dispersed northward and eastward across Texas into Louisiana and subsequently into other south-central states. The nine-banded armadillo, for example, did not arrive in Louisiana from Texas until early in this century (Lowery, 1974), whereas the Virginia opossum (which now can be found anywhere in the south-central states) already lived as far north and east as Georgia more than 20,000 years ago (Ray, 1967). As a result of the historic dispersal pattern of this faunal element, the only area of the seven-state region where it is possible to find all these species is central Louisiana (see pages 43, 103, 113, 117, 165, 167, and 189).

Three "locally distributed" species occur in the south-central states:

Elliot's short-tailed shrew, *Blarina hylophaga*
Baird's pocket gopher, *Geomys breviceps*
Texas mouse, *Peromyscus attwateri*

As mentioned earlier, the distributions of these species in the south-central region (pages 63, 157, and 175) and elsewhere are too restricted to permit assignment to a recognized faunal element.

Finally, 26 "Widespread" species occur in the south-central region:

Little brown myotis, *Myotis lucifugus*
Silver-haired bat, *Lasionycteris noctivagans*
Big brown bat, *Eptesicus fuscus*
Eastern red bat, *Lasiurus borealis*
Hoary bat, *Lasiurus cinereus*
Townsend's big-eared bat, *Plecotus townsendii*

Beaver, *Castor canadensis*
Deer mouse, *Peromyscus maniculatus*
Muskrat, *Ondatra zibethicus*
Porcupine, *Erethizon dorsatum*
Coyote, *Canis latrans*
Gray wolf, *Canis lupus*
Red fox, *Vulpes vulpes*
Gray fox, *Urocyon cinereoargenteus*
Black bear, *Ursus americanus*
Raccoon, *Procyon lotor*
Long-tailed weasel, *Mustela frenata*
Mink, *Mustela vison*
Badger, *Taxidea taxus*
Striped skunk, *Mephitis mephitis*
River otter, *Lutra canadensis*
Mountain lion, *Felis concolor*
Bobcat, *Lynx rufus*
Wapiti or elk, *Cervus elaphus*
White-tailed deer, *Odocoileus virginianus*
Bison, *Bos bison*

The superimposed distributions of these species in the seven south-central states (Map 11) show few patterns other than avoidance of the coastal marshes of southern Louisiana. It is noteworthy that the list of species with widespread ranges includes only one small rodent (the ubiquitous deer mouse). The remainder are 6 species of bats (which generally are more mobile than other mammals), 3 large rodents, 13 carnivores, and 3 large ungulates. Four of the species (beaver, raccoon, mink, and white-tailed deer) occur throughout the south-central states, and three (the gray wolf, river otter, and mountain lion) did so in the past. The gray wolf, elk, and bison have been extirpated from the region.

In a second attempt to understand patterns of distribution in the south-central states, data were compiled on the number of species of each order of mammals and of each faunal element in each state in the region (Table 1). These data are based on actual, documented distributions (as summarized in accounts of species) and not on hypothetical distributions (as depicted in some maps).

The Rodentia is represented by more native species (35) in this region than any other mammalian order. Not surprisingly, rodents make up about one-third of the mammalian species in each state in the region. The number of rodent species present is greater in states containing mountains than in states bordering the Gulf. The Chiroptera and Carnivora are next in

Map 11. *Superimposed distributions of 26 Widespread species of mammals in the south-central states.*

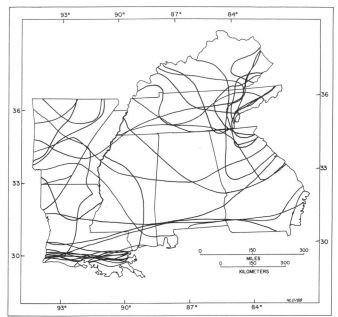

number of species represented, but they show no obvious trends. These orders are followed by the Insectivora, which is represented by more species in the Appalachian Highlands (therefore, in Georgia, Kentucky, and especially Tennessee) than in other physiographic divisions. Other orders are represented by few species of mammals and show no apparent geographic trends.

The overall pattern shown by numbers of species of native mammals in the seven south-central states reflects the importance of mountains to the biodiversity of the region. The most mountainous state, Tennessee, has the greatest number of mammalian species (77). Next are the other mountainous states (Georgia with 69 species, Arkansas with 68, and Kentucky with 67). The Gulf states (Alabama with 60 species, Mississippi with 55, and Louisiana with 54) have comparatively depauperate mammalian faunas.

These trends are more meaningful when discussed in terms of faunal elements. With one exception (the New England cottontail, the distribution of which extends into Alabama), mammals in the Appalachian and Boreomontane faunal elements reach the south-central region from the North only in Tennessee, Georgia, and Kentucky. Tennessee is the only south-central state in which it is possible to find all representatives of these

Table 1. Taxonomic and Zoogeographic Representation of Mammals in the South-Central States

Order/Faunal element	Total No. of Species	Alabama No. (%)	Arkansas No. (%)	Georgia No. (%)	Kentucky No. (%)	Louisiana No. (%)	Mississippi No. (%)	Tennessee No. (%)
Didelphimorphia	1	1 (1.7)	1 (1.5)	1 (1.4)	1 (1.5)	1 (1.9)	1 (1.8)	1 (1.3)
Insectivora	14	5 (8.3)	6 (8.8)	9 (13.0)	8 (11.9)	4 (7.4)	4 (7.3)	12 (15.6)
Chiroptera	17	16 (26.7)	16 (23.5)	14 (20.3)	14 (20.9)	11 (20.4)	15 (27.3)	14 (18.2)
Xenarthra	1	1 (1.7)	1 (1.5)	1 (1.4)	0 (0.0)	1 (1.9)	1 (1.8)	1 (1.3)
Lagomorpha	6	4 (6.7)	3 (4.4)	4 (5.8)	3 (4.5)	2 (3.7)	2 (3.6)	4 (5.2)
Rodentia	35	18 (30.0)	23 (33.8)	24 (34.8)	23 (34.3)	18 (33.3)	17 (30.9)	26 (33.8)
Carnivora	18	13 (21.7)	15 (22.1)	13 (18.9)	15 (22.4)	14 (25.9)	13 (23.6)	16 (20.8)
Artiodactyla	3	2 (3.3)	3 (4.4)	3 (4.3)	3 (4.5)	3 (5.6)	2 (3.6)	3 (3.9)
TOTAL	95	60	68	69	67	54	55	77
Appalachian	7	1 (1.7)	0 (0.0)	4 (5.8)	4 (6.0)	0 (0.0)	0 (0.0)	7 (9.1)
Austral	17	16 (26.7)	13 (19.1)	16 (23.2)	12 (17.9)	12 (22.2)	13 (23.6)	13 (16.9)
Boreal	4	2 (3.3)	1 (1.5)	2 (2.9)	3 (4.5)	0 (0.0)	2 (3.6)	4 (5.2)
Boreomontane	8	0 (0.0)	0 (0.0)	5 (7.2)	3 (4.5)	0 (0.0)	0 (0.0)	8 (10.4)
Campestrian	3	0 (0.0)	2 (2.9)	0 (0.0)	1 (1.5)	1 (1.9)	0 (0.0)	1 (1.3)
Chihuahuan	4	0 (0.0)	4 (5.9)	0 (0.0)	0 (0.0)	1 (1.9)	0 (0.0)	0 (0.0)
Eastern	16	15 (25.0)	15 (22.1)	14 (20.3)	16 (23.9)	11 (20.4)	13 (23.6)	16 (20.8)
Neotropical	7	6 (10.0)	6 (8.8)	6 (8.7)	3 (4.5)	7 (13.0)	7 (12.7)	4 (5.2)
Local	3	0 (0.0)	3 (4.4)	0 (0.0)	0 (0.0)	2 (3.7)	0 (0.0)	0 (0.0)
Widespread	26	20 (33.3)	24 (35.3)	22 (31.9)	25 (37.3)	20 (37.0)	20 (36.4)	24 (31.2)
TOTAL	95	60	68	69	67	54	55	77

faunal elements (and also of the Boreal faunal element). At the other extreme, species of the Neotropical faunal element apparently dispersed into our region through Louisiana and Mississippi, and only three of those taxa range as far north as Kentucky. Mammals of the Austral and Eastern faunal elements are widespread in all seven states, the former best represented in Alabama and Georgia and the latter in Kentucky and Tennessee. Arkansas is the only state in which it is possible to find all four taxa of the Chihuahuan faunal element and all three "locally distributed" species. The Campestrian faunal element shows no pattern. Finally, about one-third of the native mammals in each of the seven states are of Widespread species.

All mammals possess the ability to modify their environment slightly. For example, many dig burrows or construct nests to serve as places of shelter. Some others, such as the beaver, may modify their environment even more. Man, however, is the only mammal with immense power to modify the environment—creating lakes where streams and forests formerly existed, growing crops on land that once supported diverse plant communities, even causing global warming and its potentially horrendous consequences (flooded coastlines, changed climates, and mass extinctions, to name three). More than at any time in the past, the distribution, abundance, and even survival of all species, including man, depend on responsible use of the immense power wielded by humans.

Good baseline data on biodiversity under prevailing environmental conditions still are sorely needed for many areas in the south-central states, as they are for other regions of the United States. Such data will be essential in assessing the impact of future environmental perturbations. It is hoped that this book will stimulate additional study of the mammalian component of biodiversity in the south-central states.

Mammals of the South-Central States

CHECKLIST OF LAND MAMMALS

The 95 species of native mammals (excluding man) that occur in the seven south-central states, or occurred there within historic time, are listed here by page number for the convenience of users of this book. Eight species of free-living mammals introduced to the region (marked with an asterisk) also are included. Orders, families, and genera are arranged in traditional phylogenetic sequence, but species within each genus are listed alphabetically, as they also appear in the text following.

ORDER CHIROPTERA
Family VESPERTILIONIDAE

Family MOLOSSIDAE

ORDER XENARTHRA
Family DASYPODIDAE

ORDER LAGOMORPHA
Family LEPORIDAE

ORDER RODENTIA
Family SCIURIDAE

KEY TO ORDERS OF MAMMALS

1. First toe on hind foot thumblike, opposable; marsupium present in females; incisors 5/4 ....Didelphimorphia
1'. First toe on hind foot not thumblike or opposable; marsupium absent; incisors never more than 3/3 2
2. Forelimbs modified for flight ....Chiroptera
2'. Forelimbs not modified for flight 3
3. Upper incisors absent; feet with hooves .... Artiodactyla
3'. Upper incisors present; feet with claws 4
4. Toothrows continuous (no conspicuous diastema); canines present 5
4'. Toothrows with conspicuous diastema between incisors and cheek-teeth; canines absent 6
5. No obvious caniniform teeth present; size small ....Insectivora
5'. Canines obvious and conspicuously larger than adjacent teeth; size medium to large ....Carnivora
6. Ears of approximately same length as or longer than tail; incisors 2/1 .... Lagomorpha
6'. Ears much shorter than tail; incisors 1/1 ....Rodentia

Order Didelphimorphia

Opossums

Didelphimorphia is one of 10 orders of mammals (including both living and extinct groups) that collectively are termed *marsupials*. Until a recent revision by Marshall *et al.* (1990), all marsupials were included in a single order, the Marsupialia. By the new classification, three orders of Recent marsupials occur in South America, and one of those three, the Didelphimorphia, occurs in North America; all other Recent marsupials are restricted to the Australian region.

Recent representatives of the order Didelphimorphia are assigned to just one family (the Didelphidae), 13 genera, and about 75 species, only one of which exists as far north as the United States. Aside from the egg-laying monotremes of Australia and New Guinea, didelphimorph marsupials are the most primitive of all living mammals, known first from the late Cretaceous period of South America.

Members of this order primitively possess three premolars and four molars in each upper and lower jaw (the reverse of the primitive condition in placental mammals), and the number of upper and lower incisors is never equal. The dental formula of *Didelphis,* for example, is 5/4, 1/1, 3/3, 4/4, total 50, more permanent teeth by six than in any other terrestrial mammal in the south-central states. Other features of didelphimorph (and other) marsupials include offspring that are relatively undeveloped at birth, a pouch (marsupium) in females in which the young develop, a bifid reproductive tract in females, and a bifurcate penis in males located posterior to the scrotum.

Didelphis virginiana

Virginia Opossum

Distribution. This species occurs commonly throughout the south-central states. It ranges naturally from southeastern Canada to Costa Rica, and westward to the Plains States. Opossums have been introduced successfully into several areas of western North America.

Description. Tail long, usually white-tipped, scaly, sparsely haired, and prehensile; ears naked; snout pointed; legs short; thumbs opposable. Dorsum usually dark grayish or grizzled grayish overall, venter paler and lacking guard hairs. Total length, 650–900; tail, 250–370; hind foot, 55–80; ear, 45–55; weight, 1.5–5 kg (usually 2–3.5).

Natural History. Opossums generally prefer open deciduous forest near permanent water, but they also live in heavy forest, marshland, woodlots, shrub thickets, forest edge habitats, and agriculturalized areas. Ready access to water apparently is a requisite for location of home sites, which are in such places as abandoned burrows of other mammals, brushpiles, and hollows in logs or trees, and beneath farm outbuildings. The opossum's nest consists of packed leaves and other dead vegetation transported to the site in its curled, prehensile tail.

Two litters, one in early winter and the other in spring, are typical in this region, although females in extreme southern areas occasionally bear three. Four to 20 or more young in an early stage of development are born after 12 or 13 days of gestation. The tiny young climb directly into the female's pouch and there attach firmly to a teat. Females normally have only 13 mammae, and neonates that fail to attach to one quickly perish. Young remain in the marsupium for about two months, and stay with the female for another month or more before dispersing. Mortality is high among young opossums; the life-span of the species in the wild rarely exceeds two years.

Opossums are primarily nocturnal. Home ranges usually fall between 10 and 20 acres, but may be 100 acres or more. *D. virginiana* is eaten by humans in some areas of the South and occasionally is hunted in northerly areas for its pelt, which is not especially valuable. Its foods include invertebrates, fruits and other vegetative matter, bird eggs, and small vertebrates, some of which it catches alive. Carnivores and large raptors prey on opossums, and many are killed along roadways by vehicles. They host a variety of ecto- and endoparasites.

Selected References. Gardner (1973, 1982); McManus (1974); Seidensticker *et al.* (1987).

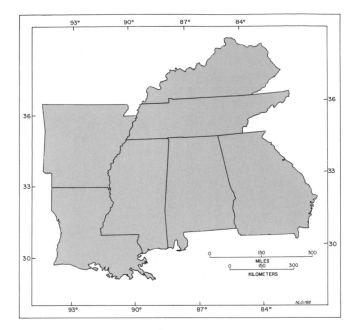

Photo courtesy L. C. Watkins

Order Insectivora

Insectivores

Although many are highly specialized, insectivores are the most primitive of living placental mammals, and represent the general stock from which more advanced placentals are thought to have evolved. The fossil record of the order extends back to late Cretaceous times in North America, some 75 to 80 million years ago. Living insectivores are found on all continents except Antarctica and Australia; in South America, however, they are restricted to the northwestern regions.

Extant members of the order Insectivora are classified in 6 families, comprising 61 genera and approximately 365 species. Two families are known in the south-central states: Soricidae (shrews), with 4 genera and 11 species; and Talpidae (moles), with 3 monotypic genera. All Insectivora have the primitive five-toed mammalian feet, and most have retained a well-developed, W-shaped pattern of cusps on the molars. The identities (that is, whether incisors, canine, or premolars) of certain simple, conical teeth in representatives of the family Soricidae are uncertain; therefore, these teeth, which number three to five above and one below on each side, are referred to as unicuspids in the key and accounts that follow. In addition to insects, insectivores consume other invertebrates such as earthworms, slugs, snails, and centipedes, and some species eat small vertebrates as well as fungi and plant material.

Key to Insectivores

1. Front feet more than twice as broad as hind feet, highly developed for burrowing; zygomatic arches and auditory bullae present (Talpidae) 2
1'. Front feet less than twice as broad as hind feet, not especially adapted for burrowing; zygomatic arches and auditory bullae absent (Soricidae) 4
2. Tail more than 50 in length; fleshy tentacles on snout; first upper incisors projecting noticeably anteriorly .... *Condylura cristata*
2'. Tail less than 50 in length; no fleshy tentacles on snout; first upper incisors not projecting anteriorly 3
3. Tail essentially naked; auditory bullae complete; total of 36 teeth .... *Scalopus aquaticus*
3'. Tail densely haired; auditory bullae incomplete; total of 44 teeth .... *Parascalops breweri*
4. Tail short, less than 30 percent of length of head and body (except in some *Notiosorex*); three, four, or five unicuspids in each upper jaw; if

five unicuspids present, first two much larger in bulk than third (second the largest) and fifth not visible in lateral view 5

4'. Tail relatively long, 30 percent or more of length of head and body; five unicuspids in each upper jaw, three or five visible in lateral view; first two unicuspids not much larger than third and fourth, or if so, second not larger than first; fifth unicuspid small but visible in lateral view (in all except *S. hoyi*) 9

5. Dorsal pelage pale grayish; three upper unicuspids; teeth lightly pigmented .... *Notiosorex crawfordi*

5'. Dorsal pelage brownish to grayish black; four or five upper unicuspids; teeth relatively heavily pigmented 6

6. Dorsal pelage brownish to grayish brown, venter noticeably paler; four unicuspids in each upper jaw, three visible in lateral view; weight less than 8 g (usually less than 6) .... *Cryptotis parva*

6'. Dorsal pelage dark grayish to grayish black, venter about same color; five unicuspids in each upper jaw, four visible in lateral view; weight more than 8 g (usually more than 10) 7

7. Total length rarely less than 112; condylobasal length rarely less than 21.5; occurring in western parts of Kentucky and Tennessee southward to northeastern Alabama and central Georgia .... *Blarina brevicauda*

7'. Total length rarely exceeds 112; condylobasal length 21.5 or less (usually less than 21.0); occurring in western and southern parts of south-central states 8

8. Total length more than 100; condylobasal length 20.0 or more, weight about 15 g .... *Blarina hylophaga*

8'. Total length usually less than 100; condylobasal length usually less than 20.0; weight about 10 g .... *Blarina carolinensis*

9. Pelage dark grayish brown to blackish dorsally; feet fringed with stiff, whitish hairs; hind foot more than 19; condylobasal length usually more than 19.5 .... *Sorex palustris*

9'. Pelage brownish to slate gray dorsally; feet not fringed with stiff hairs; hind foot less than 18; condylobasal length less than 19.5 10

10. Total length usually more than 110; condylobasal length more than 17.5 11

10'. Total length usually less than 100; condylobasal length less than 17.0 12

11. Length of tail averaging 60–70 percent of length of head and body; posterior border of infraorbital foramen behind space between first and second upper molars; third unicuspid larger than fourth .... *Sorex fumeus*

11'. Length of tail averaging 80–90 percent of length of head and body;

posterior border of infraorbital foramen even with or anterior to space between first and second upper molars; third unicuspid equal to or slightly smaller than fourth .... *Sorex dispar*

12. Length of hind foot usually 10 or less; third upper unicuspid compressed, disklike; only three upper unicuspids visible in lateral view .... *Sorex hoyi*

12'. Length of hind foot usually 11 or more; third upper unicuspid not compressed; five upper unicuspids visible in lateral view 13

13. Third upper unicuspid smaller than fourth; length of tail usually less than 32; longest hairs (unworn) at tip of tail 2–3 in length .... *Sorex longirostris*

13'. Third upper unicuspid larger than fourth; length of tail usually more than 32; longest hairs (unworn) at tip of tail 4–6 in length .... *Sorex cinereus*

Sorex cinereus

Masked Shrew

Distribution. This species has a broad range over much of northern North America and also has been reported in Siberia. In the south-central states, *S. cinereus* is known to exist in extreme southeastern Kentucky, eastern Tennessee, and northeastern Georgia. It is found immediately to the north of the Ohio River in Illinois, Indiana, and Ohio, and probably occurs in northern Kentucky.

Description. One of smaller *Sorex* of region, about same size as *S. longirostris* and slightly larger than *S. hoyi*. Pelage dark brownish in summer, paler on sides, and grayish white ventrally; longer, somewhat paler, and slightly bicolored in winter. Total length, 80–100; tail, 32–45; hind foot, 10–13; weight usually 3–5 g. Ear small and nearly concealed in pelage as in other *Sorex*.

Natural History. In this region, the masked shrew primarily inhabits moist forests, particularly in areas with heavy leaf mold and rotting logs or tall grasses or sedges. Individuals may be active at any time of day or night, and like other shrews, the species does not hibernate in the cold months. The masked shrew may excavate shallow burrows, especially under leafy cover, but it heavily utilizes the burrows and trails of other small mammals. This voracious eater consumes a broad array of invertebrates, including beetles, bugs, ants, flies, grasshoppers, crickets, earthworms, spiders, centipedes, snails, and slugs. It also eats small vertebrates on occasion, and fungus in winter months.

The masked shrew weaves spherical nests, three to four inches in diameter, from grasses and leaves, locating them under rocks, stumps, fallen logs, and debris, and in similar sites. The species breeds throughout the warm months, from late winter to midautumn. Four to 10 young are born after a gestation period of 19 to 22 days. Neonates are dark pink, naked, and more or less fully formed at birth, weighing from a quarter to a third of a gram, and are raised by the female alone. Females bear two or more litters annually.

Shrews have relatively few natural enemies. Raptorial birds, particularly owls, regularly take masked shrews; other reported predators include snakes, large frogs, fish, short-tailed shrews, and weasels. Large carnivores probably kill shrews on occasion but may not eat them because of their malodorous scent glands. Their life-span is less than two years.

Selected References. Forsyth (1976); van Zyll de Jong (1983).

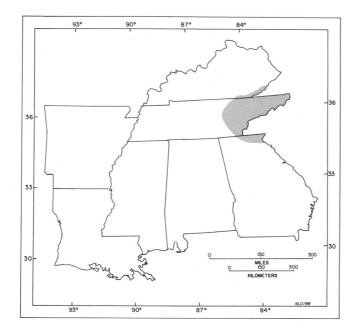

Photo courtesy H. S. Korber

Sorex dispar

Long-Tailed or Rock Shrew

Distribution. The long-tailed shrew has been recorded only in eastern North America, from Maine and adjacent New Brunswick south in the Appalachian chain to eastern Tennessee. It may be looked for also in extreme southeastern Kentucky and in the mountainous areas of northeastern Georgia.

Description. Medium-sized *Sorex* most closely resembling *S. fumeus,* with slender body. Dorsum slate-gray throughout year, venter only slightly paler; tail long, well furred, nearly unicolored. Total length, 110–135; tail, 48–65; hind foot, 13–16; weight, 3–8 g.

Natural History. The long-tailed shrew lives primarily in two mostly wooded habitats—under and among rocks, particularly on talus slopes, and along cool, rocky, mountain streams, where it frequently is taken in the same traplines as the water shrew (*S. palustris*). It evidently favors moss-covered rocks on moist, cool, wooded slopes. In some places, man-made talus slopes (in one case below a mine and in another resulting from road construction) have provided a suitable environment. The long tail may serve as a balancing aid in climbing over and among rocks, and the slender body permits the rock shrew to enter and navigate small interstices in subterranean rocky areas. Other species of small mammals commonly associated with the long-tailed shrew are *S. cinereus, S. fumeus, Peromyscus maniculatus, Clethrionomys gapperi, Microtus chrotorrhinus,* and *Napaeozapus insignis.*

The food habits of this shrew are poorly known, but it appears to subsist primarily on invertebrates. Those thus far reported are centipedes, beetles, flies, spiders, and crickets. This shrew apparently has a more restricted diet than either *S. cinereus* or *S. fumeus.* Its rostrum is slender, the incisors are procumbent, and the cranium is flattened, all adaptations that permit this shrew to pluck small food items from narrow crevices. This and other shrews must consume large quantities of food relative to their size to compensate for their high rate of metabolism. Some shrews may eat nearly their weight in food each day. This shrew probably has few natural enemies, owls being the most significant.

Little is known of the reproductive biology of *S. dispar.* Reproductively active males have been collected from April through August; reproductively active females have been taken from May through August. Two gravid females from Pennsylvania carried five fetuses each, whereas two from New York bore two fetuses each.

Selected References. Jackson (1928); Kirkland and Van Deusen (1979); Kirkland (1981).

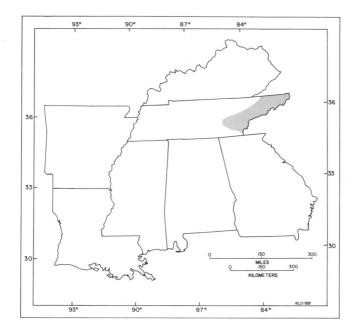

Photo courtesy R. W. Barbour

Sorex fumeus

Smoky Shrew

Distribution. This species is known only in eastern North America, from southeastern Canada (westward to Lake Superior) southward in the south-central states to central and eastern Kentucky and Tennessee, and northern Georgia.

Description. Medium-sized among *Sorex* of south-central region, about same size as *S. dispar* and smaller than *S. palustris.* Dorsal pelage dull brownish in summer, grayish to almost blackish in winter; venter slightly paler, sometimes with silvery tinge; tail bicolored. Total length, 105–120; tail, 40–50; hind foot, 12–15; weight, 6–10 g.

Natural History. The smoky shrew is principally an inhabitant of the cool, shaded forest floor in both coniferous and deciduous woodlands but also is known to occupy such habitats as swamps and bogs, grassy swales, rocky slopes, and even relatively dry places. Favored microhabitats include areas of thick leaf mold and litter on friable soils, moss-covered rocks, old decaying logs and stumps, and brushpiles. *Blarina* and other species of *Sorex* are common mammalian associates.

The food of *S. fumeus* consists of a wide variety of invertebrates, some vegetable matter, and the fungus *Endogone.* Most often consumed are adult chilopods, earthworms, moths, and beetles, as well as various larvae. When foraging, these shrews utter an almost indiscernible twitter; when alarmed, they issue a high-pitched grating note. Like other shrews, they probably emit sounds above the range of human hearing. Bobcats, foxes, weasels, hawks, and owls have been reported as predators. Principal parasites are nematodes internally and mites, chiggers, and fleas externally.

Smoky shrews may not construct tunnels and runways, but they readily use those of other small mammals. They build spherical nests three to four inches in diameter, from mammal hair and vegetative matter, locating them under stumps and logs, in hollows, beneath fallen debris on the forest floor, and within tunnels. The breeding season extends through the warm months, from March to October; females are thought to bear two or three litters annually. Litter size ranges from two to eight, averaging five. These shrews probably breed in their first year. Like other soricids, after a post-juvenile molt adult smoky shrews molt twice annually—from winter pelage to that of summer in spring, and from summer to winter pelage in late summer or early autumn. Their maximum life-span is about 18 months, but few smoky shrews survive longer than 6 months.

Selected Reference. Owen (1984).

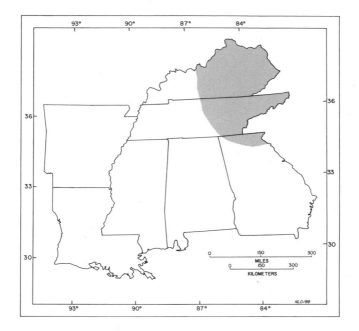

Photo courtesy H. S. Korber

Sorex hoyi

Pygmy Shrew

Distribution. This shrew has a broad range in boreal North America, from Alaska to northern Quebec and Labrador southward to the Great Lakes region, and in the Rocky and Appalachian mountain chains. In the south-central states, it presently is reported only in eastern and central Tennessee and one adjacent locality in Georgia, but probably is more widely distributed.

Description. Smallest of North American mammals. Dorsum reddish brown to grayish brown, grayer in winter; sides paler than back; venter whitish to grayish. Overall appearance somewhat tricolored; tail relatively short and bicolored. Total length, 78–90; tail, 27–34; hind foot, 8–10; weight, 2–4 g. Because of its small, compressed, third upper unicuspid (not visible in lateral view), this shrew was classified for many years in a separate genus, *Microsorex.*

Natural History. Over its considerable geographic distribution, the pygmy shrew seemingly tolerates a wide variety of ecological situations, but the species probably prefers mesic habitats. Its recorded locality in Georgia, for example, is in selectively logged hardwood forest, in an area of rocky outcrops and small cliffs near a stream.

Like other soricids, pygmy shrews are active year-round. They are good climbers and when disturbed can run rapidly. These shrews burrow in soft substrates such as litter and loose soil, especially under fallen logs, stumps, and other debris, but they also readily use the burrows and tunnels of other animals. Their food consists mostly of invertebrates. Their predators probably are much the same as for other small shrews.

Little is known of reproduction in *S. hoyi,* but it evidently is limited to the warm months. Pregnant and lactating females have been found in July and August; fetal counts range from three to nine. There are no data to suggest that more than one litter is produced per female or that females breed in their first year of life.

Like many shrews, this species is difficult to capture by conventional means. Use of pitfalls has proven a particularly good way to take specimens. A common technique is to bury empty cans flush with the ground, placing them in natural runs such as along logs or bases of rocky outcrops. Care should be taken to remove or cover the cans when not in use.

Selected References. Diersing (1980); Long (1974); Tims *et al.* (1989).

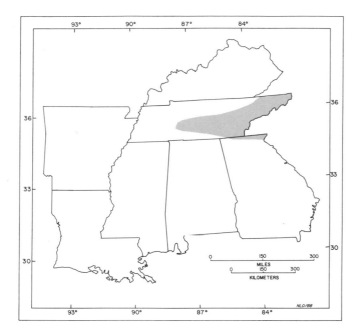

Photo courtesy J. O. Whitaker, Jr.

Sorex longirostris

Southeastern Shrew

Distribution. As its vernacular name implies, this species inhabits the southeastern United States, from Maryland and Florida westward through the southern parts of the Great Lakes states to Oklahoma. It is known to live in all seven states of the south-central region.

Description. Small shrew about size of *S. cinereus.* Dorsum brownish to reddish brown; venter paler, sometimes tending toward ochraceous; tail indistinctly bicolored. Total length, 78–92; tail, 26–33; hind foot, 10–13; weight, 3–6 g. This species differs from *S. cinereus* in having smaller skull but broader rostrum; teeth not so heavily pigmented, and third unicuspid usually smaller than fourth.

Natural History. This species has been reported in a variety of habitats, ranging from bogs and marshes to upland grassy areas and forest, and even bare hillsides and dry upland hardwoods. It seems to favor moist or wet areas bordering swamps, marshes, lakes, and streams. These shrews usually are associated with a heavy ground cover of leaves and litter, grasses, sedges, or low-growing brushy vegetation. Nests consisting of dried leaves have been found in or under rotting logs and beneath debris—in one case a piece of cardboard. Gravid females have been taken from the last of March to early October. Such a protracted breeding season suggests that they bear more than one litter annually. The known number of fetuses per pregnancy ranges from one to six, averaging four. It has not been established whether the young breed in their first year. In a study in Alabama, the population of this shrew was estimated at 12 to 18 animals per acre.

Important foods of *S. longirostris* are spiders, insects (especially larvae of Lepidoptera), centipedes, slugs, snails, earthworms, and some vegetable matter. Like some other shrews, southeastern shrews may eat more than their own weight daily. Owls are their most significant predators, but domestic cats have been reported to take fair numbers of this species in some areas. Known parasites include 25 species of mites and 1 species of flea externally, and nematodes, cestodes, and protozoans internally.

A southeastern shrew kept in captivity burrowed in moist soil and was active at all hours. It occasionally emitted a series of soft, birdlike chirps. The high frequency of these chirps (20,000 cycles per second) suggests that this species, like certain other mammals, might echolocate. It defecated in only one corner of the enclosure.

Selected References. French (1980*a*, 1980*b*, 1982).

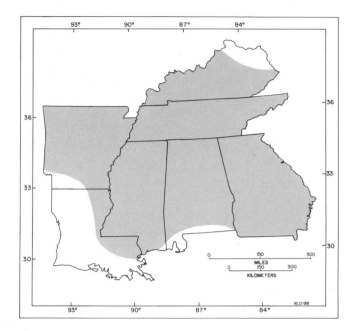

Photo courtesy T. W. French

Sorex palustris

Water Shrew

Distribution. The water shrew has a broad range over boreal North America, from southern Alaska to Quebec and Labrador, throughout much of the mountainous western United States, in the Great Lakes region and Northeast, and southward in the Appalachian chain. In the region covered, *S. palustris* is known only in the mountains of eastern Tennessee.

Description. Largest *Sorex* in south-central states; semiaquatic. Fur dense and soft, blackish to grayish brown dorsally, sometimes iridescent; venter paler, silvery white to grayish; pelage bicolored overall. Feet fringed with stiff, whitish hairs as adaptation for swimming; hind feet relatively broad. Total length, 135–155; tail, 58–71; hind foot, 18–20; weight, 8–18 g.

Natural History. This shrew, as its vernacular name implies, usually is found near permanent water, such as bogs, swamps, lakes, and rivers. Cold, fast-running streams bordered by overhanging banks, roots, and rocks provide its preferred habitat throughout most of its range. Specimens have been taken, however, in mixed forest several hundred yards from water. Along the West Prong of Little Pigeon River, one recorded locality in Tennessee, water shrews were found beneath overhanging banks and in rock crevices at elevations between 3,700 and 4,700 feet. These shrews are excellent swimmers and divers, moving easily along the bottoms of streams and pools in search of food. They are said to be able to run for short distances on the surface of the water as well. Their dense pelage is resistant to soaking.

Secretive and rarely seen, water shrews are mostly nocturnal. Their diet consists primarily of aquatic insects and their larvae, but these shrews also eat other invertebrates, small fish and other vertebrates, and some vegetable matter. As in shrews generally, their sight is poorly developed, but their senses of smell and touch are acute. There is a maturational molt from juvenile pelage to an adult coat of the appropriate season. Thereafter, there are two seasonal molts annually.

Breeding takes place from late winter to early autumn. Females may produce two or three litters annually; litter size ranges from five to eight young, averaging six. Females may bear a litter in their first year, but males are not active until the year after their birth. The normal life-span is about 18 months.

Selected Reference. Beneski and Stinson (1987).

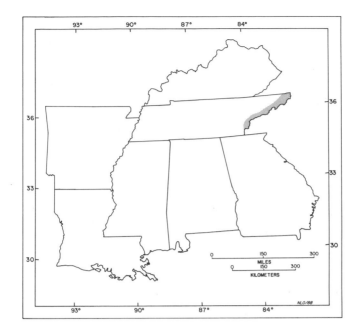

Photo courtesy R. W. Barbour

Blarina brevicauda

Northern Short-Tailed Shrew

Distribution. This species inhabits the northeastern United States and adjacent Canada, west to Nebraska and Saskatchewan. In the south-central states, it is found in most of Kentucky and Tennessee, northeastern Alabama, and south to central Georgia, where its range overlaps that of the smaller *B. carolinensis.*

Description. Largest shrew of south-central region, and largest of three species of *Blarina* in region; heavy bodied with short tail. Dorsum grayish to grayish black, venter only slightly paler. Total length, 110–135; tail, 21–32; hind foot, 14–18; weight, 20–30 g.

Natural History. Short-tailed shrews are the most common insectivores over most of the seven-state region. They occupy a broad variety of habitats, including woodlands, grasslands, brushy fencerows, and marshy areas. Populations vary both seasonally and annually but usually range from 3 to 20 shrews per acre. Much higher densities have been reported, however. Home ranges of males may be four and a half acres in extent, those of females smaller. Burrows and tunnels are at two different levels—some are but an inch or two below the surface or under logs, vegetation, or litter, whereas others are much deeper, up to 20 inches below the surface. The two levels of the same burrow system are joined at irregular intervals. These shrews also use burrows and trails of other mammals.

Short-tailed shrews may forage at any time, but much of their activity is nocturnal or in periods of subdued light. Like other shrews, they move about with seeming rapidity but little actual speed, with the tail elevated. They construct both resting nests and larger breeding nests from vegetative material, the latter four to eight inches in diameter and resembling hollow balls. Their diet includes a variety of invertebrates—larval and adult insects, snails, slugs, spiders, centipedes, millipedes, and earthworms—small vertebrates, the fungus *Endogone,* and plant material. *B. brevicauda* can be trapped easily using rolled oats as bait.

The breeding season of *Blarina* begins in late winter and continues through the warm months, although there may be a lull in early summer and midsummer. Litter size ranges from 4 to 10 young, averaging 6 or 7. The gestation period is 21 to 22 days. Females from early litters may breed in the year of birth. Longevity rarely exceeds two years.

Selected References. George *et al.* (1986); Jones *et al.* (1984).

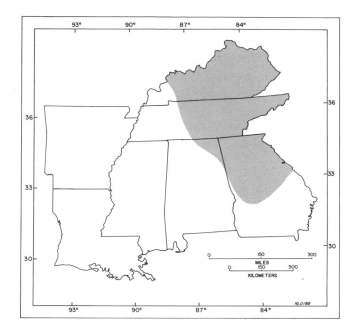

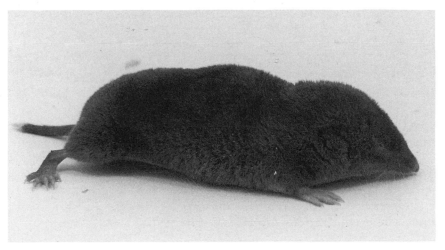

Photo courtesy E. C. Birney

Blarina carolinensis

Southern Short-Tailed Shrew

Distribution. This shrew is found from Florida westward to Texas, and north to southern Illinois and Virginia. It lives throughout the southern part of the south-central region, northward through eastern Arkansas and the western parts of Kentucky and Tennessee. It is sympatric with *B. brevicauda* in central Georgia and with *B. hylophaga* in northwestern Louisiana and adjacent Arkansas.

Description. Smallest of three species of *Blarina* in south-central states; miniature of *B. brevicauda.* Total length, 85–100; tail, 16–22; hind foot, 10–14; weight to 10 g. The shrew illustrated on the right is *B. carolinensis.*

Remarks. For many years, the three species of *Blarina* occurring in the south-central states were thought to represent a single species. In the past decade or so, however, studies of morphological and chromosomal differences among populations suggest recognition of at least three species. There also is good evidence of distinctive fossil histories.

Selected References. George *et al.* (1982); Jones *et al.* (1984); Schmidly (1983).

Blarina hylophaga

Elliot's Short-Tailed Shrew

Distribution. Elliot's short-tailed shrew currently is reported in Iowa and Nebraska southward to Texas. In the south-central states, it is known only in western and central Arkansas and northwestern Louisiana.

Description. Medium-sized of three species of *Blarina* in south-central states; resembles *B. brevicauda.* Total length, 103–120; tail, 19–25; hind foot, 12–16; weight, 13–17 g.

Remarks. This species is a medium-sized *Blarina,* larger than *B. carolinensis* but smaller than *B. brevicauda.* There is some overlap of measurements, however, between *B. hylophaga* and the other species of *Blarina,* and examination of chromosomes may be needed to confirm identifications. Thus identification of these shrews is best left to specialists. *B. hylophaga* seems to be more an inhabitant of mesic riparian woodlands and forest edge then *B. carolinensis,* which is most common in forests with a dense understory (frequently honeysuckle) and heavy leaf litter.

Selected References. George *et al.* (1981, 1982); Jones *et al.* (1984); Moncrief *et al.* (1982).

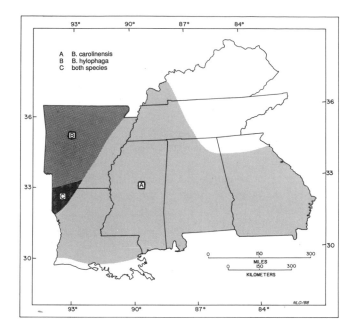

Photo courtesy R. Altig

Cryptotis parva

Least Shrew

Distribution. This shrew lives in the eastern United States, westward to eastern Colorado, and southward through eastern and central Mexico to eastern Panama. In the south-central states, the species is found in all but southeastern Louisiana.

Description. Small, solidly built shrew with short tail; somewhat resembling small *Blarina* but usually paler in color and possessing only four unicuspids. Dorsum dark brownish, sometimes reddish brown, in winter, paler brownish to grayish brown in summer; venter grayish. Total length, 72–90; tail, 13–18; hind foot, 9–12; weight, 3.5–6.5 g.

Natural History. The least shrew is not dependent on mesic habitats, being a creature of grasslands and other upland areas, weedy fencerows, fields and roadsides, meadows, and the like. It is a common small mammal in many places. It seeks refuge in shallow burrows of its own or of other mammals, and under refuse, fallen logs, and rocks, where it constructs nests, four to five inches in diameter, of dried grasses and leaves. *C. parva* is a social shrew, perhaps even colonial, as several individuals frequently nest together (31 were found in a nest under a log in Texas). These shrews utter clicks and high-pitched chirps, as well as other sounds inaudible to humans.

This species feeds on both animal and plant material. Important in its diet are adult and larval insects, earthworms, spiders, centipedes, slugs, and snails. A least shrew may consume 60 to 100 percent of its body weight daily. Owls are its primary predators; others are hawks, snakes, and carnivores such as spotted skunks. Chiggers, mites, and fleas are frequent external parasites. Little is known of this shrew's population dynamics. In a study in Tennessee, its home range size was estimated at half an acre.

Reproduction takes place from early spring to midautumn. Females bear several litters annually; young from early litters may breed later in the same season. Litter size ranges from two to seven young, but is normally four to six. Gestation lasts 21 to 23 days. Young are born blind and naked, and weigh about one-third of a gram. They mature rapidly, their eyes open in about 14 days, and they reach essentially adult size in two to three weeks. Juvenile pelage is thin and fuzzy in comparison with that of adults. Known longevity is 21 months, but few individuals survive longer than a year.

Selected Reference. Whitaker (1974).

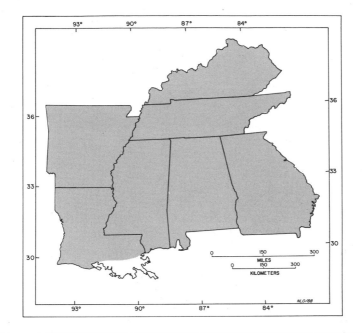

Photo courtesy T. H. Kunz

Notiosorex crawfordi

Desert Shrew

Distribution. This species is a denizen of the arid and semiarid South-west. It is found from central Mexico northward to Colorado and from California eastward to Arkansas, Oklahoma, and Texas. In the south-central region, the desert shrew is known only in northwestern Arkansas (Crawford and Washington counties).

Description. Small shrew with relatively short tail. Superficially resembles *Cryptotis parva* but has two fewer teeth (three pairs of unicuspids instead of four), less pigmented teeth (especially those in anterior part of jaw), and larger and more prominent ears. Dorsum silvery gray to grayish brown; venter slightly paler; tail well haired and distinctly bicolored. Total length, 77–98; tail, 22–32; hind foot, 9–13; weight, 3–6 g.

Natural History. The desert shrew occupies a wide variety of habitats but seems to favor semidesert shrub areas characterized by mesquite, agave, and scrub oaks, and sandsage habitats supporting yucca. In Arkansas, it was surmised that the species lived in woodrat nests located in crevices at the base of overhanging limestone escarpments. Virtually nothing is known of population dynamics in this shrew.

Like other shrews, these are exceedingly active animals; their movements are rapid and appear nervous. They emit high-pitched squeaks when fighting or under stress. They construct fluffy nests, two to six inches in diameter and with two openings, of grasses, leaves, and sometimes feathers. *Notiosorex* does not burrow. Their nests, therefore, are most often located in rock crevices, under rocks, logs, piles of lumber, and sheet metal, beneath brushpiles and other ground cover, and in woodrat "houses." The desert shrew eats a variety of vertebrates but prefers larval and adult insects. It attacks large prey by eating the legs first. Great-horned owls and barn owls are its only documented predators; cast pellets from owls are a good source of skeletal parts of this and other shrews. This shrew uses mostly metabolic water but will drink free water when available. When at rest, it falls into a deep sleep or torpor.

The reproductive season of this shrew spans the warm months of the year, from at least April through November. The known range of young per litter is three to five. Neonates are naked and blind, and the pinnae are not evident.

Selected References. Armstrong and Jones (1974); Hoffmeister (1986); Lindstedt and Jones (1980).

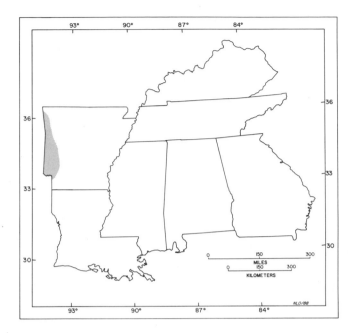

Parascalops breweri

Hairy-Tailed Mole

Distribution. This mole inhabits the northeastern United States and adjacent southeastern Canada, west to Ontario, Ohio, and eastern Kentucky, and south in the mountains and foothills to eastern Tennessee and southwestern North Carolina. In may be found in northern Georgia.

Description. Dorsum blackish, venter slightly paler; tail thick, fleshy, noticeably constricted at base, covered with long, coarse hairs. Juvenile pelage grayer and much shorter than that of adults. Snout shorter than in *Scalopus* and with median longitudinal groove on anterior half, nostrils directed laterally. Dental formula 3/3, 1/1, 4/4, 3/3, total 44. Total length, 150–175; tail, 26–35; hind foot, 17–20; weight, 40–65 g. Males slightly larger than females.

Natural History. Active both day and night, this species, like other moles, is primarily fossorial, though it forages above ground occasionally, especially at night. These typically are moles of eastern woodlands, but *P. breweri* also is found in pastures, cultivated fields, lawns, and gardens. This mole prefers sandy loam soils. Where it is sympatric with *Scalopus,* it tends to occupy higher ground and wooded areas, whereas the eastern mole prefers open country and lowlands. Like other moles, *P. breweri* does not hibernate. It constructs both foraging tunnels and deep tunnels, the latter 12 or more inches below the surface.

Breeding takes place in February and March. After an estimated gestation period of one month, females give birth to an average of four to five young in a leafy nest six to eight inches in diameter, located deep in the burrow system. There is a single litter annually. Neonates are naked except for short vibrissae; their skin is whitish and wrinkled. Young grow rapidly and probably are weaned about a month after birth. Adults molt twice annually, once in spring and again in early autumn. Longevity may be four years or more.

This mole's food consists of earthworms, larval, pupal, and adult insects, and other small animals. A captive 55-gram mole ate 66 grams of food in 24 hours. Captives will eat bird eggs and meat as well as soft-bodied invertebrates. Predators are few, the following having been recorded: domestic dogs and cats, red foxes, opossums, owls, snakes, and in one case a bullfrog. Parasites include fleas, mites, and lice externally, and roundworms and acanthocephalans internally.

Selected Reference. Hallett (1978).

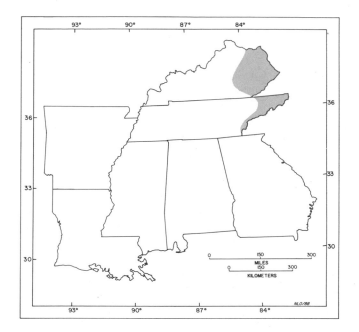

Photo courtesy R. W. Barbour

Scalopus aquaticus

Eastern Mole

Distribution. This species occurs in the eastern United States, northward to Massachusetts, Michigan (and adjacent Ontario), and Minnesota, and westward to Colorado, Texas, and northeasternmost Mexico. It is found throughout the south-central states except in southern Louisiana.

Description. Pelage silvery gray through dark brownish to blackish dorsally, paler ventrally; venter sometimes with whitish to orangish blotching. Robust mole with short, essentially hairless tail; toes of feet webbed, in contrast to *Parascalops;* nostrils directed anteriorly. Dental formula 3/2, 1/0, 3/3, 3/3, total 36. Total length, 145–195; tail, 20–38; hind foot, 17–25; weight, 65–115 g. Males are larger than females, and moles from the North and West average larger than those from the Southeast.

Natural History. This mole occupies a variety of habitats in both forested and nonforested areas. It prefers moist, loose, sandy or loamy soils. *S. aquaticus* spends most of its life underground. It digs tunnels of two kinds on well-drained sites—those near the surface, the ridges of which are familiar to most, and which are utilized for foraging; and deeper tunnels of more permanent construction, located 6 to 10 inches or more below the surface. Piles of soil, "mole hills," are thrown out of the system, especially in autumn. Individuals may be active day or night and in any season. In a study in Kentucky, male home ranges averaged 2.7 acres, but those of females were less than an acre. The systems of adjacent moles may overlap.

The eastern mole constructs nests four to six inches in diameter from grasses, leaves, and rootlets, placing them deep in the permanent tunnel system. In winter it occupies only one nest, but utilizes several in the warm months. Young moles apparently do not breed until about one year old. Thereafter, females give birth to a single litter annually, in late winter or spring, consisting of two to five (usually four) offspring. Gestation lasts about five weeks.

Eastern moles have a voracious appetite. They eat mostly earthworms and larval and adult insects, but they also consume other invertebrates and plant material. Predation on moles is minimal because they spend little time above ground. Birds of prey capture some, and carnivores and snakes probably take a few. Adults swim well, but flooding may cause death in nestlings. *S. aquaticus* has a known longevity of at least three years, more females than males attaining that age.

Selected References. Yates and Schmidly (1978); Davis and Choate (1993).

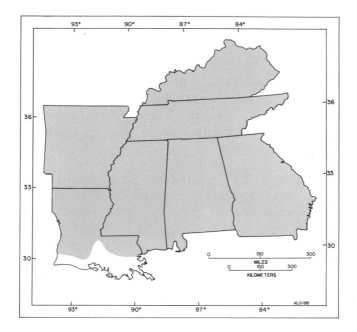

Photo courtesy R. W. Barbour

Condylura cristata

Star-Nosed Mole

Distribution. The star-nosed mole inhabits eastern Canada and the northeastern United States, west to Manitoba and Minnesota. Southwardly it is found in the Appalachian chain to eastern Tennessee and adjacent South Carolina and possibly northeasternmost Georgia, and on the coastal plain to southeastern Georgia.

Description. Pelage blackish both dorsally and ventrally, dense and shiny. Nose ringed by 22 fleshy appendages; tail relatively long, constricted at base, covered with coarse, blackish hairs. Dental formula as in *Parascalops;* bones of cranium noticeably thin. Total length, 160–205; tail, 60–83; hind foot, 25–30; weight, 35–70 g.

Natural History. This is the rarest of the three species of moles found in Great Smoky Mountains National Park. Its preferred habitats are moist woodlands and meadows, swamps, and bogs. *C. cristata* is both diurnal and nocturnal but seems to be most active at night and early in the morning. Numerous multiple captures from the same burrow systems are on record, suggesting that this mole is gregarious, possibly even colonial. It is less fossorial than other moles and is an excellent swimmer, spending much time in the water. It is active on or under snow and has been observed swimming under ice. It may spend more time in water in winter than in summer.

These moles usually construct tunnels near water—lakes, marshes, or streams. The tunnels vary from an inch or so to about two feet in depth. Burrowing is most pronounced around rocks, fallen logs, and roots of large trees, and tunnels sometimes have openings under water. Like other moles, this mole is prompt in repairing damaged runways. It builds its nests of leaves and grasses at a natural high place in the system to avoid flooding. Nests used for rearing young are larger than nests of single adults. Females are thought to bring forth only one litter annually, in spring or early summer, consisting of two to seven young (averaging five). The young leave the nest when they weigh about 30 grams.

Star-nosed moles feed chiefly on aquatic annelids and insects but also consume terrestrial earthworms, grubs, and other invertebrates. Hawks and owls are their main predators, but carnivores, snakes, and large fish probably take a few. Nematodes and cestodes have been reported as endoparasites; mites and fleas are known ectoparasites.

Selected Reference. Petersen and Yates (1980).

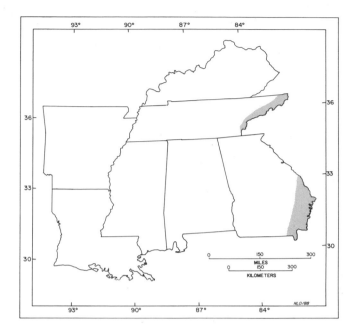

Photo courtesy G. C. Hickman

Order Chiroptera

Bats

Bats constitute the only group of mammals that is truly volant. They are inhabitants of boreal, temperate, and tropical regions around the world, north to the treeline in the Holarctic and including all of Africa, Australia, and South America, and many oceanic islands, such as Hawaii and New Zealand. Modern chiropterans are divided into two suborders: Megachiroptera, of the Old World tropics; and Microchiroptera, having the same range as the order. They make up 17 families, about 170 genera, and some 900 species. Only two families, Vespertilionidae (16 species) and Molossidae (1 species), are known in the south-central states.

All bats in this region are insectivorous, and their potential source of food thus is drastically reduced in the northern states in winter. Two strategies developed to meet this situation are migration many miles southward to warmer environs, where food is available, and hibernation, in which bats become torpid in a protected place in the cold months. Members of a few species evidently both migrate and hibernate, but not much is known of this dual response to cold weather.

The chiropteran flying surface consists of the wing membrane and the uropatagium, or interfemoral membrane. These double-layered extensions of the body skin encompass the forelimbs, the hind limbs except the feet, and in all species in the south-central states some or all of the tail. Elongated bones of the fingers and hand support the wing membrane with the exception of the thumb, which is relatively small and the only digit of the manus that bears a claw.

The earliest known bats are represented by isolated teeth from the Paleocene of Europe, but the earliest known skeleton, not much different from that of a modern microchiropteran, is from the Eocene of Wyoming. Bats probably are related to early insectivores, and some modern species retain primitive W-shaped cusps on the molars that do not differ significantly from the pattern found in the Insectivora. The number of teeth in bats varies from 20 to 38, but the range in those known from the seven-state region is 30 to 38. Some bats live a surprisingly long time for their size, up to 30 years or more.

Key to Bats

1. Tail extending conspicuously beyond posterior border of uropatagium; anterior border of ear with horny bumps; lower incisors bifid (Molossidae) .... *Tadarida brasiliensis*
1'. Tail not extending conspicuously (5 at most) or at all beyond poste-

rior border of uropatagium; anterior border of ear smooth; lower incisors trifid (Vespertilionidae) 2

2.   Single pair of upper incisors (incisors 1/3); total number of teeth 30 or 32 (if 32, minute premolar present internally between upper canine and P4, and dorsal surface of uropatagium noticeably furred) . 3

2'.   Two pair of upper incisors (incisors 2/3); total number of teeth 32 to 38 (if 32, dorsal surface of uropatagium essentially naked) 7

3.   Premolars 1/2; overall color dark brown; uropatagium essentially naked, with but a few fine hairs .... *Nycticeius humeralis*

3'.   Premolars 1/2 or 2/2; overall color not dark brown; dorsal surface of uropatagium noticeably furred at least on anterior half 4

4.   Dorsal pelage some shade of yellowish; premolars 1/2 (minute premolar lacking between upper canine and P4); dorsal surface of uropatagium noticeably furred only on proximal half
     .... *Lasiurus intermedius*

4'.   Dorsal pelage not yellowish; premolars 2/2 (minute premolar present internally between upper canine and P4); dorsal surface of uropatagium more or less furred throughout 5

5.   Dorsal pelage dark brownish and heavily frosted with white, hoary in appearance; forearm more than 45; greatest length of skull more than 17 .... *Lasiurus cinereus*

5'.   Dorsal pelage reddish or dark mahogany faintly tipped with whitish; forearm less than 45; greatest length of skull less than 15 6

6.   Dorsal pelage reddish (males somewhat darker than females); lacrimal ridge prominent .... *Lasiurus borealis*

6'.   Dorsal pelage mahogany faintly tipped with whitish; lacrimal ridge barely evident .... *Lasiurus seminolus*

7.   Dorsal pelage blackish and lightly frosted with whitish or, if not, ear tremendously enlarged (28 or more from notch); premolars 2/3, total number of teeth 36 8

7'.   Dorsal pelage not blackish and frosted with white, ear not enlarged (21 or less from notch); premolars 1/2, 2/2, or 3/3, total number of teeth 32, 34, or 38 10

8.   Dorsal pelage blackish frosted with white; dorsal surface of uropatagium furred proximally from a third to half its length; ear from notch less than 15 .... *Lasionycteris noctivagans*

8'.   Dorsal pelage brownish or brownish gray; dorsal surface of uropatagium essentially naked, with but a few fine hairs; ear from notch 28 or more 9

9.   Upper incisors unicuspid; hairs on toes not extending noticeably beyond claws; venter tan ....*Plecotus townsendii*

9'. Upper incisors bicuspid; hairs on toes extending well beyond claws; venter grayish ....*Plecotus rafinesquii*

10. Dorsal surface of uropatagium thinly but clearly furred on proximal third; premolars 2/2, total number of teeth 34 ....*Pipistrellus subflavus*

10'. Dorsal surface of uropatagium essentially naked, with but a few fine hairs; premolars 1/2 or 3/3, total number of teeth 32 or 38 11

11. Total length more than 110 (averaging 120); greatest length of skull more than 18; premolars 1/2, total number of teeth 32 ....*Eptesicus fuscus*

11'. Total length less than 110 (usually less than 100); greatest length of skull less than 18; premolars 3/3, total number of teeth 38 12

12. Wing membrane attached at ankle; forearm usually more than 40; greatest length of skull usually more than 15.5 .... *Myotis grisescens*

12'. Wing membrane attached at base of toe; forearm usually less than 40; greatest length of skull usually less than 15.5 13

13. Ears and membranes dark brownish to blackish, contrasting noticeably with color of dorsum, distinct dark facial mask; forearm less than 34; hind foot small, usually 8 or less ....*Myotis leibii*

13'. Ears and membranes brownish, not contrasting noticeably with color of dorsum, no distinct facial mask; forearm more than 34; hind foot usually 9 or more 14

14. Ear relatively long, usually 16–17 from notch; tragus long (about 9), tapering to a pointed tip; greatest length of skull averaging more than 15.0 .... *Myotis septentrionalis*

14'. Ear of moderate length, usually 13–15 from notch; tragus moderate in length (6–7), less tapered at tip; greatest length of skull rarely exceeding 15.0 15

15. Braincase low, rising only gradually from rostrum; hairs on hind foot not extending beyond toes; calcar strongly keeled ....*Myotis sodalis*

15'. Braincase higher, rising moderately to abruptly from rostrum; hairs on hind foot extending beyond toes; calcar not keeled or only indistinctly so 16

16. Braincase rising moderately abruptly from rostrum; dorsal pelage glossy in appearance, ventral pelage not tipped with white or tan .... *Myotis lucifugus*

16'. Braincase rising abruptly from rostrum; dorsal pelage "woolly" in appearance, ventral pelage tipped with white or tan .... *Myotis austroriparius*

Table 2. Dental Formulae of Bats of the South-Central States

Genus	Incisors	Canines	Premolars	Molars	Total
Eptesicus	2/3	1/1	1/2	3/3	32
Lasionycteris	2/3	1/1	2/3	3/3	36
Lasiurus	1/3	1/1	1–2/2	3/3	30–32*
Myotis	2/3	1/1	3/3	3/3	38
Nycticeius	1/3	1/1	1/2	3/3	30
Pipistrellus	2/3	1/1	2/2	3/3	34
Plecotus	2/3	1/1	2/3	3/3	36
Tadarida	1/3	1/1	2/2	3/3	32

* *L. intermedius* lacks the peglike upper premolar present in other species of *Lasiurus* treated in this book.

Figure 1. *Anatomy of a generalized bat.* Courtesy Michael J. Harvey

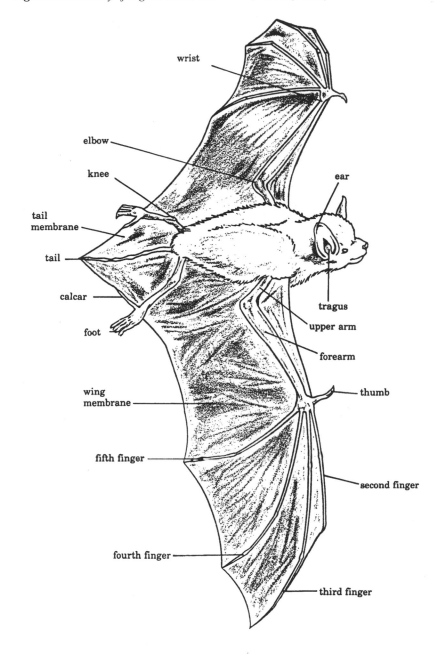

Myotis austroriparius

Southeastern Myotis

Distribution. As the vernacular name implies, this species occurs in the southeastern United States, ranging westward to northeastern Texas and adjacent Oklahoma, and northward to the southern parts of Indiana and Illinois. It is found in every state in the south-central region.

Description. Dorsum usually grayish to brownish, but varying to bright orange-brown; females somewhat more brightly colored than males; little or no contrast in color between base and tip of hairs; venter paler than dorsum, tan to whitish; pelage somewhat woolly in appearance. Medium-sized myotis; no keel on calcar; feet with long hairs extending beyond toes. Skull with abruptly rising rostrum and inflated braincase. Total length, 78–92; tail, 34–42; hind foot, 8–11; ear, 12–15; forearm, 36–41; weight, 4–9 g.

Natural History. This species is active year-round in the southern parts of its range but may hibernate six to seven months in the North. Hibernacula are in caves, mines, and buildings, where *M. austroriparius* has been found singly, in small groups, and in compact clusters of up to 100 bats. Several other species of bats may share its retreat. Hibernating bats awaken from time to time and occasionally move about. In the South, bats may go into torpor for a few days when daily temperatures drop below about 40°F.

Maternity colonies are formed in early spring in the southern states of the region, later to the north. Males are solitary or form small groups at this time of year, but some may join colonies of females and young in summer. Caves afford optimal roost sites, but mines and other man-made structures also are used, as are hollow trees. Bats leave their roosts early in the evening, proceeding to nearby water, usually a stream or pond, to drink before foraging. They fly low when feeding. Most breeding takes place in autumn, followed by delayed fertilization. Unlike many other species of *Myotis,* *M. austroriparius* bears twins as a rule; these are born in mid- to late spring depending on latitude. Neonates weigh little more than one gram; they become fully volant in five to six weeks.

Mites, batflies, and chiggers are known ectoparasites, and trematodes are reported endoparasites. Recorded enemies include opossums, cockroaches, several species of snakes, and raccoons. Destruction or alteration of roosting sites by man poses a major threat.

Selected References. Jones and Manning (1989); LaVal (1970).

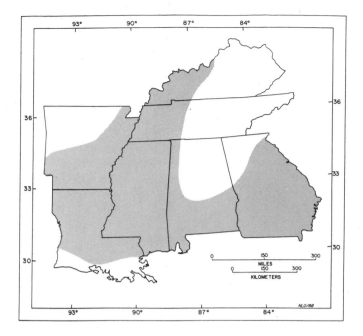

Photo courtesy R. W. Barbour

Myotis grisescens

Gray Myotis

Distribution. This myotis is a species of the southeastern United States, occurring from the Florida Panhandle northward to Illinois, Indiana, and Ohio, and westward to northeastern Oklahoma and adjacent Kansas. In the south-central states, it has been reported in Alabama, Arkansas, Kentucky, Mississippi, and Tennessee, and may occur also in western Georgia.

Description. Largest myotis in region. Dorsum grayish brown, pelage relatively sparse and decidedly woolly in appearance; venter grayish white. Wing membrane attached at ankle rather than at base of toes as in other species of this genus. Total length, 90–107; tail, 32–47; hind foot, 9–13; ear, 12–16; forearm, 40–45; weight to 12 or more g.

Natural History. This endangered species utilizes deep caves both as hibernacula in winter and as roosting sites in summer. It occasionally uses man-made structures that resemble caves, such as large storm sewers, but surprisingly there are no reports of *M. grisescens* in abandoned mines. Hibernating sites range in temperature from 42° to 52°F. Females form maternity colonies in spring, which can number from a few hundred bats to several hundred thousand, most often in large, deep, vertical caves. Males and barren females roost in different parts of the same shelter or in others nearby. Populations of the gray bat have declined markedly in the last decade or so, principally because of commercialization, destruction, and vandalism of caves. Also, these and other insectivorous bats are susceptible to indirect poisoning through use of insecticides. Migrations of a few hundred miles from summer haunts to winter retreats are known (these bats rarely use the same retreat in both summer and winter).

In the warm months, gray bats leave daytime retreats at dark and forage primarily over water—along streams and around ponds and lakes. Foraging flights may be as long as 15 miles. Mayflies are a major food source. *M. grisescens* has few enemies other than man.

Breeding takes place in autumn, before the bats go into hibernation, but some mating probably occurs over winter. Females become impregnated with stored sperm when they arouse from torpor in spring. A single offspring, weighing 2.5 to 3 grams, is born in June. Young mature rapidly and are volant in 20 to 25 days. The known life-span is 16.5 years.

Selected References. Harvy (1986); Tuttle (1975, 1976*a*, 1976*b*, 1979); Tuttle and Stevenson (1977).

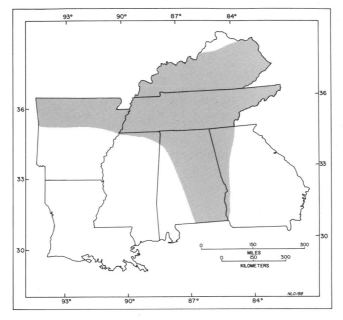

Photo courtesy R. W. Barbour

Myotis leibii

Eastern Small-Footed Myotis

Distribution. The eastern small-footed myotis has a discontinuous range from the Ozarks of Arkansas, Missouri, and Oklahoma eastward to the Appalachian region, and hence northward to the New England states and adjacent southeastern Canada. Formerly, *M. leibii* and its western counterpart, *M. ciliolabrum,* which occupies a broad range in the western United States and adjacent parts of Canada and Mexico, were regarded as conspecific.

Description. Smallest myotis in eastern North America. Yellowish brown dorsally, shiny tips on hairs, giving an overall burnished appearance; paler and more buffy ventrally; distinct, blackish facial mask; ears and membranes dark blackish brown, contrasting noticeably with pelage. Calcar keeled. Total length, 75–85; tail, 32–39; hind foot, 7–9; ear, 13–15; forearm, 30–34; weight, 3.5–6 g.

Natural History. This myotis is considered one of the rarest species of bats in the eastern United States. It is known as a saxicolous species. It is restricted primarily to rocky habitats (thus its spotty distribution in many areas)—sites with rock fissures, caves, and abandoned mines. It tends to roost and hibernate singly or in small groups rather than in large congregations, wedged into fissures or crevices in cool, dry caves or mines. It uses a variety of man-made structures as daytime retreats in the warm months, and like its western counterpart, it also may roost under rocks, in abandoned swallow nests, and even in holes in banks and hillsides. Females with young usually roost alone, but small maternity colonies—of about 10 adult females—have been reported.

These bats emerge from daytime retreats early in the evening, while there still is some light in the western sky, and forage slowly over streams and ponds and along cliffs, ledges, and wooded areas, rarely more than 20 feet above the ground. One study found that *M. ciliolabrum* masticates its insect food to a much finer degree than this and other species. *M. leibii* may interrupt its foraging activities several times for periods of rest, when it may become semitorpid.

Most mating takes place in autumn prior to hibernation as in other hibernating bats, sperm being stored in the female until fertilization in late winter or early spring. Females give birth to one offspring, which weighs about one gram, in May or June.

Selected References. Barbour and Davis (1969); Mohr (1933, 1936); van Zyll de Jong (1985).

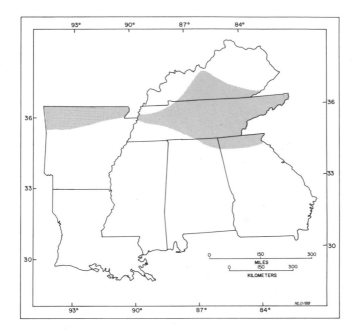

Photo courtesy R. W. Barbour

Myotis lucifugus

Little Brown Myotis

Distribution. This species has the broadest range of any North American myotis, occurring from coast to coast and from Alaska to Mexico. It is known in all states in the south-central region except Louisiana but is uncommon in many areas.

Description. Medium-sized myotis. Dorsum dark brown, pelage sleek and glossy, often with metallic sheen; venter paler, sometimes slightly grayish; ears and membranes brownish. No keel on calcar. Total length, 83–99; tail, 33–42; hind foot, 9–12; ear, 13–16; forearm, 34–40; weight, 5.5–9.5 g.

Natural History. This species is one of the best-known American bats because of its broad distribution and because it is colonial and common in many places. It evidently is less abundant in the southern parts of its range than farther to the north. Maternity colonies, numbering up to several thousand females, begin forming in spring, frequently in warm buildings, including attics of occupied houses. They may use the same maternity sites year after year. Males and barren females roost singly or in small groups in the warm months. As is the case for most bats, all roosting sites are near available water. Dispersal from winter hibernacula ranges from short distances to 300 miles or more.

These myotis begin to forage at late dusk, frequenting the same areas night after night. The usual flight pattern is over water—lakes, ponds, streams, and rivers—and along woodland borders. *M. lucifugus* eats a variety of insects, including flies, moths, and small beetles. It eats small insects in flight but lands to consume larger prey. Its summer retreats are in man-made structures and tree hollows, behind loose bark, and in caves and crevices.

Hibernation takes place from October to late March or April. Caves and mines with relatively high humidity and temperatures from 40° to 60°F are typical hibernacula. These bats hibernate singly or in small clusters, hanging from the walls or ceiling or wedging themselves into cracks and crevices. Several other species of bats frequently share their hibernating sites.

Most mating takes place directly before hibernation, but copulating pairs may be found in hibernacula throughout the winter. A single young (rarely twins) is born in mid- or late spring. Known longevity for the little brown myotis is slightly more than 30 years, the longest life-span recorded for any bat.

Selected Reference. Fenton and Barclay (1980).

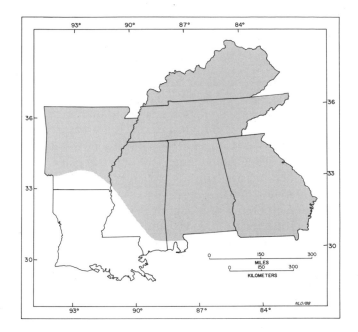

Photo courtesy T. H. Kunz

Myotis septentrionalis

Northern Myotis

Distribution. This is a northern bat that is not particularly common in the south-central states. It is recorded as far south as the Florida Panhandle, however, and in the seven-state region it is found in much of Alabama, Arkansas, and Georgia, in most of Kentucky and Tennessee, and in northeastern Mississippi. Elsewhere, the northern myotis ranges across southern Canada and the northern United States east of the Rockies.

Description. Medium-sized myotis with relatively long ears and long, pointed tragus. Dorsum dull brownish; venter pale brownish to pale grayish brown; ears and membranes only slightly darker than upper parts. Calcar slightly keeled. Total length, 78–96; tail, 32–35; hind foot, 8–10; ear, 16–18; forearm, 32–37; weight, 5.5–9.5 g.

Natural History. The biology of *M. septentrionalis* is not as well known as that of some other, more abundant species of myotis. These bats hibernate in caves and mines, usually wedging themselves into fissures or crevices in walls or ceilings. They occasionally hang torpid in the open, sometimes in association with *M. lucifugus, M. leibii,* and *Pipistrellus subflavus.* Hibernation probably lasts from October to March or April; bats may disperse 100 miles or more from hibernacula.

Maternity colonies of up to 30 females form in spring. At that time of year, *M. septentrionalis* frequently forms daytime retreats in abandoned or little-used buildings, but also may roost behind loose tree bark or shutters of buildings, beneath shingles, in tree holes, and even in birdhouses. Males and barren females roost singly or in small groups in the warm months. Day and night roosts (between foraging activities) probably are in different places. Foraging begins just after dark and continues, after a lull, to just before dawn. Flight of these bats over ponds, streams, and trees has been recorded. A study in Missouri found that this species foraged mainly over forest on hillsides and ridges rather than over riparian woodland, frequenting areas under the forest canopy and just above shrub level.

Little is known about reproduction in this species. Females bear a single young in late spring or early summer. Lactation may continue into August, but most young bats are weaned earlier, about a month after birth. Like other bats, adults of this species molt once a year (reproductively active females last) in early summer or midsummer. Known longevity from banding records is 18.5 years.

Selected References. Fitch and Shump (1979); van Zyll de Jong (1985).

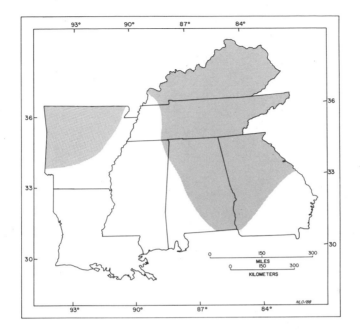

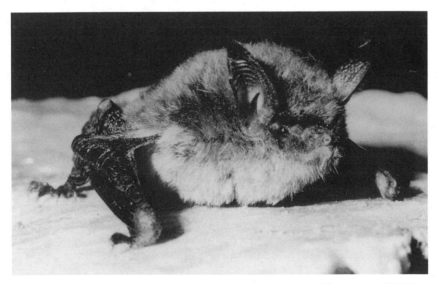

Photo courtesy T. H. Kunz

Myotis sodalis

Social Myotis

Distribution. This is a species of the east-central United States, occurring from central New England westward to Iowa, Missouri, and Oklahoma, and southward to northern Florida. In the south-central region, it is found in Kentucky and Tennessee, northern Arkansas, northwestern Mississippi, and parts of Alabama and probably Georgia.

Description. Medium-sized myotis with small but evident keel on calcar. Dorsum varying in color but usually dull chestnut gray to dark pinkish gray, the individual hairs tricolored; venter somewhat paler with pinkish white appearance overall; hairs on hind foot short and inconspicuous. Total length, 77–95; tail, 35–43; hind foot, 8–10; ear, 13–15; forearm, 36–41; weight usually 5–8 g.

Natural History. This myotis is listed as endangered by the United States Fish and Wildlife Service because of documented declining populations and human disturbance of roosting sites. The species is most common, at least in hibernacula, in southern Indiana, Kentucky, and the Ozarks of Missouri and adjacent Arkansas. It is sometimes referred to as the "Indiana myotis."

This bat hibernates in caves, mostly in tight clusters, occasionally in association with *M. lucifugus.* Like some other species, *M. sodalis* swarms around hibernacula before dispersal in spring and before entry into torpor in autumn. Males enter hibernation later than females, ordinarily in November, and leave the hibernaculum later in spring, usually in mid-April. *M. sodalis,* like many other hibernating species, may be active within a cave from time to time over winter or may move between hibernacula.

Females form small maternity colonies in spring, roosting in tree hollows and behind loose slabs of bark. Males and barren females seek roosts away from maternity groups. A single offspring is born in June or early July and is weaned in 25 to 35 days. Known longevity in this species exceeded 20 years in one instance, and there are several records of 13 to 14 years.

This bat's nocturnal foraging patterns frequently are over or near water. In one study conducted in Indiana, these bats were observed searching for insect prey near the foliage of riparian and floodplain trees from about 6 feet above the ground to as high as 100 feet. Their food consists primarily of small, soft-bodied insects, such as moths and flies, but also includes some beetles and hard-bodied dipterans. Among documented predators are mink, screech owls, and black rat snakes.

Selected Reference. Thomson (1982).

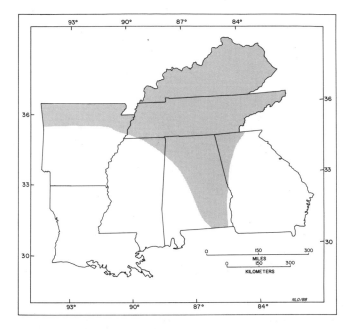

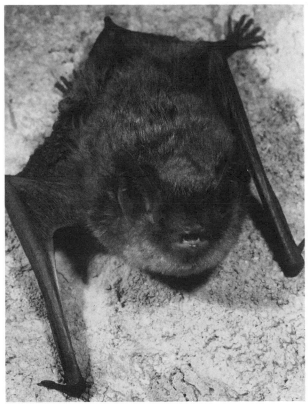

Photo courtesy R. W. Barbour

Lasionycteris noctivagans

Silver-Haired Bat

Distribution. This migratory species occurs from southwestern Alaska to northeastern Mexico, and is known in all but the southernmost parts of the United States. It has been recorded in all states in the south-central region.

Description. Strikingly attractive bat with silky dark brownish to blackish dorsum, pelage washed with silvery white; venter paler and with silvery wash less pronounced; uropatagium furred on basal half above; membranes blackish brown. Total length, 90–106; tail, 38–45; hind foot, 7–10; ear, 14–17; forearm, 38–43; weight 8.5–12.5 g.

Natural History. This bat probably is not resident in the south-central states in summer, migrating to more northerly forested regions instead. Thus, it is to be looked for in the region only in the colder months and as a migrant in spring and autumn.

The usual day roost in summer, of individual bats and females with young, is behind a loose piece of bark or in a tree hollow, abandoned bird nest, or dense foliage. These bats hibernate in a variety of shelters, including buildings, caves and mines, crevices in cliffs, and hollow trees. Migrants favor more open places for temporary roosts, such as sheds and other outbuildings, and piles of lumber, fenceposts, railway ties, and bricks. Little is known of wintering habits of *Lasionycteris,* and whether these bats are active at that time of year in the South has not been determined. Many apparently hibernate after migrating southward, but most records from the region evidently are of actual migrants.

The silver-haired bat is an early forager in at least some areas, and may be seen flying at early dusk. Its periods of activity may depend in part on those of competing species. Its slow flight pattern makes *L. noctivagans* one of the easiest species to shoot on the wing, and it is easily trapped in mist nets as well. Its insect food consists mostly of moths, midges, and small beetles, but this bat is an opportunistic feeder.

Silver-haired bats breed in autumn and store sperm through the winter. Ovulation and fertilization occur in late April and May, and one or two young, usually two, are born after 50 to 60 days of gestation. Neonates are naked, have ears folded at birth, and weigh slightly less than two grams. Females carry young on occasion, but apparently only to move them from one site to another.

Selected Reference. Kunz (1982).

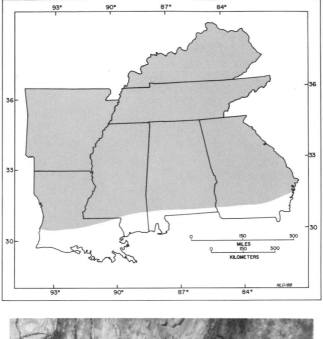

Photo courtesy R. W. Barbour

Pipistrellus subflavus

Eastern Pipistrelle

Distribution. As the vernacular name implies, this bat ranges across eastern North America, west to Nebraska and Texas, and from southeastern Canada southward to Honduras. It is found in all seven south-central states.

Description. One of smallest bats in temperate North America (about same size as *M. leibii*). Dorsal pelage varying from reddish brown through yellowish brown to pale grayish brown; venter paler; ears not markedly contrasting with dorsum; membranes somewhat darker than dorsum, uropatagium furred dorsally, sometimes thinly, on basal third. Total length, 75–90; tail, 33–41; hind foot, 8–10; ear, 12–14; forearm, 31–35; weight, 4–8 g.

Natural History. This is a hibernating species. Little is known of its movements from winter quarters to the warm-weather range, but *P. subflavus* evidently is not a strong seasonal migrant. Its hibernacula generally are caves, mines, deep rock crevices, and relatively warm, humid buildings. Torpid bats roost singly or in small clusters in the open, beads of water forming on them from the humid surroundings. They move frequently within the hibernaculum. Torpor lasts from October to April for females, to May for males.

In the warm months, these bats may continue to occupy winter retreats, but most roost in tree hollows and in high tree foliage; small maternity colonies have been found in buildings as well. In any event, they do not disperse great distances from winter quarters. Swarming with other bats near hibernacula has been observed in late summer and early autumn. This species is thought to begin nightly foraging relatively early, coursing over lakes, streams, and ponds, along the forest edge, and in other open woody habitats. Daytime torpor in summer has been recorded.

This is a common bat in many areas. It is an opportunistic feeder, 16 general insect groups having been recorded as dietary items in a study in Indiana. Of these, leafhoppers, beetles, and dipteran flies amounted to almost 50 percent of volume. Parasites include several kinds of trematodes, chiggers, and macronyssid, spinturnicid, and myobiid mites.

Females give birth to one to three young (usually two) from late May through early July. The neonates are pinkish and naked, with eyes closed and pinnae folded. Postjuvenile molt takes place in late summer; thereafter adults molt once annually. Known longevity is 14.8 years.

Selected Reference. Fujita and Kunz (1984).

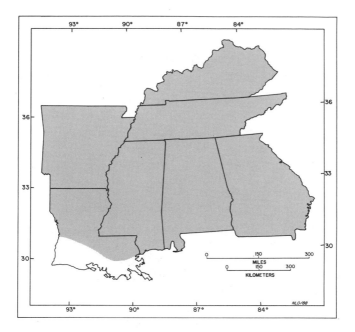

Photo courtesy R. J. Baker

Eptesicus fuscus

Big Brown Bat

Distribution. This bat has a broad range, from southern Canada to northern South America, and is found on many islands of the Antilles. It is closely related to, and may be conspecific with, *E. serotinus,* which ranges widely in Eurasia. *E. fuscus* is found throughout the south-central region except in southern Louisiana.

Description. One of larger North American bats. Dorsum dark brown; venter paler brownish; ears and membranes blackish brown. Total length, 112–130; tail, 38–50; hind foot, 9–13; ear, 16–20; forearm, 42–50; weight, 13–25 or more g. Females average 5 percent larger than males.

Natural History. Because this species is conspicuous, colonial, and common over much of its range, much is known of its habits. When active, these bats tend to be early fliers readily recognized by their relatively slow and steady flight. They are easily shot on the wing at dusk as well as captured in mist nets. They may be active intermittently through the night, with return to the day roost at early dawn. Some audible chattering can be heard from these bats in flight. They forage over water, around wooded clearings, and along riparian vegetation. They consume a variety of insects; in one study, stomach contents included mostly beetles, flies, moths, true bugs, and cicadellids.

The big brown bat's warm-weather roosts typically are in man-made structures but may be in caves, mines, hollow trees, and crevices, or behind loose bark. Males and barren females are mostly solitary in summer, but gravid females form maternity colonies that may number several hundred. Big brown bats occupy some sites in both summer and winter, but summer haunts may be 50 or more miles removed from winter retreats. The latter usually are in caves, mines, buildings, storm sewers, or other man-made structures, normally in environments only a few degrees above freezing. Torpid bats hang singly or in aggregations exceeding 100 individuals, or wedge themselves into cracks, crevices, or holes in the walls or ceiling of the hibernaculum. There is some movement within and between hibernacula.

These bats copulate in autumn and ovulate in spring. Females give birth to two offspring, weighing three to four grams each, in late May or June. The young become volant in about four weeks. Known longevity in this species is 19 years.

Selected References. Barbour and Davis (1969); Goehring (1972); Kunz (1974); Kurta and Baker (1990).

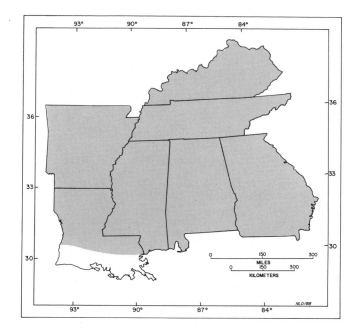

Photo courtesy N. L. Olson

Lasiurus borealis

Eastern Red Bat

Distribution. Until recently, this species was thought to occupy a broad area in temperate North America southward well into South America. Now it is known to occur only in the eastern United States and southeastern Canada, west to Wyoming, Colorado, and Texas, and south to eastern Mexico. A closely related species, *L. blossevillii,* occurs elsewhere within the range of red bats in western North America.

Description. Medium-sized bat with relatively long, pointed wings. Dorsum usually bright reddish orange to chestnut, females duller in color than males; venter paler, more yellowish than dorsum; uropatagium completely furred dorsally. Ears short, rounded, furred outwardly; membranes dark brownish, ears pale; conspicuous yellowish white shoulder and wrist patches. Total length, 108–125; tail, 45–60; hind foot, 8–10; forearm, 37–42; weight, 6–14 g (pregnant females to 20 g or more).

Natural History. Members of the genus *Lasiurus* are referred to as "tree bats" because females with young and individual bats roost in vegetation in the warm months, usually in trees. There they hang from twigs, leaf petioles, or small limbs during the day, resembling dead leaves. They apparently prefer maples and elms in many places but frequently use clumps of Spanish moss in the South. In the northern part of its range the red bat is a seasonal migrant, but in the south-central region it is active all year in some areas, such as in Louisiana, and is alternately active and torpid (in colder weather) in others, such as Kentucky. During torpidity, its retreats probably are in hollow trees and under loose bark.

Eastern red bats select daytime roosts with an open space below them and initiate flight simply by dropping from the roost. These bats emerge early, while the sun still lingers in the western sky, flying high above the ground until darkness, when they descend to forage; the area hunted may be the same night after night. Females evidently return unerringly to their young, which they leave at the roost site. Solitary bats frequently return to the same roost for several consecutive days.

Most breeding apparently takes place during southward migration in autumn, and copulation in flight has been observed. Females with one to five young have been reported; four is the norm, more offspring than are known for any other bat.

Selected Reference. Shump and Shump (1982*a*).

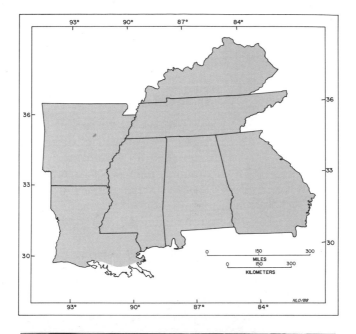

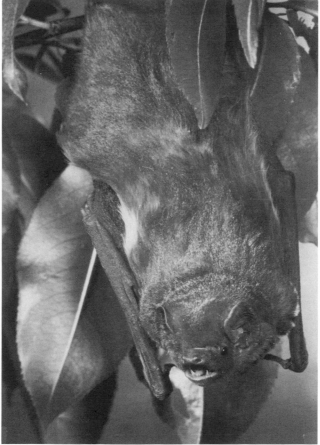

Photo courtesy R. W. Barbour

Lasiurus cinereus

Hoary Bat

Distribution. This species has a broad North American range, from Canada southward to Guatemala. Isolated subspecies occur also in South America and on the Hawaiian Islands. Because this strong flyer is migratory, extralimital records are not uncommon, and hoary bats have been taken on South Hampton Island in the Canadian arctic, on Iceland, Hispaniola, and Bermuda, and even on the Orkney Islands, off Scotland. *L. cinereus* can be found throughout the south-central region except in coastal Louisiana and Mississippi.

Description. Largest bat of south-central region. Ears short, broad, rounded, and furred externally; tragus blunt as in other species of *Lasiurus*. Dorsal pelage varying from yellowish brown to mahogany, heavily frosted with silvery white, imparting hoary appearance; venter whitish to yellowish brown; uropatagium furred. Wings long and narrow, membranes blackish brown; yellowish white patch on shoulder, cream-colored spot on wrist. Total length, 133–150; tail, 48–62; hind foot, 11–14; ear, 17–20; forearm, 52–57; weight averaging 25 g.

Natural History. This bat is strongly migratory, and at least some migrants travel in groups. Breeding probably takes place during autumnal migration. Some of these bats evidently overwinter in the southern states, migrating northward in spring, but others seem to be year-round residents; juveniles and post-lactating females are on record from Louisiana, for example. Warm-weather residents, however, are only females and their young, males moving to higher latitudes.

Like its relatives, the hoary bat spends the day concealed in a roost in trees or shrubs, usually 10 to 15 feet above the ground. The site is well covered but open underneath to facilitate initial flight. Except for females with young (and possibly in migration), hoary bats roost singly. They normally leave daytime quarters after dark but sometimes can be seen flying at late dusk. They emit a chattering during flight readily heard by humans. After an initial period of activity, the bats roost until additional foraging later in the night. Like other bats, females carry young only to move them. Few ectoparasites have been taken from this and other noncolonial bats.

Females bear two young in late spring. These are capable of flight in four to five weeks. Molt from juvenile pelage takes place in late summer; thereafer, there is one molt per year in summer.

Selected Reference. Shump and Shump (1982*b*).

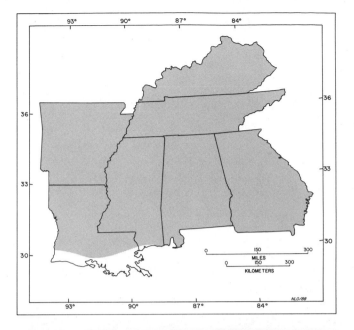

Photo courtesy R. W. Barbour

Lasiurus intermedius

Northern Yellow Bat

Distribution. This bat is found in the southeastern United States, northward along the Eastern Seaboard to Virginia and New Jersey and westward to Texas, in the lowlands of eastern and western Mexico, and southward to Honduras. A related species is known in Cuba. In the south-central region, *L. intermedius* ranges from central Georgia westward through north-central Louisiana.

Description. Relatively large bat, smaller than *L. cinereus* but larger than *L. borealis* and *L. seminolus,* about size of *E. fuscus;* ears more pointed than in other *Lasiurus.* Dorsum silky and yellowish to yellowish brown, even yellowish gray; venter paler yellowish; membranes brownish; uropatagium furred on proximal half; no patches on shoulders and wrists. Females, which average larger than males, have four mammae, as in other species of *Lasiurus.* Total length, 121–132; tail, 51–60; hind foot, 8–11; ear, 15–17; weight to about 20 g.

Natural History. Northern yellow bats typically inhabit forested areas near permanent water. They frequent both coniferous and deciduous woodlands. They often select clumps of Spanish moss as roosting sites but roost in trees as well. They have been found in palm groves in Florida. Most are solitary, but congregations of up to 50 have been reported. A group of northern yellow bats was found in a retreat among dried cornstalks hanging from the sides of a large, open shed in Mexico. Small maternity colonies may form in spring and summer. The species is active year-round except on the coldest nights of the winter months, although these bats have been found in torpor in the northernmost part of their range.

The northern yellow bat's food consists of a variety of insects. Flies, homopterans, dragonflies, beetles, bugs, and hymenopterans made up the bulk of its diet in one study. It typically forages about 15 feet above the ground in areas with few trees. Macronyssid mites are its only reported ectoparasite. Remains of this bat have been found in castings of the barn owl.

The sexes apparently are separated except during breeding, which probably takes place in autumn and winter. Females have two to four offspring (the average was 3.4 in a study in Florida). Neonates have a forearm length of about 16 and weigh approximately 3 grams. Volant young have been taken as early as June.

Selected Reference. Webster *et al.* (1980).

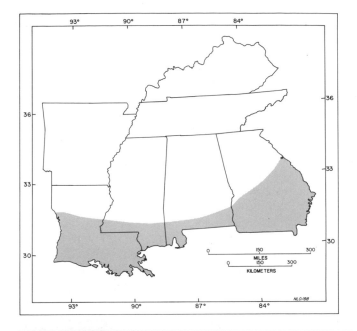

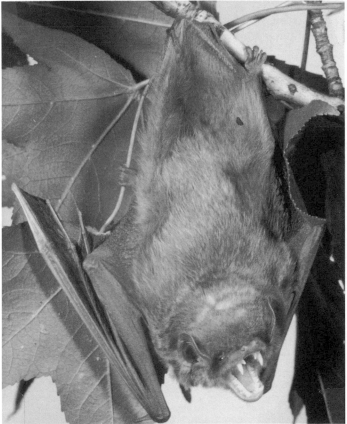

Photo courtesy R. W. Barbour

Lasiurus seminolus

Seminole Bat

Distribution. The seminole bat is a southeastern species that occurs from Florida to Virginia westward to southeastern Oklahoma and eastern Texas. There are extralimital records from southernmost Texas, New York, Pennsylvania, and Bermuda, and a questionable report from Veracruz in eastern Mexico. In the south-central region, *L. seminolus* is found northward to southern Tennessee.

Description. Strongly resembles *L. borealis,* of which it was thought to be a color phase for many years but from which it differs in color and cranial details. Dorsum deep mahogany, lightly frosted; venter slightly paler, especially posteriorly, where color is pale reddish orange; whitish spots on shoulders and wrist at base of thumb; dorsal aspect of uropatagium furred, much more densely on proximal half. Total length, 90–110; tail, 35–50; hind foot, 8–10; ear, 10–13; forearm, 37–43; weight, 8.5–12.5 g.

Natural History. This is the most abundant bat in much of the south-central region. It prefers Spanish moss as a roosting site, only one or two individuals retreating to the same clump. Clumps with a southwestern exposure seem to be favored, probably because they best permit preflight warming from the sun. Roosts usually are 5 to 20 feet above the ground. The Seminole bat inhabits wooded areas, both of deciduous and coniferous trees. It forages mostly at tree-top level in forested areas, although it also flies over water courses and forest clearings, and along forest edge. Migratory behavior has not been demonstrated for *L. seminolus,* but there may be some slight adjustments between its winter range and its summer haunts. These bats are active in the colder months but do not forage when the temperature drops below about 60°F.

This species feeds almost exclusively on insects, nearly all of which it catches in flight. In studies in Florida, dipterans, beetles, dragonflies, and hymenopterans were found to make up the bulk of its diet. The bats eat some prey in flight but readily alight to devour large insects. As with other members of the genus *Lasiurus,* few parasites have been recorded for this species.

Fetal counts range from two to four. The mean was 3.3 in a sample of 21 from Florida. Four fetuses carried by one female totaled six grams in weight. Parturition takes place in late May and early June.

Selected Reference. Wilkins (1987).

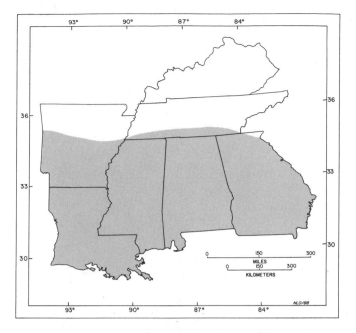

Photo courtesy R. W. Barbour

Nycticeius humeralis

Evening Bat

Distribution. The evening bat is found in all seven of the south-central states. It ranges northward to New Jersey and the southern part of the Great Lakes region, westward to Nebraska, Kansas, Oklahoma, and Texas, and southward in eastern Mexico to Veracruz. A related species occurs on Cuba.

Description. Medium-sized bat that superficially resembles *E. fuscus* or a large myotis but differs from both in dental formula. Dorsum dark brownish, hairs plumbeous basally; venter paler, sometimes tawny; ears and membranes dark brown to blackish. Total length, 80–96; tail, 30–40; hind foot, 7–9; ear, 12–14; forearm, 30–37, weight 7–14 g.

Natural History. The evening bat is a species typical of the eastern deciduous forest and a common, widely distributed bat in much of the south-central region. Its day roosts are in hollows of trees, under loose slabs of bark, and in a variety of man-made structures such as outbuildings, church belfries, cisterns, and even attics of occupied older homes. This species is a communal occupant of roosts, sometimes in company with *Eptesicus fuscus* or *Tadarida brasiliensis.* It is active year-found, at least in the southern states of the region covered, but apparently migrates southward in winter from Kentucky and other northern areas, and torpid bats have been found in southern Arkansas. Thick layers of fat accumulated in summer and autumn provide the energy needed for migration or hibernation. Much remains to be learned of the habits of this bat in winter. This species never is found in mines or caves.

Evening bats leave their daytime roosts at late dusk to course over clearings, farm ponds, and other open water, or along forest edge in search of insects. Rarely do they fly above tree-top level. *N. humeralis* is rather slow and deliberate in flight, and is easily shot on the wing in the evening light and trapped in mist nets. Its diet consists of a variety of insects, including moths, beetles, flies, bugs, and flying ants. Mites and batbugs parasitize this species externally, cestodes, nematodes, and trematodes internally. Like many other bats, it has a well-developed sense of homing; individuals removed 100 miles or more from their home roosts have returned to them within a few days. Females bear one to three young, usually twins, in early June. There is one report of four fetuses found in a female in Alabama. Known longevity of this relatively short-lived bat is not much more than five years, and average longevity is only two years.

Selected References. Watkins (1972); Watkins and Shump (1981).

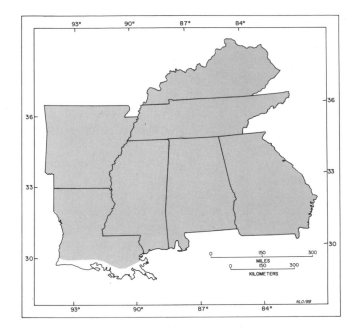

Photo courtesy R. W. Barbour

Plecotus rafinesquii

Rafinesque's Big-Eared Bat

Distribution. This is a bat of the southeastern United States. It is found from Florida northward to North Carolina, West Virginia, and the southern parts of the southern Great Lakes states, and westward to southeastern Oklahoma and eastern Texas. It is reported in each of the seven south-central states.

Description. Pale-colored bat of medium size with tremendously enlarged ears and two large lumps on snout. Dorsum brownish gray overall, individual hairs dark brown to blackish basally, pale reddish to brownish distally; venter whitish. This species differs from *P. townsendii* in having first upper incisors bicuspid, hairs on feet projecting beyond toes, venter whitish instead of tan, and dorsum more grayish and with distinctly bicolored hairs. Total length, 85–105; tail, 43–50; hind foot, 9–12; ear, 28–37; forearm, 38–45; weight, 8–13 g.

Natural History. This is one of the least-known bats in the South. It is colonial, like many other chiropterans. Colonies range in size from several bats to 100 or more; females usually outnumber males in such groups. In the warm months, these bats seek shelter in unoccupied buildings, abandoned mines and wells, and other man-made structures, behind loose bark, and in caves, crevices, hollow trees, and similar retreats. Size and location of colonies are related to roost temperatures. *P. rafinesquii* hibernates in the cold months, perhaps only for brief periods in the southern part of its range, generally singly or in small groups; its hibernacula are more open and lighted than those of most other bats. Torpor may occur for a few days at a time in summer as well.

This bat forages after dark, returning to daytime quarters before first light; unlike most other bats, it is not crepuscular. Little is known of the insect composition of its diet. Several species of snakes are known predators, capturing these bats as they roost, and small carnivores probably also take some. As in other North American bats, there is a single annual molt, which takes place in late spring and early summer.

Copulation occurs in autumn and winter; females give birth to a single young in late spring. Neonates weigh about 2.5 grams and are naked, but quickly acquire a dark juvenile pelage, which is replaced by adult pelage in about three months. Young possess permanent dentition and become volant by three weeks of age. Known longevity is slightly more than 10 years.

Selected Reference. Jones (1977).

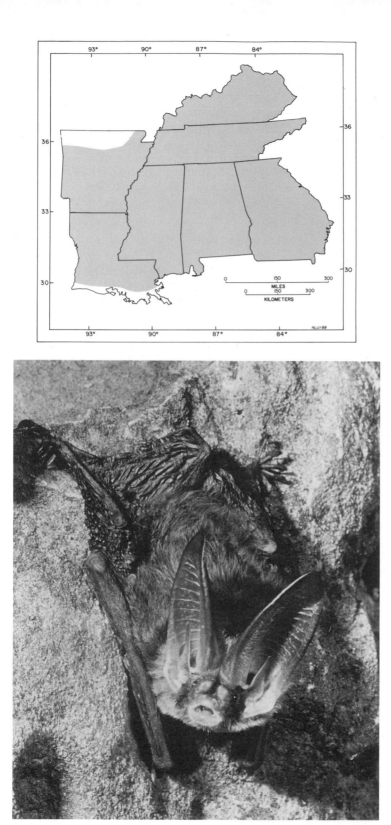

Photo courtesy R. W. Barbour

Plecotus townsendii

Townsend's Big-Eared Bat

Distribution. This species, which has a broad range in western North America, from southern Canada to southern Mexico, is known in the south-central region only in isolated areas of northwestern Arkansas and east-central Kentucky. These represent distinctive subspecies, the western population also occurring in southern Missouri and the eastern race known additionally in Virginia and West Virginia. Possibly only a thousand or so of these bats occur in the south-central states.

Description. Like *P. rafinesquii*, this is a medium-sized, brownish-colored bat with large ears and two large, fleshy lumps on the snout. Dorsum pale to dark brown, venter pale brown. Differences between *P. townsendii* and *P. rafinesquii* given in account of latter. Total length, 95–115; tail, 42–54; hind foot, 10–13; ear, 32–38; forearm, 40–45; weight, 7–12 g.

Natural History. Townsend's big-eared bat is a cavernicolous species. It is never found far from caves or abandoned mines, which it uses exclusively for hibernacula. The species inhabits such areas in summer also, but may utilize man-made structures as well. In hibernation, these bats normally seek relatively cold places, frequently near the mouth of the hibernaculum. They hibernate in clusters or singly, hanging by one foot with ears curled like the horns of a ram and wings wrapped around the body. This is a relatively sedentary bat, long-distance migrations from hibernating sites to summer haunts being unknown.

This big-eared bat generally is a late flyer, leaving roosts well after dark. It feeds primarily on small moths but may consume other insects as well. Recorded endoparasites are nematodes, cestodes, and trypanosomes. Ectoparasites include a conspicuous winged batfly, a wingless batfly, ticks, chiggers, and several kinds of mites. Known longevity of *P. townsendii* from banding records is 16.4 years.

Mating takes place in autumn and over winter; females mate in their first year, but males do not reach sexual maturity until the year following their birth. Gestation lasts from 56 to 100 days after fertilization, depending on temperature and varying periods of torpor in females. A single young is born naked in late spring, with eyes closed and with enlarged ears and feet. Young bats are capable of flight at two and a half to three weeks of age and are weaned by six weeks.

Selected Reference. Kunz and Martin (1982).

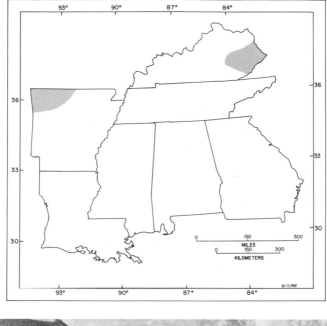

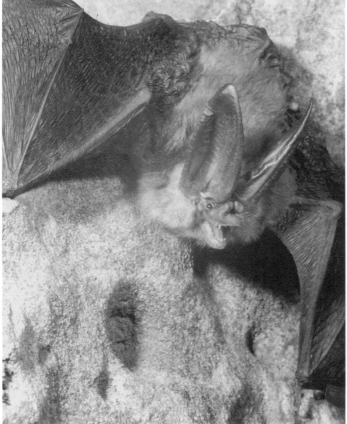

Photo courtesy R. W. Barbour

Tadarida brasiliensis

Brazilian Free-Tailed Bat

Distribution. This free-tailed bat has a broad range, from North Carolina, South Dakota, and Oregon southward through Middle America into much of South America. It also is found in the Antilles. It is a breeding resident of the southern part of the south-central region, with records of autumn wanderers to the north of that area.

Populations of free-tailed bats in the southeastern United States, known by the subspecific name *T. brasiliensis cynocephala,* differ in several important morphological and behavioral characteristics from populations of *T. brasiliensis* elsewhere in the range of the species. It is quite possible, therefore, that the two represent different species.

Description. Unique among bats of south-central states in that tail is free of uropatagium for about half its length. Dorsum dark brownish to blackish brown, venter paler, membranes dark brown; dorsal pelage has velvety texture. Wings long and narrow; deep vertical grooves on upper lip; conspicuous fleshy bumps on ears. Total length, 92–105; tail, 30–42; hind foot, 7–10; ear, 12–14; forearm, 30–37; weight, 7–14 g.

Natural History. This is a colonial species and a common bat throughout much of the South. It roosts primarily in buildings but has been taken behind shutters, in hollow trees, and from similar retreats. In this region, *T. brasiliensis* is essentially nonmigratory and does not hibernate, although summer and winter quarters may be in different places. The greatest distance of recorded seasonal movement for banded individuals in Louisiana is 84 miles. Nursery colonies in the warm months may contain several thousand bats.

These free-tailed bats leave roosting sites a few minutes after sunset to drink and then course far and wide in search of insect food. They are capable of rapid flight (more than 25 mph) sustained for long periods at altitudes of 9,000 feet or more. They feed almost exclusively on small moths, which they catch on the wing. On cold nights not all bats leave the roost to forage, and those that do may return within an hour or two as the ambient temperature drops. Breeding probably takes place in March, after which time the sexes segregate, and females give birth to a single young in June that is blind and naked. The young mature rapidly but do not fly until about five weeks of age, later than many vespertilionids. Gestation lasts 11 to 12 weeks.

Selected References. Barbour and Davis (1969); Wilkins (1989).

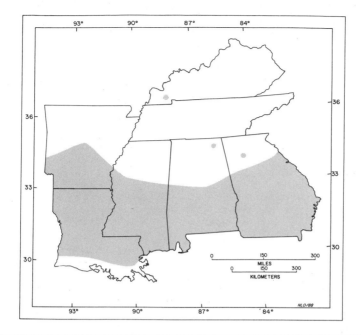

Photo courtesy N. L. Olson

Order Xenarthra

Xenarthrans

Members of this order, for which the name Edentata formerly was used, are grouped in four Recent families, all restricted to the New World: Dasypodidae (armadillos), Myrmecophagidae (anteaters), Bradypodidae (three-toed tree sloths), and Megalonychidae (two-toed tree sloths and the relatively recently extinct ground sloths). All modern groups are restricted to tropical environments except dasypodids, which also inhabit temperate regions in both North America and South America. The fossil record of xenarthrans dates back to the Paleocene in South America, some 60 million years ago.

Incisor and canine teeth are absent in Xenarthra, and cheekteeth are either absent (myrmecophagids) or, if present, subcylindrical and peglike, lacking enamel, and single-rooted. Only dasypodids have deciduous teeth. The number of cervical vertebrae varies from five to nine, depending on the group—megalonychids have five to seven, myrmecophagids and dasypodids have seven, and bradypodids have eight or nine. All members of the order have long, sharp, recurved claws. Living xenarthrans make up 13 genera and about 30 species.

Dasypus novemcinctus

Nine-Banded Armadillo

Distribution. In North America, the nine-banded armadillo occurs northward to southern Nebraska, westward to western Texas, New Mexico, and southeastern Colorado, and eastward through the south-central states to South Carolina and Florida. Both natural dispersal and introductions account for the distribution in this region. The species has not yet dispersed into the cooler areas of the south-central states. It also ranges southward into South America.

Description. Resembles no other mammal in region. Most of animal covered dorsally by bony carapace consisting of scapular shield, nine flexible bands (thus the vernacular name), and pelvic shield; bony plate on head; tail encased in series of bony rings; remainder of body covered with tough skin that contains hard scales on lower legs and feet; all toes heavily clawed; cheekteeth, 28–36. Dorsum generally grayish brown; venter paler. Total length, 620–800; tail, 245–365; hind foot, 75–100; ear, 30–40; weight to about 8 kg, but usually 3.5–5.

Natural History. This species is found principally in woodlands, at forest edge, on savannas, and in scrubby and brushy areas. Its diet consists mostly of insects, their larvae, and other invertebrates, but it also consumes fruits, mushrooms, berries, eggs of ground-nesting birds, and probably a few small vertebrates. Armadillos do not hibernate, and their northward distribution thus is limited by climate (in terms of both the physiology of the animals themselves and the availability of food). Nevertheless, there has been a rather dramatic northward dispersal of the species within historic time, which presumably is continuing.

Because of their protective armor, armadillos have few natural enemies. They can run with surprising speed, generally seeking safety in dense underbrush or among rocks or fallen timbers, or in burrows. When caught in the open, they can curl up in such a way that the bony carapace provides substantial protection. Armadillos dig their own burrows and also dig and root in the ground in search of food. Active burrows, which frequently are on a slope, usually have several entrances, only one of which is used regularly. Armadillos construct nests of leaves and other vegetation in the burrows or under natural shelters such as large rocks and tree roots. Armadillos have poor eyesight and also exhibit a defense mechanism of jumping when startled. Many are killed on roadways each year by vehicles that would have passed over them without effect had they not jumped. They swim well and also have been seen crossing small bodies of water by walking on the bottom.

Breeding takes place in summer, but implantation of the fertilized egg usually is delayed about 14 weeks. A delay of up to two years has been recorded in captive animals. Normally four young, developed from the same fertilized egg and thus identical quadruplets, are born in late winter or early spring after a gestation of 120 days. The neonates are precocial; they reach sexual maturity in one year and may live as long as four years.

Selected References. Humphrey (1974); McBee and Baker (1982); Zimmerman (1990).

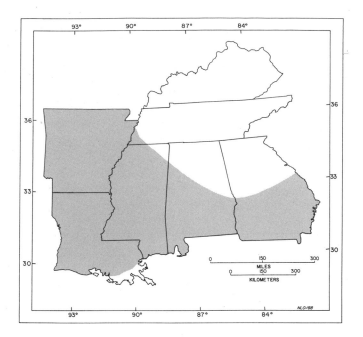

Photo courtesy R. W. Manning

Order Lagomorpha

Lagomorphs

The order Lagomorpha comprises two living families, the Ochotonidae (pikas) and the Leporidae (hares and rabbits). Only representatives of the latter are found in the south-central states, though lagomorphs are distributed almost worldwide, occurring all across the Northern Hemisphere, including Greenland and many arctic islands, in the northern half of South America, and throughout Africa and southeastern Asia. They have been introduced onto Australia and New Zealand and elsewhere. There are 12 modern genera and about 65 Recent species. Two genera and six species of leporids are found in the seven-state region here considered.

The fossil history of this order can be traced back to late Paleocene times, but its relationships to other groups have been in question. Once considered a suborder of Rodentia (Duplicidentata), lagomorphs subsequently have been thought related to a number of other mammalian groups, including marsupials, insectivores, primates, artiodactyls, and other ungulate assemblages. More recently, it has come to be accepted that Rodentia and Lagomorpha probably share a common ancestral stock, divergence taking place in the early Cenozoic. Members of both orders have an enlarged pair of incisors, both above and below, and a broad diastema between the incisors and the cheekteeth. However, lagomorphs have a small pair of upper incisors behind the first pair, and their pattern of mastication of food with the cheekteeth is a transverse grinding uncharacteristic of rodents. Furthermore, the skulls of lagomorphs are fenestrate and some of the larger long bones are hollow—both adaptations to lighten the body load for rapid locomotion. The dental formula of Recent species is 2/1, 0/0, 3/2, 2–3/3, total 26 or 28 (all species in the south-central region have 28 teeth).

Key to Lagomorphs

1. Interparietal bone distinct, not fused to parietals; hind foot 115 or less 2
1'. Interparietal bone indistinct, completely fused to parietals; hind foot usually 120 or more (except in smallest *Lepus americanus*) 5
2. Greatest length of skull more than 76; hind foot rarely less than 100 .... *Sylvilagus aquaticus*
2'. Greatest length of skull less than 76; hind foot rarely more than 95 . 3
3. Anterior extension of supraorbital process small and blunt, or essentially absent; postorbital process fused to skull only at posterior tip, if

at all; auditory bulla smaller than foramen magnum; black spot between ears .... *Sylvilagus transitionalis*

3'. Anterior extension of supraorbital process rounded or pointed but
always present; postorbital process fused to skull for half or more its
length; auditory bulla larger than foramen magnum; no black spot
between ears 4

4.   Tail dingy bluish to grayish ventrally; postorbital processes fused to
skull for five-sixths of length or throughout .... *Sylvilagus palustris*

4'. Tail whitish ventrally; postorbital processes fused to skull only in posterior half .... *Sylvilagus floridanus*

5.   Ear less than 90; tail less than 60; no anterior projection of supraorbital process .... *Lepus americanus*

5'. Ear more than 90; tail more than 60; pronounced anterior projection
of supraorbital process .... *Lepus californicus*

Figure 2. *Dorsal views of skulls of* Lepus americanus *(left) and* Sylvilagus pal-ustris *(right). Note that the interparietal bone at the posterior end of the skull is separate from the parietals in* Sylvilagus *but fused with the parietals in* Lepus. *Modified from Hall (1981).*

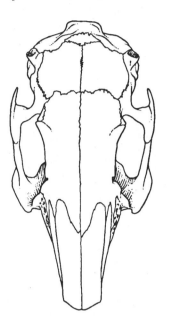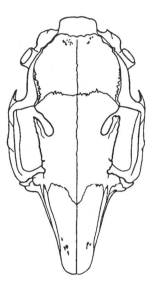

Sylvilagus aquaticus

Swamp Rabbit

Distribution. The swamp rabbit is found throughout much of the south-central region, being absent in parts of Georgia, southeastern Alabama, and eastern Kentucky and Tennessee. It ranges westward to southeastern Kansas and the eastern parts of Oklahoma and Texas, and northward to southern Illinois and adjacent Indiana.

Description. Largest member of genus *Sylvilagus.* Dorsum brownish, blackish brown middorsally; nape with dull rusty patch; venter and underside of tail whitish; upper surface of hind feet tan. Total length, 450–540; tail, 60–75; hind foot, 95–115; ear, 60–80; weight, 1.65–2.65 kg.

Natural History. This rabbit is a denizen of floodplain forests, wooded bottomlands, briar and honeysuckle patches, and canebrakes. It favors damp to wet substrates and readily swims to escape predators or to move from one area to another. Its presence is indicated by piles of fecal pellets. These rabbits are mostly nocturnal, as are all other species of *Sylvilagus,* spending the day in a self-made depression or "form" in a grassy area, beneath a bush or other ground vegetation, or in a hollow log or tree. Swamp rabbits utilize elevated objects such as stumps or hummocks as defecation sites. They eat a variety of plant material, including grasses, sedges, shrubs, and twigs and bark of trees.

Swamp rabbits probably breed year-round, at least in the southern parts of their range. Females are polyestrous, and ovulation is induced. The gestation period is 35 to 40 days, after which a litter of one to six (averaging three) blind, helpless, thinly furred young are born, weighing about 60 grams each. The young are reared in a nest under a fallen log or roots of a tree. Their eyes open after about a week, and they begin to leave the immediate area of the nest in two weeks. Females have postpartum estrus and may produce four or five litters annually. Swamp rabbits born early in the season may breed the same year. The average adult life-span has been estimated at 1.8 years.

Home ranges vary in size with habitat and season, but most fall between 2 and 20 acres. Unlike other rabbits, *S. squaticus* has few predators, the most significant being humans. Flooding poses a problem, especially to young. Nematodes, cestodes, and trematodes have been reported as endoparasites; fleas, ticks, and mites are known ectoparasites.

Selected Reference. Chapman and Feldhamer (1981).

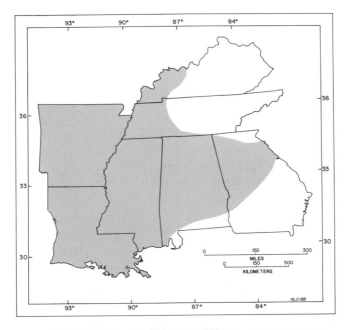

Photo courtesy R. H. Maslowski

Sylvilagus floridanus

Eastern Cottontail

Distribution. The most widespread member of the genus *Sylvilagus,* this species occurs throughout the eastern United States, northward to southernmost Canada and westward almost to the Rocky Mountains. It is found also in the American Southwest, and southward through much of Latin America. It inhabits each of the states in the south-central region.

Description. Medium-sized cottontail; dorsum grayish to brownish, sprinkled with blackish hairs; nape rust-colored; venter whitish except in throat region, which is brownish, feet whitish. Total length, 390–450; tail, 40–60; hind foot, 85–105; ear, 50–60; weight, 0.8–1.5 kg.

Natural History. The eastern cottontail is a familiar North American mammal because of its broad range, its high visibility and abundance in many areas, and its importance as a game species. It is primarily a denizen of eastern deciduous forests and forest edge habitats, but it also lives in grasslands, along weedy fencerows, and in similar habitats. It has become commensal with humans around farms and even in cities. Its nests are slanted holes in the ground beneath overhead cover, usually lined with stems, fur, or leaves. Much of its activity is crepuscular and nocturnal, but it may be active in daytime as well. Forbs and grasses make up much of its diet in the warm months; in winter, in addition to such greens as may be available, these rabbits browse on twigs and tree bark. They obtain most of their water from food.

The breeding season of the eastern cottontail extends throughout the year in much of the south-central region. Females give birth annually to as many as seven litters of one to nine young (usually three to five) after a gestation period of about 30 days. Postpartum estrus occurs. Neonates weigh 35 to 45 grams. Their eyes open seven to eight days after birth, and they are able to leave the fur-lined nest in about two weeks; they gain full independence at four to five weeks of age.

Eastern cottontails are primarily solitary animals, although they sometimes seem colonial when populations are high. Home ranges of females are 5 to 15 acres, those of males somewhat larger. Ranges overlap broadly, though breeding females may be territorial. Densities of up to five rabbits per acre have been reported. Countless numbers are killed each year by vehicles on roadways, and many fall prey to carnivores and raptors.

Selected References. Chapman *et al.* (1980); Hill (1972).

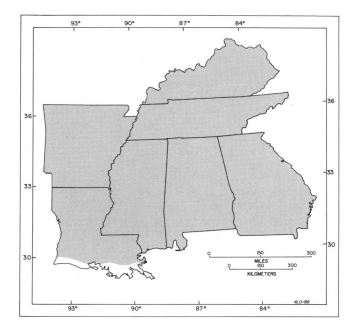

Photo courtesy J. K. Jones, Jr.

Sylvilagus palustris

Marsh Rabbit

Distribution. This species inhabits the southeastern United States, occurring from southeastern Virginia southward through the eastern parts of North and South Carolina, eastern and southern Georgia, and Florida, thence westward through the Florida Panhandle to Mobile Bay in southern Alabama. Its range abuts that of *S. aquaticus* in Georgia and Alabama.

Description. Larger than *S. floridanus* but smaller than *S. aquaticus*. Dorsum dark reddish brown to blackish brown; venter whitish centrally, pale grayish brown to buff elsewhere; tail dingy gray or bluish gray ventrally (white in other species of *Sylvilagus*); feet slender, reddish to buffy. Total length, 410–450; tail, 30–40; hind foot, 85–95; ear, 45–55; weight, 1.0–2.2 kg.

Natural History. Like other species of *Sylvilagus,* the marsh rabbit generally is nocturnal in its habits. It spends daylight hours resting in a "form," a usually well hidden depression dug out with the aid of the long claws on its front feet. *S. palustris* lives primarily in and around marshes and swamps, including brackish water along the East Coast. These rabbits are excellent swimmers and readily take to water. They feed on a variety of lowland plants, such as cattails, rushes, and cane, and also consume twigs and leaves of trees, shrubs, and woody vines. This and other lagomorphs practice coprophagy. Availability of water seems to be the most important limiting factor in distribution of this species.

Marsh rabbits are hunted by humans both for sport and for food. They are preyed upon by great horned owls, harriers, and other birds of prey, small carnivores, and alligators, and the young are eaten by large snakes. Internally they harbor cestodes and nematodes, whereas ticks, fleas, and botflies are known ectoparasites. Destruction of suitable habitats by man is the only long-term threat to the marsh rabbit.

Both males and females are sexually active year-round. The gestation period has been estimated at between 30 and 37 days. Fully adult females give birth to several litters annually (five or six in some instances); litter size ranged from three to five young in a study in Georgia. The altricial neonates are born in a nest lined with grass and fur situated in a depression on the surface of the ground. They do not leave the immediate vicinity of the nest until weaned.

Selected Reference. Chapman and Wilner (1981).

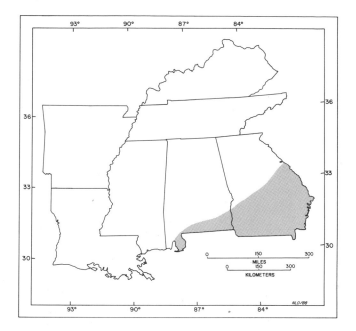

Photo courtesy J. N. Layne

Sylvilagus transitionalis

New England Cottontail

Distribution. This cottontail is known only in the eastern United States, from near the Canadian border in New Hampshire southward in the Appalachians to northeastern Alabama and northern Georgia. In the seven-state region, it occurs also in southeastern Kentucky and eastern Tennessee.

Description. Medium-sized cottontail resembling *S. floridanus,* with which it is sympatric and with which it is known to hybridize. Dorsum pinkish buff to ochraceous buff, overlain with distinct blackish wash; black spot usually located between ears; venter whitish. Ears relatively short and rounded, shorter than those of *S. floridanus.* Supraordinal process short or obsolete; postorbital process thin and tapering, rarely in contact with skull posteriorly; bullae small. Total length, 385–430; tail, 35–58; hind foot, 89–97; ear, 54–63; weight, 0.7–1.0 kg.

Natural History. This rabbit is primarily an inhabitant of dense woodlands and mountainous areas. It does, however, live at sea level in the northern part of its distribution. Its home range, which may shift seasonally, encompasses from about half an acre to two acres or more, sometimes linearly. This cottontail tends to be secretive, rarely straying far from suitable cover, and most of its activity is nocturnal. In summer, more than half of its diet consists of grasses and clovers. Other foods include herbaceous plants and shrubs, twigs, buds, seeds, and fruit. Like other lagomorphs, *S. transitionalis* engages in coprophagy, reingesting green fecal material.

Females produce two or three litters annually, of 3 to 8 young per litter (averaging 5.2 in one study). The gestation period is 28 days. Young are born blind and helpless in a nest lined with fur and grass. Nests are located in depressions in the ground, covered over by a cap of grasses and fur that is itself covered over by twigs and leaves when the female is away. The female begins nest building about 72 hours prior to parturition. Lactation continues about 16 days, after which the young eat solid food. Sex ratios of young were essentially equal in one study, but males outnumbered females by about two to one in another.

Fleas, ticks, and occasionally botflies are known external parasites, and numerous internal parasites have been reported. Potential predators include several carnivores and large raptorial birds; however, not straying far from cover serves as some protection against predation.

Selected Reference. Chapman (1975).

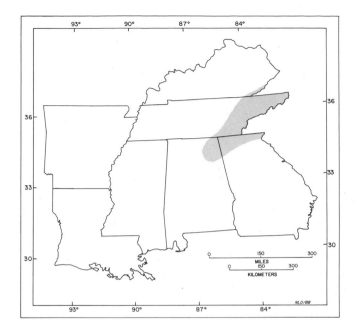

Photo courtesy J. F. Parnell

Lepus americanus

Snowshoe Hare

Distribution. This is a lagomorph of boreal North America. It ranges across Canada and Alaska, except in the extreme north, and occurs also in the mountains of the western United States, and across North Dakota through the Great Lakes region to New England. Formerly it was found in the Appalachian chain southward to eastern Tennessee.

L. americanus was found within historic times in the mountains of eastern Tennessee but has not been recorded there for many years. The well-known mammalogist Remington Kellogg wrote in 1939 that these "hares were formerly present in the mountainous district extending from Mount Guyot to White Rock, Cocke County [Tennessee]." He noted that local residents often saw them in the cold months and recognized them because they turned white in winter. They usually were found in "rhododendron thickets near the summits of peaks."

Description. Smallest New World member of genus *Lepus*. In summer, dorsum rusty brown with blackish brown wash, especially middorsally; nose dark brown, nostrils edged with white; venter white to grayish white; ears tipped with black; tail blackish above, whitish below. In winter, pelage white except for black-tipped ears. Total length, 370–460; tail, 25–45; hind foot, 110–140; ear, 62–80; weight, usually 1.0–2.3 kg.

Natural History. The snowshoe hare occupies wooded habitats, including secondary growth and brushy areas. This animal is crepuscular and nocturnal, resting in a secluded "form" during the day. Its foods consist mainly of succulent green plants in summer and woody vegetation in winter. Populations vary greatly, reaching a peak every 9 or 10 years, followed by a drastic reduction in numbers. Populations of several carnivores, especially the lynx, that depend on *L. americanus* as a principal food source suffer accordingly. This hare is of considerable economic interest, being hunted for food and sport and for its pelt.

Females give birth to three or four litters annually of one to seven young (usually two to five). Gestation lasts about 35 days. The breeding season extends from early spring through late summer. Young, like those of other hares, are precocial, being well furred and having eyes open at birth; young of rabbits, by contrast, are altricial. Snowshoe neonates are fully active within a week and weaned when about three weeks old.

Selected References. Bittner and Rongstad (1982); Keith and Windberg (1978); Kellogg (1939).

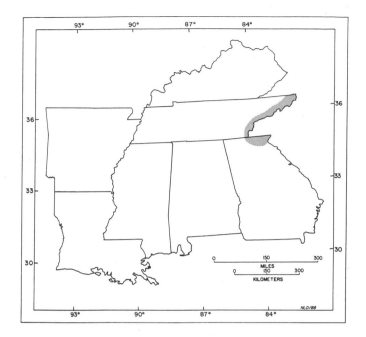

Photo courtesy H. S. Korber

Lepus californicus

Black-Tailed Jackrabbit

Distribution. This jackrabbit has a broad range in semiarid western North America. It is found from central Mexico northward to Montana and Washington west of the Continental Divide and to South Dakota in the East. In the seven-state region, it has invaded western Arkansas within historic times apparently in response to land-clearing operations.

Description. Largest leporid of south-central states. Dorsum grayish or grayish brown overall, washed with wavy blackish markings; sides grayish; venter white; tail with black dorsal stripe above that extends onto back, white below. Total length, 535–585; tail, 70–90; hind foot, 120–135; ear, 110–125; weight, 1.5–3.5 kg.

Natural History. This jackrabbit is a denizen of open country—grasslands with scattered shrubs, yucca, and cacti, rangelands, and some cultivated areas. In Arkansas, it inhabits pastures and cropland cleared of timber. These hares avoid wooded areas and those covered with heavy brush. They emerge at night to feed on grasses, forbs, and crops, especially alfalfa; in winter they eat dry vegetation, twigs, buds, and even cacti. Their home ranges may be as large as two square miles but are much smaller in good habitat. Like other lagomorphs, they void two kinds of feces—hard, dry pellets at night and soft, green pellets by day. They reingest the latter, which are a source of vitamins, and synthesize them intestinally.

Jackrabbits can run 35 to 40 miles per hour over short distances. This speed, coupled with keen eyesight, hearing, and smell, is their principal means of detecting and avoiding predators. Nevertheless, coyotes, foxes, eagles, and large hawks prey on them, and weasels, hawks, and owls take a toll on young. By day, these hares rest in a simple "form," hollowed out anew each morning, frequently at the base of a shrub but oftentimes in open grassland. Here they lie, motionless and with ears laid back, but ever alert to flee, at the last moment, any approaching danger. Extremely dense populations of this jackrabbit may occur during periods of drought.

Breeding occurs throughout the year, especially when green vegetation is available. Females bear one to four litters a year of one to eight young. Ovulation is induced. Gestation lasts 41 to 47 days. Neonates are precocial, being well furred and mobile, and having open eyes. They begin to eat solid food by the tenth day. Longevity of eight years has been reported.

Selected References. Hansen and Flinders (1969); Jones *et al.* (1983); Tiemeier *et al.* (1965).

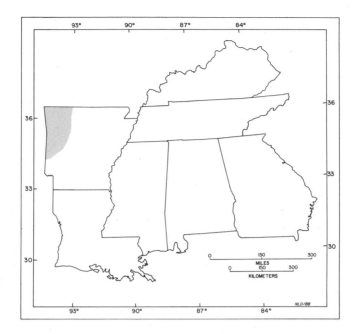

Photo courtesy K. Steibben

Order Rodentia

Rodents

Fossils of rodents date from the late Paleocene, about 60 million years ago. Rodents probably share a common ancestral stock with rabbits and allied groups, as explained in the ordinal account of the Lagomorpha. Rodents constitute the most diverse group of living mammals, making up more than 30 families, approximately 490 genera, and some 1,600 species. Members of the order occur naturally on all major land masses except New Zealand and Antarctica, and some species have been introduced widely within historic times by humans.

Rodents are characterized by a single pair of ever-growing incisors above and below, a distinct diastema between the incisors and the cheek-teeth, and a dental formula that never exceeds 1/1, 0/0, 2/1, 3/3, total 22. Most rodents are strictly terrestrial, but some are semiaquatic, some are fossorial, some are scansorial, and some are true gliders. The diet of many rodents is primarily herbivorous, but some also eat insects and other small animals. Some rodents are strictly seasonal breeders, whereas others breed more often, some year-round.

Seven families of Rodentia are native to the south-central states (we here refer all cricetine rats and mice to the family Muridae and jumping mice to the family Dipodidae) and an eighth, Myocastoridae, has been introduced. Thirty-five indigenous and four introduced species of rodents are treated in this book; two noninterbreeding subspecies of *Peromyscus maniculatus* are included separately. The key to rodent families is followed by keys for the individual families (Sciuridae, Geomyidae, Muridae, and Dipodidae) that contain more than one species occurring in this region.

Key to Families of Rodents

1. Modified for semiaquatic life, hind feet webbed; lower incisor more than 6.0 in width at alveolus 2
1'. Not especially modified for semiaquatic life (except *Ondatra* and *Neofiber*), hind feet not webbed; lower incisor less than 5.5 in width at alveolus 3
2. Tail flattened dorsoventrally, its breadth approximately 25 percent of its length; infraorbital canal smaller than foramen magnum
    . . . . Castoridae
2'. Tail not flattened dorsoventrally, its breadth less than 10 percent of its length; infraorbital canal larger than foramen magnum
    . . . . *Myocastoridae
3. Sharp quills on dorsum and tail; infraorbital canal larger than foramen magnum . . . . Erethizontidae

3'.   No quills on any part of body; infraorbital canal never larger than foramen magnum 4
4.   Hairs on tail usually distichous; skull with distinct postorbital processes .... Sciuridae
4'.   Hairs on tail not distichous; skull lacking distinct postorbital processes 5
5.   External fur-lined cheek pouches present; cheekteeth 4/4 6
5'.   No external fur-lined cheek pouches; cheekteeth 4/3 or 3/3 7
6.   Tail more than three-fourths length of head and body; hind feet larger than forefeet; tympanic bullae exposed on posterodorsal part of skull
      .... Heteromyidae
6'.   Tail much less than three-fourths length of head and body; hind feet smaller than forefeet; tympanic bullae not exposed on posterodorsal part of skull .... Geomyidae
7.   Tail much longer than head and body; hind feet noticeably elongate; cheekteeth 4/3 (*Zapus*) or 3/3 (*Napaeozapus*) .... Dipodidae
7'.   Tail about equal in length to or shorter than head and body; hind feet not noticeably elongate; cheekteeth 3/3 .... Muridae

Key to Sciurids

1.   Skin between forelimbs and hind limbs noticeably loose, forming gliding membrane; narrow interorbital region V-shaped 2
1'.   Skin between forelimbs and hind limbs not noticeably loose; interorbital region not V-shaped 3
2.   Hairs of venter white to base; total length less than 260; greatest length of skull less than 36 .... *Glaucomys volans*
2'.   Hairs of venter gray, white only at tips; total length more than 260; greatest length of skull more than 36 .... *Glaucomys sabrinus*
3.   Size large, length of hind foot more than 70; skull relatively massive, greatest length more than 70 .... *Marmota monax*
3'.   Size smaller, length of hind foot less than 65; skull smaller and relatively delicate, greatest length less than 70 4
4.   Dorsal pelage striped; infraorbital foramen (no extensive canal) piercing zygomatic plate .... *Tamias striatus*
4'.   Dorsal pelage not striped; distinct infraorbital canal passing between zygomatic plate and rostrum 5
5.   Total length less than 400; greatest length of skull less than 55; anterior border of orbit opposite P4 ....*Tamiasciurus hudsonicus*
5'.   Total length more than 400; greatest length of skull more than 55; anterior border of orbit opposite M1 6
6.   Pelage grayish overall dorsally, white ventrally; tips of hairs on tail

white throughout; premolars usually 2/1 (P3 much reduced and occasionally absent) .... *Sciurus carolinensis*

6'.   Pelage variable overall dorsally, orangish brown to dark grayish with a
blackish head, and depending on geographic origin, buff, whitish or
orangish ventrally; tips of hairs on tail not white throughout; premolars 1/1 .... *Sciurus niger*

Key to Geomyids

1.   Nasals hourglass-shaped (constricted near middle); occurring in Alabama and Georgia .... *Geomys pinetis*
1'.   Nasals not hourglass-shaped; occurring in Arkansas and Louisiana
.... *Geomys breviceps*

Key to Murids

1.   Annulations of scales easily visible on sparsely haired tail; cheekteeth
with three longitudinal rows of cusps 2
1'.   Annulations of scales on tail nearly or completely concealed by pelage (except in *Neofiber* and *Ondatra*, which are semiaquatic); cheekteeth with two longitudinal rows of cusps or prismatic 4
2.   Total length less than 200; greatest length of skull less than 25; occlusial surface of upper incisors notched in lateral view ... *Mus musculus*
2'.   Total length more than 300; greatest length of skull more than 35;
occlusial surface of upper incisors smooth in lateral view 3
3.   Tail longer than head and body; usually 10 mammae in females; temporal ridges on skull strongly bowed outward posteriorly
.... *Rattus rattus*
3'.   Tail about same length as or shorter than head and body; usually 12
mammae in females; temporal ridges on skull approximately parallel
.... *Rattus norvegicus*
4.   Total length more than 215; greatest length of skull usually more
than 30; maxillary toothrow usually more than 4.3 5
4'.   Total length less than 215; greatest length of skull usually less than
30; maxillary toothrow usually less than 4.3 9
5.   Underfur dense and woolly, modified for semiaquatic life; tail flattened laterally or rounded, sparsely haired, scaly; posterior margin of
orbit shelflike and nearly right-angled 6
5'.   Underfur not dense and woolly; tail rounded and generally covered
with hair; posterior margin of orbit not shelflike or right-angled 7
6.   Total length more than 400; tail laterally flattened; greatest length of
skull more than 55 .... *Ondatra zibethicus*
6'.   Total length less than 400; tail rounded; greatest length of skull less
than 55 .... *Neofiber alleni*

7.   Dorsal pelage harsh, grizzled brownish to dark grayish; tail much shorter than head and body; cheekteeth cuboid, third molar not much smaller than first; zygomatic plate with strong anterodorsal projection .... *Sigmodon hispidus*

7'.   Dorsal pelage smooth, grayish brown to dark buffy brown; tail not much shorter than head and body; cheekteeth elongate, third molar noticeably smaller than first; zygomatic plate lacking anterodorsal projection 8

8.   Hind foot less than 35; greatest length of skull less than 36; cusps on upper molars prominent, more or less opposite each other; palatine vacuities extending posteriorly to, or beyond, first upper molars .... *Oryzomys palustris*

8'.   Hind foot more than 35; greatest length of skull more than 36; molars semiprismatic, with deep re-entrant angles; palatine vacuities not extending posteriorly to first upper molars .... *Neotoma floridana*

9.   Cheekteeth cuspidate; tail more than 45 percent total length 10

9'.   Cheekteeth prismatic; tail less than 35 percent total length 20

10.   Face of upper incisor conspicuously grooved; greatest length of skull less than 22.5 11

10'. Face of upper incisor smooth; greatest length of skull more than 22.5 14

11.   First primary fold of third upper molar at least as long as second, both folds extending more than halfway across crown of tooth; worn occlusal surface of left third lower molar S-shaped; tail usually more than 80 .... *Reithrodontomys fulvescens*

11'. First primary fold of third upper molar distinctly shorter than second, extending less than halfway across crown of tooth; worn occlusal surface of left third lower molar C-shaped; tail less than 80, usually 70 or less 12

12.   Distinct labial ridge, often with cusplets, on first two lower molars; ranges over most of south-central region ......*Reithrodontomys humulis*

12'. No labial ridge on lower molars; in south-central region occurs only in Arkansas 13

13.   Tail distinctly bicolored, with dark stripe above, shorter than head and body; breadth of braincase 9.6 or (usually) less .... *Reithrodontomys montanus*

13'. Tail not distinctly bicolored, about equal in length to head and body; breadth of braincase 9.5 or (usually) more ... *Reithrodontomys megalotis*

14.   Ears same color as head, reddish to golden buff; posterior palatine foramina nearer posterior edge of palate than anterior palatine foramina .... *Ochrotomys nuttalli*

14'. Ears different in color from head, somewhat more grayish and usually rimmed with white; posterior palatine foramina about equidistant between anterior palatine foramina and posterior edge of palate .. 15

15. Size relatively large; hind foot 22 or more; greatest length of skull averaging more than 28 16

15'. Size smaller; hind foot 22 or (usually) less; greatest length of skull averaging less than 28 17

16. Dorsum pale brownish buff, venter whitish overall; tail longer, averaging about 100; braincase more inflated, breadth more than 13 .... *Peromyscus attwateri*

16'. Dorsum dark buffy brown, venter dull white to tawny grayish overall; tail shorter, averaging about 80; braincase less inflated, breadth less than 13 .... *Peromyscus gossypinus*

17. Hind foot usually 18 or less; greatest length of skull less than 25; tail averaging about 40 percent of total length 18

17'. Hind foot usually 19 or more; greatest length of skull more than 25; tail averaging more than 40 percent of total length 19

18. Dorsum pale buffy gray; tail sharply bicolored with narrow middorsal brownish stripe; palatine foramina 4.7 or less .... *Peromyscus polionotus*

18'. Dorsum dark brownish; tail distinctly bicolored but lacking narrow middorsal stripe; palatine foramina averaging about 5.0 ....*Peromyscus maniculatus bairdii*

19. Tail averaging 85, distinctly bicolored; rostrum not much expanded laterally at base .... *Peromyscus maniculatus nubiterrae*

19'. Tail averaging 80, darker above than below but not distinctly bicolored; more or less pronounced lateral bulbous expansion at base of rostrum ....*Peromyscus leucopus*

20. Tail short, approximately same length as hind foot; distinct groove on face of upper incisor .... *Synaptomys cooperi*

20'. Tail relatively long, longer than hind foot (only barely so in some *Microtus pinetorum*); face of upper incisor smooth or at most with shallow, faint groove 21

21. Dorsum with broad reddish to reddish brown stripe, contrasting with grayish flanks; posterior border of palate shelflike .... *Clethrionomys gapperi*

21'. Dorsum lacking reddish to reddish brown stripe, more or less same color as flanks; posterior border of palate rounded or with median spine 22

22. Nose yellowish to orangish; third upper molar with four re-entrant angles on each side .... *Microtus chrotorrhinus*

22'. Nose essentially same color as dorsum, not yellowish or orangish; third upper molar with three or fewer re-entrant angles on each side 23

23. Dorsal pelage molelike (soft and smooth), reddish to reddish brown;

tail less than 29; skull wide and flat; last upper molar with two re-entrant angles on each side .... *Microtus pinetorum*

23'. Dorsal pelage relatively coarse, grizzled brownish to blackish; tail more than 26 (usually more than 29); last upper molar with two or three re-entrant angles on each side, if two then skull high and narrow 24

24. Venter buff to ochraceous; third upper molar with two re-entrant angles on each side .... *Microtus ochrogaster*

24'. Venter silvery to grayish; third upper molar with three re-entrant angles on each side .... *Microtus pennsylvanicus*

Key to Dipodids

1. Tip of tail usually white; flanks with distinct orangish tinge; cheek-teeth 3/3 .... *Napaeozapus insignis*

1'. Tip of tail not white; flanks olivaceous; cheekteeth 4/3
.... *Zapus hudsonius*

Table 3. Dental Formulae of Rodents of the South-Central States

Genus	Incisors	Canines	Premolars	Molars	Total
Tamias	1/1	0/0	1/1	3/3	20
Marmota	1/1	0/0	2/1	3/3	22
Sciurus	1/1	0/0	2/1	3/3	22
Tamiasciurus	1/1	0/0	1/1	3/3	20*
Glaucomys	1/1	0/0	2/1	3/3	22
Geomys	1/1	0/0	1/1	3/3	20
Chaetodipus	1/1	0/0	1/1	3/3	20
Castor	1/1	0/0	1/1	3/3	20
Oryzomys	1/1	0/0	0/0	3/3	16
Reithrodontomys	1/1	0/0	0/0	3/3	16
Peromyscus	1/1	0/0	0/0	3/3	16
Ochrotomys	1/1	0/0	0/0	3/3	16
Sigmodon	1/1	0/0	0/0	3/3	16
Neotoma	1/1	0/0	0/0	3/3	16
Clethrionomys	1/1	0/0	0/0	3/3	16
Microtus	1/1	0/0	0/0	3/3	16
Neofiber	1/1	0/0	0/0	3/3	16
Ondatra	1/1	0/0	0/0	3/3	16
Synaptomys	1/1	0/0	0/0	3/3	16
Mus	1/1	0/0	0/0	3/3	16
Rattus	1/1	0/0	0/0	3/3	16
Zapus	1/1	0/0	1/0	3/3	18
Napaeozapus	1/1	0/0	0/0	3/3	16
Erethizon	1/1	0/0	1/1	3/3	20
Myocaster	1/1	0/0	1/1	3/3	16

* A vestigial second upper premolar sometimes is present in *Tamiasciurus*.

Tamias striatus

Eastern Chipmunk

Distribution. This chipmunk is an inhabitant of the deciduous forests of eastern North America, from southeastern Canada almost to the Gulf Coast, and westward to Manitoba, the eastern Dakotas, and eastern Oklahoma. The species occurs in at least portions of all seven south-central states.

Description. One of smallest sciurids of region. Dorsum prominently marked with five dark brownish, two whitish, and two orangish to brownish stripes; rump yellowish brown to orangish; white facial stripes on either side of eye; venter white; tail grizzled brownish above, orangish below, with grayish border. Total length, 230–280; tail, 75–105; hind foot, 34–38; ear, 17–21; weight, 90–130 g.

Natural History. This sciurid occupies wooded areas with a dense canopy and sparsely covered forest floor, as well as open brushy habitats, ravines, and deciduous growth along stream borders. It is reasonably tolerant of humans and may live in wooded suburban areas and the vicinity of farmsteads. Both sexes vocalize, and the characteristic chirps can be heard when these strictly diurnal animals are active. Chipmunks hibernate during the colder months of the year.

Home ranges vary from less than 100 square yards to more than 2 acres, depending on habitat and season. Populations as high as 20 per acre have been reported, but the norm is about 10 per acre in optimal habitat, fewer elsewhere. Burrow systems, up to 30 feet long and 3 feet deep, have one or more large storage chambers. The nest chamber is lined with leaves. The burrow entrance usually is located at the base of a tree, bush, or rock, or among exposed roots. These chipmunks readily climb in search of food or to escape harm but rarely nest above ground.

The eastern chipmunk's diet consists principally of seeds and nuts, some of which are cached. Insects, other invertebrates, and fungi also are important foods, and this chipmunk occasionally eats small vertebrates. Its enemies include hawks, weasels, foxes, bobcats, and snakes. Females bear one or two litters of two to eight young (usually four or five) after 31 or 32 days of gestation. Young from the first litter are born in late March and April, those from the second (if produced) in midsummer. Twelve years is the known longevity in confinement, eight in the wild, although the average life-span is much shorter.

Selected Reference. Snyder (1982).

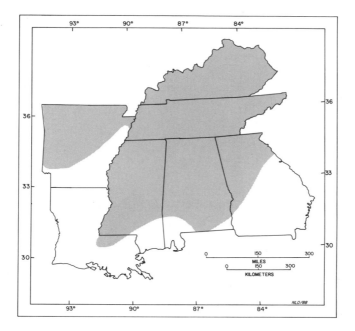

Photo courtesy E. C. Birney

Marmota monax

Woodchuck

Distribution. The woodchuck occupies a broad range in temperate and sub-boreal North America, from eastern Alaska all across central Canada, and south in the eastern United States to southern Arkansas and central Alabama.

Description. Largest sciurid of south-central region, heavy bodied, with relatively short tail and limbs. Dorsum grizzled brownish except whitish around nose; venter somewhat paler than dorsum, feet dark brown to blackish, tail darker than dorsum. Head broad and relatively short, ears relatively small and rounded, tipped with whitish. Adults molt once a year in summer. Total length, 500–650; tail 120–160; hind foot, 70–90; ear, 25–32; weight, which varies seasonally in all hibernating sciurids, 2.5–5.4 kg.

Natural History. This species hibernates for four to five months during the winter. It is an animal of the forest edge, rarely found in deep woods or in open fields or pastures far removed from brushy fencerows or other cover. It often is seen in wooded suburban areas. Woodchucks are almost strictly herbivorous. They eat a variety of weedy plants but seem especially fond of legumes like clover and alfalfa. They also eat fruits such as apples and berries, as well as row and garden crops when available. This is a sport and game mammal in many areas and an agricultural pest in others; the meat is said to be delicious if properly prepared.

The woodchuck is an excellent digger, and its burrows, identified by a mound at the mouth, frequently are extensive. They may reach 4 feet or more in depth and about 30 feet in length, and usually have two or three entrances, at least one a well-concealed escape route. These diurnal animals are solitary, except for females with young, and are strongly territorial. They are sometimes referred to as "whistle pigs" because of the cry they emit when excited or in danger. Like other sciurids, woodchucks host a variety of parasites. Large carnivores prey on them, and hawks occasionally take young.

Breeding takes place upon emergence from hibernation in spring. Females bear a single litter of two to nine young (usually four or five) after a gestation period of 31 to 33 days. Neonates are blind and helpless at birth, and weigh about 30 grams. They remain in the maternal burrow for about four weeks.

Selected References. Grizzell (1955); Lee and Funderburg (1982).

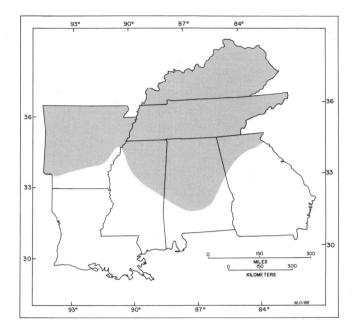

Photo courtesy R. W. Barbour

Sciurus carolinensis

Eastern Gray Squirrel

Distribution. This gray squirrel is endemic in eastern North America, occurring from Quebec southward to Florida, and westward to Manitoba in the North and Texas in the South. It is found throughout the south-central states except in southernmost Louisiana.

Description. Medium-sized of three tree squirrels in region. Easily distinguished from *S. niger,* with which it is broadly sympatric, by its overall grayish color dorsally, whitish color ventrally, and whitish to pale grayish-tipped hairs on tail, although color variants occur. Total length, 420–480; tail, 200–230; hind foot, 50–68; ear, 23–31; weight, 350–650 g.

Natural History. This squirrel is typical of hardwood forests in the eastern United States, but it also lives in mixed forests and in city parks and similar habitats in urban areas. Gray squirrels are diurnal and may be seen any time of day, but most activity is in the early morning and late afternoon. Like the fox squirrel, *S. carolinensis* has two kinds of nests, one built of leaves and grasses in a tree cavity or hollow, and the other a ball of leaves and twigs woven in the open between small branches or in the fork of a branch. The latter are occupied principally by young and by adults in warm weather. Gray squirrels are heavily parasitized, supporting fleas, lice, mites, ticks, and botfly larvae externally, and cestodes, nematodes, trematodes, protozoans, and spiny-headed worms internally.

These squirrels forage for food both in trees and on the ground. Their diet includes seeds, fruits, buds, flowers, leaves, inner bark, and some insects, bird eggs, and young birds. Nuts, such as acorns, walnuts, and beechnuts, also are harvested in late summer and autumn and buried singly or in small lots, most to be relocated in winter by the squirrel's keen sense of smell. This caching activity, known as "scatter hoarding," is an important means of seed dispersal. Some wooded areas provide an inadequate variety of foods to support sizable populations of this squirrel.

This squirrel and the fox squirrel are important game animals. Both are active year-round. Females produce two litters annually, one in late winter and the other in summer. A litter consists of one to eight young (usually two to four). The gestation period is about 44 days. Young gray squirrels are weaned at about six weeks of age, and females are capable of producing young when about one year old.

Selected References. Allen (1952); Flyger and Gates (1982*a*); Uhlig (1955).

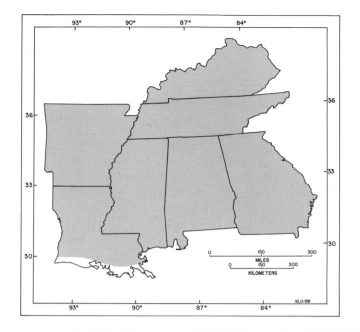

Photo courtesy W. E. Clark

Sciurus niger

Fox Squirrel

Distribution. Principally a native of deciduous and mixed forests in the eastern United States, the fox squirrel ranges westward along river systems to the base of the Rockies, and from southernmost Canada to northernmost Mexico. It occurs throughout the south-central region except in extreme southern Louisiana.

Description. Largest tree squirrel of region. Color variable geographically from pale grayish dorsally with black head in East to brownish orange with paler orangish to yellowish orange belly in West; some southern populations have white ears and feet and partially white faces; black (melanistic) fox squirrels are not uncommon. Total length, 490–620; tail, 230–340; hind foot, 50–70; ear, 19–30; weight to 1.2 kg.

Natural History. Although the fox squirrel favors mature deciduous and pine-oak woodlands, it also is found in open forests, at the forest edge, and in woodlots and riparian timber. Unlike the gray squirrel, the fox squirrel tends to be more active at midday than in morning and late afternoon. Its diet consists of acorns, pine seeds, and other nuts when seasonally available, but it consumes a wide variety of plant and animal foods, including fruits and corn and other grains. Like the gray squirrel, it practices scatter hoarding. Home ranges are three-dimensional, tend to be elliptical, and average between 12 and 50 acres (but may be as large as 100 acres), depending on season, habitat, sex, and age.

Fox squirrels forage more on the ground than gray squirrels and thus are more susceptible to predation by terrestrial carnivores. Owls and hawks also prey on them. These are popular game animals, and hunters take thousands each year. Parasites found on this species are the same as those of the gray squirrel. Occasional fox squirrels have scabies or mange caused by a skin-infecting mite.

These squirrels locate their nests in a tree cavity or construct them of leaves, twigs, Spanish moss, or other plant material in branches of a tree or against the trunk. Occasionally they build nests in stumps, and they readily use nest boxes. They have two reproductive peaks each year, in late winter and mid- to late summer. Litters range from one to six young, averaging three. The gestation period is about 45 days. Young are weaned at about three months of age.

Selected References. Moore (1957); Packard (1956); Weigl *et al.* (1989).

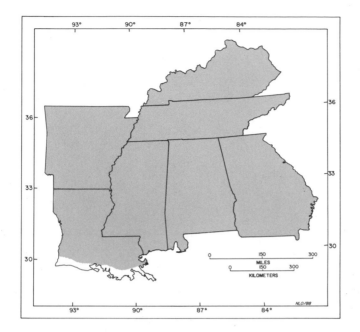

Photo courtesy L. Miller

Tamiasciurus hudsonicus

Red Squirrel

Distribution. This squirrel occupies coniferous and mixed conifer-hardwood forests all across Canada to Alaska, and south in the western mountains to Arizona and New Mexico, in the Great Lakes region to southern Indiana, and in the Appalachian chain to eastern Tennessee, northeasternmost Georgia, and northwestern South Carolina.

Description. Smallest of tree squirrels in south-central region. Dorsum dark reddish brown and venter white to grayish white, separated by blackish lateral stripe; prominent white ring around eye; tail somewhat darker dorsally than back. Total length, 300–350; tail, 110–140; hind foot, 42–54; ear, 20–25; weight averaging 225 g.

Natural History. The red squirrel, sometimes referred to as a "boomer" or "mountain boomer" locally, inhabits primarily spruce-fir forests in the warm months but may be found at somewhat lower elevations in winter. It is a common inhabitant of Great Smoky Mountains National Park, although populations fluctuate considerably. It usually locates its den sites in natural hollows of trees or enlarged woodpecker holes but also uses stumps, rock piles, and other ground-level refuges. One squirrel may occupy several dens within its range. Its diet consists of fruits, berries, seeds, nuts, buds, mushrooms, other plant parts, and occasionally animal material. Its enemies include mustelids—especially marten and fisher where they occur—and other carnivores, raptorial birds, and snakes.

This species is more territorial than its larger relatives. Males vigorously defend breeding territories, vocally and by pursuit; males and females may defend smaller, contiguous territories in the colder months. These squirrels are active by day and in all seasons. Their home ranges usually cover three to six acres. They cache food for winter use, frequently in conspicuous piles termed *middens.* Such larders may contain hundreds of food items, mostly conifer cones and nuts from deciduous trees.

Like other tree squirrels, *T. hudsonicus* is noisy and conspicuous during courtship. Females usually produce two litters a year. The period of gestation is 35 to 40 days. Litters consist of 1 to 10 young, usually 3 to 5, which are born naked, hairless, and with eyes and ears closed. Offspring are weaned at about day 50. Longevity of 10 years has been reported in captivity, but animals that reach maturity in the wild probably survive 3 or 4 years. Like most other squirrels, adult red squirrels molt twice a year.

Selected References. Flyger and Gates (1982*b*); Layne (1954); Smith (1968, 1970, 1978).

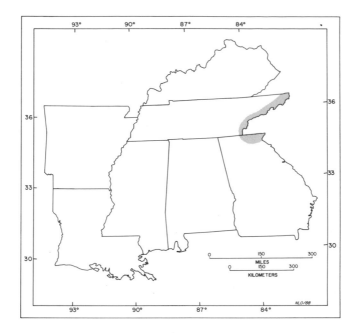

Photo courtesy R. B. Fischer

Glaucomys sabrinus

Northern Flying Squirrel

Distribution. This flying squirrel is found across boreal North America from Alaska to Labrador, and southward in the mountains of the west, to the Great Lakes region, and in the Appalachians to extreme eastern Tennessee, where it is uncommon.

Description. Larger of two New World flying squirrels. Pelage richly colored and relatively thick. Dorsum cinnamon brown to smoky brown, sides of head smoky gray with darker eye ring; venter pale yellowish to ochraceous buff, the hairs gray basally and pale distally; tail grayish buff above, darker toward tip, suffused with orange ventrally. Total length, 270–300; tail, 127–142; hind foot, 35–40; ear, 20–30, weight, 75–125 g.

Natural History. This squirrel usually lives in cloud-shrouded spruce-fir, mixed hemlock, and adjacent mature hardwood forest at higher elevations but has been taken in birch and other deciduous habitats as well, down to an elevation of about 4,000 feet. Flying squirrels are unique among American sciurids in being nocturnal. They are active throughout the year but may aggregate for warmth in winter.

These squirrels usually locate their nests in tree cavities, but occasionally build external shelters about the size of a soccer ball. They line their nests with finely shredded bark, moss, lichens, feathers, grass, and other available materials. Females normally produce two litters annually, one in later winter and another in midsummer. Gestation lasts 37 to 42 days. Young frequently number two to four per litter, but the range is one to six. Neonates weigh five to six grams, are naked, and have eyes and ears closed, but the gliding membrane is clearly evident. Young are weaned when about 60 days old. Normal longevity probably is less than four years.

These squirrels forage in trees or glide gracefully to the ground, where they search for food in leaf litter. Their home ranges average two to three acres; population densities range from one squirrel per six or seven acres to five per acre in excellent habitat. Their diet includes nuts and seeds, buds, fruits, insects, fungi, lichens, and occasionally small vertebrates. Their food-storing behavior is poorly known; caching may not be practiced. Principal predators include owls, hawks, mustelids, canids, and felids. Lice, fleas, mites, ticks, nematodes, cestodes, and protists are known parasites. Escape from predators involves a series of long glides to the bases of trees along a predetermined path.

Selected Reference. Wells-Gosling and Heaney (1984).

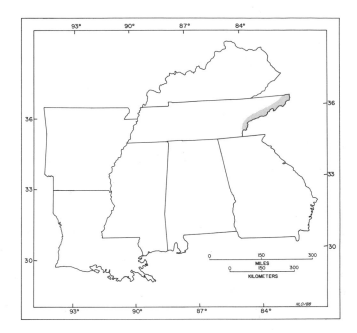

Photo courtesy N. M. Gosling

Glaucomys volans

Southern Flying Squirrel

Distribution. This species ranges throughout the eastern United States, save for southwestern Florida and southernmost Louisiana, westward to Minnesota, Nebraska, and Texas. It also occurs in southeasternmost Canada and in isolated montane populations in Mexico, Guatemala, and Honduras. *G. volans* is found in all seven south-central states.

Description. Smaller than *G. sabrinus*, not so richly colored; pelage silky. Dorsum drab brownish or brownish gray; venter cream-colored, hairs whitish to base; tail pale brownish above, not dark tipped, paler below. Total length, 220–250; tail, 80–110; hind foot, 28–33; ear, 15–20; weight, 40–80 g.

Natural History. This flying squirrel favors mature broad-leaved forests, but it also inhabits mixed coniferous-deciduous woodlands. Flying squirrels do not actually fly; rather, they glide gracefully, using the outstretched fold of skin between their legs (patagium) as the gliding surface along with the flattened tail. In this manner, they can travel 100 feet or more from near the top of one tree to the base of another as a means of movement to and from foraging areas and to escape predators. Like its northern relative, *G. volans* forages both in trees and on the ground.

Females normally breed from midsummer to early winter, bringing forth litters of one to seven young, most often two or three, from late August or September to as late as March. Gestation lasts about 40 days. Newborns are pink and hairless, and have eyes and ears closed; they weigh between three and five grams. Young are weaned in six to eight weeks. Captives have lived 13 years, but the average life-span of wild adults is much shorter.

This species is dependent on tree hollows and nest boxes for denning. These squirrels do not hibernate but may be relatively inactive during periods of cold or inclement weather. Population densities vary with habitat but usually approximate one to three or four squirrels per acre. Breeding females are territorial, but in winter, groups may den together, presumably to conserve energy. Their staple foods are nuts of deciduous trees such as oak and hickory, but they also consume seeds, berries, fruits, buds, bark, blossoms, fungi, lichens, insects, bird eggs, and small vertebrates. They cache nuts for winter use.

Selected References. Dolan and Carter (1977); Linzey and Linzey (1979); Raymond and Layne (1988); Sawyer and Rose (1985).

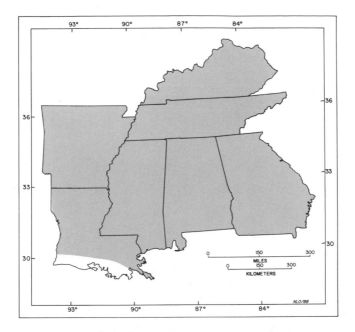

Photo courtesy New York Zoological Society

Geomys breviceps

Baird's Pocket Gopher

Distribution. This pocket gopher ranges from east-central Oklahoma and adjacent eastern Texas southward to the Gulf Coast and eastward to the Mississippi River. In the south-central region, it inhabits the southern two-thirds of Arkansas and the western half of Louisiana.

Description. Adapted for living underground. Front legs stout, with well-developed claws for digging; eyes and ears small. External fur-lined cheek pouches present. Pelage usually dark brownish dorsally, somewhat paler ventrally; irregular white spotting frequent. Melanistic individuals not uncommon, but albinos rare. Tail sparsely haired. Similar to plains pocket gopher except for diploid number of chromosomes (74 in *G. breviceps,* 70 or 72 in *G. bursarius*). Total length, 190–250; tail, 60–75; hind foot, 25–30; weight, 200–400 g. As in other gophers, males appreciably larger than females.

Natural History. These pocket gophers usually are found in reasonably well drained sandy and loamy soils. They dig subsurface burrows as they search for food. The burrow system contains food-storage areas, chambers for deposition of excrement, and, in the deepest part, grass-lined chambers that function as nests. During rainy periods, these gophers move their nest chambers to a higher location in the burrow system. Surface mounds of loose soil indicate the presence of the burrows, in which numerous invertebrates and occasionally small vertebrates also live. Gophers eat roots, tubers, stems, and other parts of plants, as well as some insects. The gopher's breeding season probably lasts from January at least through August. Adult males and females share the same burrow system for a short time during this period; otherwise, they are solitary except for females with young. Gestation probably lasts 40 to 50 days. Litter size ranges from one to eight young, averaging three to four. There is some indication that old females may produce two litters annually. Young gophers grow rapidly and reach sexual maturity at about three months of age.

Pocket gophers harbor few external and internal parasites. Major predators on these mammals are snakes, weasels, badgers, skunks, bobcats, coyotes, hawks, and owls. Gophers may be considered nuisances when they inhabit cemeteries, golf courses, gardens, and cultivated fields. Also, these animals may damage buried cables and plastic pipes by gnawing them. Their burrow systems, however, enhance drainage and mixing of soils.

Selected References. Bohlin and Zimmerman (1982); Heaney and Timm (1983); Sulentich *et al.* (1991).

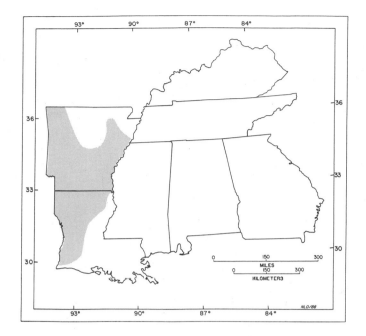

Photo courtesy R. W. Barbour

Geomys pinetis

Southeastern Pocket Gopher

Distribution. This species ranges across the southern parts of Georgia and Alabama, westward to Mobile Bay, and southward through the northern half of Florida. A related species, *Geomys personatus,* is found in southern Texas and adjacent Mexico.

Description. Typical geomyid adaptations for fossorial mode of life, with thickset body and external fur-lined cheek pouches; forelimbs strong and heavily clawed; eyes and pinnae small. Dorsum medium to dark brownish; venter pale brownish gray; tail nearly naked. Total length, 250–305; tail, 81–96; hind foot, 33–37; weight, 220–420 g. Males average 10 percent larger than females. In contrast to *G. breviceps,* this species has 42 chromosomes.

Natural History. This gopher normally is restricted to rather dry, sandy soils; however, sometimes it inhabits well-drained, gravely substrates, especially in upland areas. It may benefit from use of fire by foresters. In Alabama, *G. pinetis* has been found on gravely ridges under mixed stands of longleaf pine and oak. These rodents live in underground chambers, indicated by surface mounds of earth excavated from their burrows; they rarely emerge except to disperse. Their burrowing activities may be correlated with temperature and availability of food. Numerous species of arthropods are associated with their burrows, many of them apparently obligate commensals.

Breeding apparently takes place throughout the year, although peaks in reproductive activity (especially in females) occur in February and March and from June to August. Females may produce two litters per year. Litter size ranges from one to three young, averaging slightly less than two. Young are born by breech presentation. The eyes, ears, and cheek pouches are closed at birth. Three neonates averaged 50 mm in length and 5.8 g in weight in one case. Young wean and disperse at about one month of age. Females reach sexual maturity in four to six months. As in other gophers, the juvenile pelage is paler and not as full as that of adults. Adults probably molt twice annually.

In the south-central states covered here and in Florida, these animals frequently are referred to as "salamanders." The term *gopher* usually is applied to the gopher tortoise, *Gopherus polyphemus.* This pocket gopher harbors some ectoparasites (chewing lice) as well as a few endoparasites. Its potential predators include small mammalian carnivores, such as mink and skunks, as well as owls.

Selected Reference. Pembleton and Williams (1978).

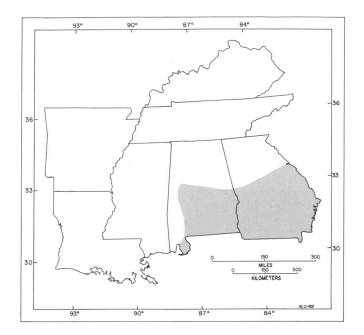

Photo courtesy S. L. Williams

Chaetopidus hispidus

Hispid Pocket Mouse

Distribution. The range of *C. hispidus* extends from southern North Dakota to central Mexico and from the Rocky Mountains to Missouri and Louisiana. In the south-central states, this species has been recorded in five parishes in west-central Louisiana, where it generally is thought to be rare.

Description. Only pocket mouse in south-central states. External fur-lined cheek pouches present. Dorsal pelage bristly, ochraceous buff interspersed with black hairs; venter white; distinct, buffy orange lateral line. Total length, 190–240; tail, 90–115; hind foot, 23–30; ear, 12–14; weight, 35–60 g.

Natural History. This poorly studied mouse inhabits a variety of grassland habitats, which frequently also support some forbs, shrubs, and trees. It occasionally lives in irrigated lands and fairly wet lowlands but most often is found in drier, upland areas. It seems to prefer sandy or sandy loam soils. Its burrows vary from simple tunnels used by immature animals to branched tunnel systems with two or more entrances occupied by adults. Hispid pocket mice are usually nocturnal but may be active beneath dense cover during the day.

This species is mostly a granivore, seeds making up more than 80 percent of its diet in some areas. Those consumed vary by season, and these mice may cache large quantities of seeds for consumption during winter. They also eat insects in season. Although these rodents are capable of torpor, they apparently do not store fat for winter months, nor do they hibernate, at least in the southern part of their range. They may remain below ground during cold weather, however.

Relatively little is known about reproduction or development in this species. Litter size ranges from 2 to 10 young, with an average of 6. Two or more litters may be produced by adult females annually, from spring through midautumn. Females breed in the year of their birth, some before they have completely shed the juvenile pelage. Nothing is known of longevity in *C. hispidus,* but it is unlikely that many of these mice survive into a second year of life.

Mammals (especially small carnivores), snakes, and owls are major predators on hispid pocket mice. They are known to harbor fleas, ticks, mites, and other ectoparasites, as well as endoparasites, such as *Trypanosoma cruzi* (the protozoan that causes Chagas' disease) and some spirochetes.

Selected References. Choate and Jones (1989); Paulson (1988).

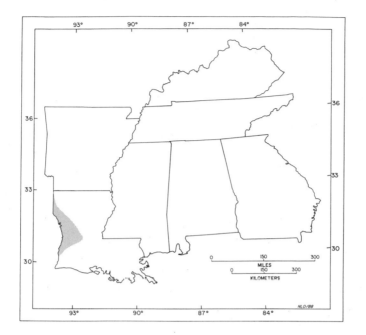

Photo courtesy R. J. Baker

Castor canadensis

Beaver

Distribution. The range of the beaver includes most of North America, from central Alaska and northern Canada to northern Mexico; it is absent from some arid portions of the Southwest. This species was extirpated before the end of the last century from many parts of the south-central region; however, through restocking programs, the beaver now inhabits suitable aquatic habitats throughout the seven states.

Description. Largest rodent in temperate North America. Heavy bodied; tail flat, paddle shaped, scaly, and nearly naked. Feet webbed; claw on second toe of hind foot split for grooming. Underfur dense, silky, with long, coarse guard hairs; pelage dark brown to reddish brown dorsally and ventrally; tail and feet black. Total length, 950–1,200; tail, 290–370; hind foot, 170–190; ear, 30–35; weight, 15–30 kg or more.

Natural History. The beaver generally is active at night, but in some places and seasons it may be observed at any time of day as well. These animals build elaborate nests and burrows. They usually construct lodges in open, quiet waters behind their dams, but occasionally they build lodges against banks or construct burrows with underwater openings to house dens and to store food. Their dams sometimes flood agricultural land by blocking canals, drainage ditches, and pipes. Beavers are herbivores; they eat leaves, branches, and bark of most kinds of woody plants that grow near water. These animals also consume numerous herbaceous plants, especially aquatic plants. The colony is the fundamental unit of the beaver population, usually consisting of four to eight related animals.

Three to five young are born, usually from April to June, after a gestation period of about 107 days. Neonates have open eyes and are fully furred. They grow and mature rather slowly; breeding begins at two years of age.

These rodents are susceptible to numerous parasites, including those that cause rabies and tularemia. Large carnivores prey on them, as do mink on young animals. Humans are, however, the major threat to the species through trapping and habitat disturbance or destruction. Beavers were reduced to low numbers throughout much of North America by 1900, but have been reintroduced over most of their former range. In the 1983–1984 season, almost 10,000 pelts were harvested in the south-central region.

Selected References. Hill (1982); Jenkins and Busher (1979); Novak (1987).

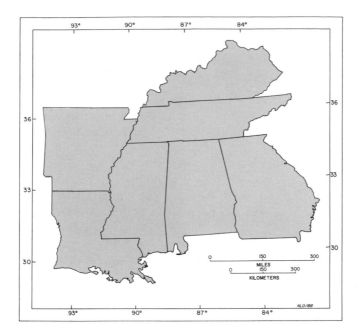

Photo courtesy J. L. Tveten

Oryzomys palustris

Marsh Rice Rat

Distribution. This species inhabits an area from southern New Jersey and eastern Pennsylvania southward to Florida and westward to Oklahoma and the Gulf Coast of Texas. It occurs throughout the south-central region except in eastern Tennessee, northern Kentucky, and north-central Arkansas.

Description. Medium-sized generalized rat. Tail about half of total length, slender, and sparsely haired without sharp bicoloration. Fur dark brown to grayish brown on dorsum, grayish white or pale buff on venter; underfur dense, soft, and water repellent. Ears and eyes moderately large. Total length, 225–250; tail, 110–140; hind foot, 25–35; ear, 12–16; weight, 45–80 g.

Natural History. This rodent inhabits wet meadows and dense vegetation bordering marshes, swamps, bayous, streams, ditches, ponds, and canals. It lives also in thick vegetation in old fields and along roadways. The marsh rice rat is a good swimmer and diver; it can swim for some distance under water, as well as on the surface. This species is primarily nocturnal but may be active during the day beneath dense cover. These rats consume seeds and parts of green plants, as well as insects, snails, and other animal materials. In marshy areas, they sometimes construct feeding platforms of stems of aquatic plants.

Marsh rice rats construct globular nests of woven grasses and leaves, placing them on high ground in dense vegetation, in shallow burrows, or beneath debris. In wet areas, they may suspend nests above the water level in thick vegetation. Rice rats also occasionally modify abandoned bird nests.

In the southern parts of this region, marsh rice rats may breed throughout the year, but breeding occurs mostly from February through November in the northern areas. Gestation takes 21 to 28 days. Females produce several litters in a year. Litter size averages four to five young, with a range of one to seven. Neonates weigh three to four grams. Growth is rapid, with weaning taking place at 11 to 13 days; sexual maturity is reached in six to eight weeks.

Ectoparasites found on this species include fleas, lice, mites, and ticks. Numerous endoparasites also are recorded, some of which apparently are obtained by the consumption of infected crustaceans and fish. Owls, hawks, snakes, and mammalian carnivores are major predators on *O. palustris*. Especially during periods of high population densities, marsh rice rats can be pests in rice-growing areas.

Selected Reference. Wolfe (1982).

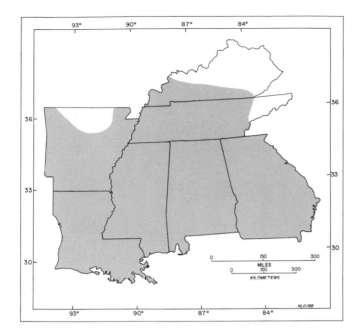

Photo courtesy R. W. Barbour

Reithrodontomys fulvescens

Fulvous Harvest Mouse

Distribution. The range of this species extends from southeastern Kansas and southwestern Missouri southward to the Gulf Cost, westward to Arizona and Sonora, Mexico, and southward across Mexico to Honduras and Nicaragua. In the south-central states, *R. fulvescens* occurs in the southwestern half of Mississippi, throughout Arkansas, and in most of Louisiana.

Description. Medium-sized harvest mouse, about equal in body mass to *R. megalotis.* Tail longer than head and body, not sharply bicolored. Dorsal pelage golden brown, with mixture of black hairs along center of back; sides cinnamon to reddish yellow; venter grayish white to buff; ears cinnamon. Upper incisors grooved as in other species of *Reithrodontomys.* Total length, 150–175; tail, 85–95; hind foot, 16–20; ear, 12–16; weight, 10–12 g.

Natural History. This species is common in fields containing tall grasses and shrubs. Other habitats include fencerows, woodland-grassland ecotonal areas, weedy gullies, and creek bottoms with rank and tangled vegetation (grasses, vines, shrubs). These mice are scansorial. Their activity is almost exclusively nocturnal, with a peak beginning just after sunset. The nest of this mouse, about the size of a baseball, is a round mass of shredded grasses, sedges, and other plant materials. It generally is placed above the ground, sometimes in an abandoned bird nest, and frequently contains a pair of mice. Seeds and small invertebrates make up most of the diet of this species; it consumes herbs and grasses occasionally. Food intake varies seasonally, depending on availability of items.

In the south-central region, this harvest mouse probably breeds throughout the year. Gestation lasts approximately 22 to 23 days. Litter size ranges from one to seven young, with two to four being the norm. Neonates weigh about two grams; they are blind and mostly hairless. Their eyes open in 9 to 12 days, and their climbing ability is apparent at 12 to 13 days; sexual maturity is attained in two to three months. Little is known of social organization in *R. fulvescens.* Densities range from less than 1 to almost 20 mice per acre, and are highest in summer and winter. Home ranges average half an acre.

Fleas are known to parasitize these animals. Hawks and owls are known predators; snakes and small mammalian carnivores probably also feed on these mice.

Selected Reference. Spencer and Cameron (1982).

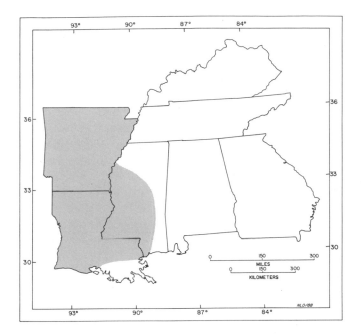

Photo courtesy R. Altig

Reithrodontomys humulis

Eastern Harvest Mouse

Distribution. This mouse inhabits much of the southeastern United States, excluding southern Florida, west to Texas and Oklahoma. It ranges throughout most of the south-central region, being absent only on the coastal plain of southern Louisiana and in north and central Arkansas.

Description. Small harvest mouse resembling *R. montanus;* tail not distinctly bicolored, less than half of total length; eyes and ears relatively small. Pelage of head and body dark brown, with some blackish hairs; fur of venter buffy to whitish to grayish white. Total length, 110–130; tail, 45–60; hind foot, 15–18; ear, 8–9; weight, 6–10 g.

Natural History. The eastern harvest mouse seems most common in old fields containing dense stands of weeds (such as goldenrod) and harsh grasses (for example, fescue and Johnson grass). This mouse is found frequently in weed-filled ditches and briar thickets and beneath tangles of honeysuckle. It apparently does not construct either runways or burrows. Except during coldest weather in the northern part of the region covered, this mouse is almost exclusively nocturnal. Seeds make up most of its diet, but it consumes green vegetation and insects on occasion.

These mice construct round nests of shredded grass and other plant materials, placing them in clumps of tall, dense vegetation or suspending them above ground in thick cover. Some mice construct several nests in a single season. *R. humulis* is not strongly territorial, and several of these mice may huddle together in cold weather to conserve energy.

In the south-central states, *R. humulis* probably breeds throughout the year, with some reduction in reproductive activity in midsummer and midwinter. Gestation lasts 21 to 22 days. Litter size ranges from one to eight young, with two or three in most litters. Neonates weigh little more than a gram. Growth of the young is rapid; weaning takes place within 4 weeks, and the mice are sexually mature and begin breeding when about 11 to 12 weeks old. Like other mice, females of this species may cannibalize their young if the nest is disturbed.

Small mammalian carnivores, as well as snakes and owls, prey on eastern harvest mice. Helminths and arthropods are common parasites of this species. As in other small rodents, there is high mortality among the young; the average life expectancy thus is only a few months.

Selected References. Dunaway (1968); Layne (1959).

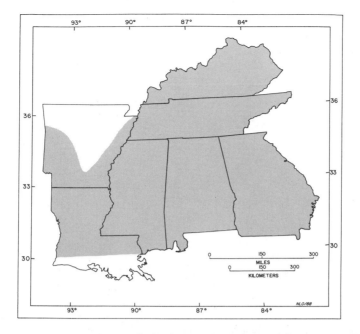

Photo courtesy R. W. Barbour

Reithrodontomys megalotis

Western Harvest Mouse

Distribution. This species ranges across western North America from southern Canada to southern Mexico and from the Pacific Coast to Indiana. In the south-central region, *R. megalotis* occurs in the upper portion of the Mississippi Alluvial Plain in northeastern Arkansas. There is some evidence that this species is extending its range as a result of deforestation practices.

Description. Tail about equal in length to head and body, somewhat bicolored; darker on top, paler on underside. Pelage on dorsum brownish overall, with some black-tipped hairs; venter dull white to grayish; ears and eyes prominent. Total length, 120–150; tail, 55–75; hind foot, 15–17; ear, 12–14; weight, 10–15 g.

Natural History. This harvest mouse is a typical inhabitant of grassy and weedy areas, such as little-used pastures, meadows, fallow fields, fencerows, roadsides, and railroad rights-of-way. It also lives in grassy habitats along borders of cultivated fields and at the edge of riparian areas. This mouse is almost entirely nocturnal. It feeds on grass and weed seeds but also consumes succulent stems of plants and some insects when available. These mice climb readily in tall grass and brush, especially in search of food. When on the ground, they frequently utilize runways and burrows of other rodents, such as those of voles and cotton rats.

The western harvest mouse constructs a spherical nest of shredded grass and other plant materials. Usually it places its nest either in a clump of dense grass above ground or on the ground in dense cover but occasionally builds in burrows. Like other south-central murids, *R. megalotis* does not hibernate.

In this region, western harvest mice probably breed throughout the year, but most activity takes place in spring and autumn. Females produce several litters annually. The gestation period is 22 or 23 days. Litter size ranges from one to nine young, averaging four. Neonates weigh about 1.5 grams at birth; they are pink and hairless, with eyes, ears, and anus closed. Young are weaned at about three weeks of age. Females usually begin breeding when six to eight weeks old but may breed only a month after birth.

Numerous endo- and ectoparasites have been reported in *R. megalotis,* including protozoans, nematodes, cestodes, fleas, and mites. Its major predators are hawks, owls, snakes, and small mammalian carnivores.

Selected Reference. Webster and Jones (1982).

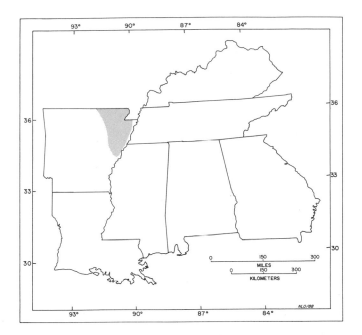

Photo courtesy T. H. Kunz

Reithrodontomys montanus

Plains Harvest Mouse

Distribution. This species ranges from southwestern North Dakota and southeastern Montana southward throughout the Great Plains to south-central Texas and to Sonora, Chihuahua, and Durango, Mexico. In the south-central states, this mouse has been recorded only in two counties in the northwestern corner of Arkansas.

Description. Small harvest mouse, about same size as *R. humulis.* Tail shorter than head and body, and sharply bicolored. Narrow dark stripe on top of tail that extends to prominent dark middorsal body stripe; dorsal pelage otherwise pale gray to buffy gray, usually sprinkled with black hairs; venter whitish. Single longitudinal groove on each upper incisor as in other harvest mice. Total length, 110–135; tail, 45–60; hind foot, 15–17; ear, 12–15; weight, 10–15 g.

Natural History. The natural history of this mouse is poorly known. It is found most frequently in open, grassy areas. Old hay fields with harsh, dense grasses seemingly are its preferred habitat in Arkansas, but this species also commonly lives in grassy areas along highways, railroads, and fencerows. This harvest mouse consumes seeds, grains, and stems of a variety of plants; insects, especially grasshoppers, also form part of its diet. It builds globular nests of fine grass and shredded plant materials, locating them in bunches of grass on the surface or above the ground, or beneath the ground in burrows.

Breeding probably occurs throughout the year, peaking in the summer months. The gestation period is about 21 days. Offspring are altricial at birth and weigh about a gram. Fur develops in about six days, and eyes open at about eight days. Young are weaned in approximately two weeks and attain adult size and pelage some five weeks after birth. These mice reach sexual maturity at about two months of age. Maximum longevity in the wild is at least 14 months.

The plains harvest mouse frequently lives in association with other species of *Reithrodontomys* and with species of several other rodent genera. Under such conditions, it usually is the least abundant member of the community of rodents. Although other species of harvest mice have been documented as hosts for various parasites, there is little information available with regard to *R. montanus.* These mice contribute to the diets of owls and other raptors, snakes, and several carnivorous mammals.

Selected Reference. Wilkins (1986).

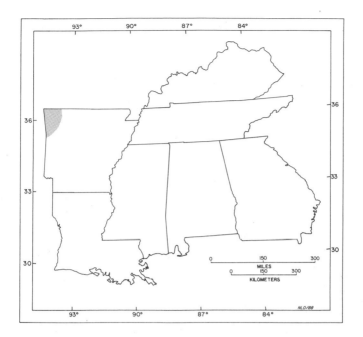

Photo courtesy J. L. Tveten

Peromyscus attwateri

Texas Mouse

Distribution. This mouse ranges from southeastern Kansas, southwestern Missouri, and northwestern Arkansas across central Oklahoma to south-central Texas between the Llano Estacado and the Balcones Escarpment. In the seven-state region, *P. attwateri* is known only in the Ozark and Ouachita mountains in the northwestern part of Arkansas. The Arkansas River valley divides the range of this mouse.

Description. Largest member of genus in region. Tail about as long as head and body, bicolored, moderately well haired, with prominent tuft at tip. Dorsal pelage grayish brown to dark brown, buffy or tawny on sides; venter whitish, hairs plumbeous at base; feet white, large; ears and eyes large. Total length, 185–220; tail, 90–110; hind foot, 22–26; ear, 18–22; weight, 20–35 g.

Natural History. In the Ozarks, this species is associated with cedar trees and grasses growing in shallow soils overlying rock. These mice are found mostly along rocky outcroppings and cliffs, usually near the base of an escarpment, where they exclude other *Peromyscus* species and may be the most common small mammal. In the Ouachita Mountains, these rodents are found most often in open pine-oak-hickory forest and woodlands on steep, dry, south-facing slopes. In this area Texas mice also live near cedar trees in dry, rocky ravines or adjacent to exposed shale beds. This mouse is an excellent climber and obtains much of its food from trees and shrubs. Acorns are an important item of its diet; it also consumes pine seeds, grass seeds, beetle larvae, crickets, and fungi. There is little documentation of parasites harbored by this species, but botfly infestations are common. Its major predators apparently include hawks, owls, snakes, and small carnivores.

Like that of some other members of the genus, the nest of the Texas mouse is a globular structure of grasses, dry leaves, and other plant fibers. It is constructed beneath tumbled rocks, in crevices, and in other natural cavities. Little is known about reproduction in this species. Breeding may occur throughout the year, but there are peaks of activity in spring and autumn. Litter size ranges from two to six young, averaging three. The normal age at which these mice begin breeding is not known. The estimated maximum life-span is 18 months; most Texas mice that survive to adulthood probably live no longer than 6 or 7 months.

Selected Reference. Schmidly (1974).

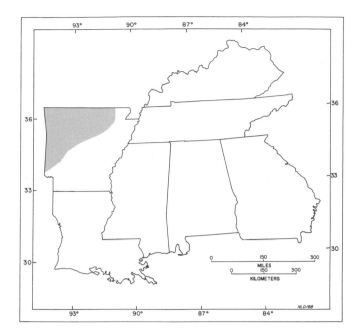

Photo courtesy R. J. Baker

Peromyscus gossypinus

Cotton Mouse

Distribution. The cotton mouse is found from southern Virginia and southern Illinois southward to Florida, and westward to Oklahoma and Texas. It ranges throughout the south-central region except in much of Kentucky, the highlands of eastern Tennessee, the northernmost part of Georgia, northern Arkansas, and the coastal plain of southern Louisiana.

Description. Relatively large mouse; darkest *Peromyscus* of seven-state region. Tail as long as or slightly longer than head and body, bicolored. Pelage dark brown dorsally, with darker area extending from shoulders to base of tail; venter and feet white. Total length, 160–205; tail, 70–97; hind foot, 22–26; ear, 16–18; weight, 20–40 g.

Natural History. This mouse inhabits dense underbrush along edges of streams and in bottomland hardwood forests, as well as suitable places in hammocks and swamps. The species occurs also in margins of cleared fields, in old fields, and in some upland forested areas. It frequently invades abandoned and little-used buildings. Cotton mice swim well, and several studies have indicated that they prefer flooded or periodically wet habitats. Cotton mice are nocturnal and are active throughout the year. They place their nests beneath fallen logs, brushpiles, and refuse and in old buildings, or may construct them above ground in clumps of thick vegetation. These mice are good climbers and thus sometimes nest in tree cavities and hollow stumps as well. They are opportunistic omnivores. Insects, spiders, slugs, and snails make up most of the diet of this species, but it also eats seeds and spores of the fungus *Endogone*. Home ranges are half an acre to an acre and a half.

The species potentially breeds year-round, but there is a marked decline in reproductive activity in the summer months. The gestation period is about 23 days. Litter size ranges from one to seven young, averaging four. Neonates weigh about two grams at birth. Pinnae unfold on about the fourth day, and eyes open between days 12 and 14. These mice are fully haired at about 10 days. They are weaned in three to four weeks and reach full adult size in about 60 days. Males begin breeding at about day 45, and females are reproductively active by about day 70.

Parasites of cotton mice include trematodes, cestodes, nematodes, mites, ticks, fleas, and botfly larvae. Predators include owls, weasels, foxes, bobcats, snakes, and feral house cats. Longevity of this species seldom exceeds one year.

Selected Reference. Wolfe and Linzey (1977).

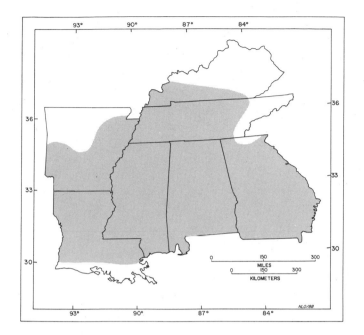

Photo courtesy R. W. Barbour

Peromyscus leucopus

White-Footed Mouse

Distribution. This mouse ranges from southern Canada and Maine southward through the eastern half of the United States to the south-central region, then west to central Arizona and south to the Yucatan Peninsula. In the south-central states, *P. leucopus* is absent only from the southern parts of Louisiana, Georgia, and Alabama, and an adjacent portion of Mississippi.

Description. Medium-sized member of genus in region. Tail shorter than head and body, indistinctly bicolored. Ears dusky brown, edged with white; pelage grayish brown to rich reddish brown dorsally, white ventrally; feet white. Total length, 160–200; tail, 65–85; hind foot, 18–21; ear, 15–18; weight, 17–30 g.

Natural History. This mouse is common in woodlands having cover in the form of fallen logs, brush piles, and rocks, and in shrubs along fence-rows and streams. It also readily invades man-made structures. These mice are nocturnal and are active throughout the year. They construct nests of dry plant material beneath logs, stones, and piles of brush and refuse, and in underground burrows. White-footed mice climb readily and thus occasionally place nests in abandoned bird and squirrel nests, and in hollow trees as well. They consume various seeds, nuts, fruits, and other plant materials, as well as insects and other small invertebrates. They may cache food, especially seeds and nuts, in burrows and near nests.

In the south-central region, the breeding season of this species extends throughout the year, with reduced activity in summer. Females produce several litters annually. Gestation lasts 22 to 23 days in nonlactating females, longer for those nursing young. Litter size ranges from one to seven young, averaging three to four. Young weigh 1.5 to 2.0 grams at birth. Juveniles have the gray dorsal pelage and sparse grayish-white ventral fur typical of all young in the genus *Peromyscus*. This is replaced by a subadult coat at 40 to 50 days of age, which is followed by molt to adult pelage. Adults are reported to molt once a year, in spring or early summer.

Botfly larvae, fleas, lice, mites, and ticks are common ectoparasites; endoparasites include tapeworms, roundworms, and flatworms. White-footed mice are significant food items for owls, weasels, foxes, bobcats, feral house cats, and snakes. They may be minor pests where grains are stored. Mortality in this species usually causes a complete population turnover annually.

Selected References. Lackey *et al.* (1985); Suttkus and Jones (1991).

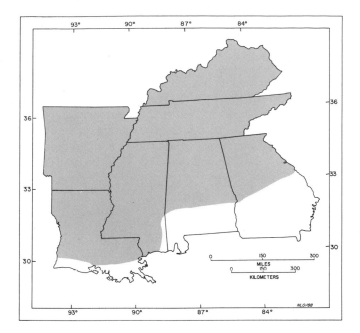

Photo courtesy R. W. Barbour

Peromyscus maniculatus bairdii

Deer Mouse

Distribution. P. maniculatus has a broad geographic distribution. The species ranges over much of central and southern Canada, throughout the United States (except parts of the Southeast), and southward to Oaxaca in southern Mexico. It includes distinctive, noninterbreeding grassland and woodland populations, which are treated separately in this book. In the south-central region, *P. m. bairdii* is found in most of Kentucky, north-central and northwest Tennessee, and north-central Arkansas. It also may be found in northwestern Mississippi.

Description. Relatively small mouse. Tail short, distinctly bicolored, dark above and white below; pelage variable dorsally, grayish brown to dark reddish brown, usually with somewhat darkened middorsal band; venter white. Total length, 125–155; tail, 40–65; hind foot, 16–20; ear, 12–16; weight, 15–26 g.

Natural History. P. m. bairdii inhabits open areas of grasses and weeds. It is especially common along grassy fencerows and roadsides and in abandoned fields. These mice invade weedy fields and various cultivated crops as well as pastureland, and may occupy human dwellings, particularly in the winter months. They generally prefer dry upland habitats. This species is nocturnal, like its relatives, with peaks of activity in early evening and before dawn. It places its nests in its own burrows or those dug by other mammals, or constructs nests on the surface of the ground, either in clumps of vegetation or beneath trash. Its diet consists mostly of seeds, but it also consumes other plant materials and small invertebrates as available. It sometimes caches seeds in burrows.

Breeding occurs throughout the year in the south-central region, and females bring forth multiple litters. Gestation requires 22 to 27 days. Litter size ranges from one to nine young, averaging between three and four. Young weigh one to two grams at birth; they are naked, with eyes closed. Their eyes open at about 14 days of age. Young are weaned in about 25 days and achieve sexual maturity at 45 to 50 days.

These mice probably seldom live more than a year in the wild. Deer mice are a staple food of owls, hawks, bobcats, weasels, mink, foxes, snakes, and other predators. Home ranges from 0.1 to about 10 acres have been reported. Local population size varies greatly, averaging three mice per acre.

Selected References. Barbour and Davis (1974); Webster *et al.* (1985).

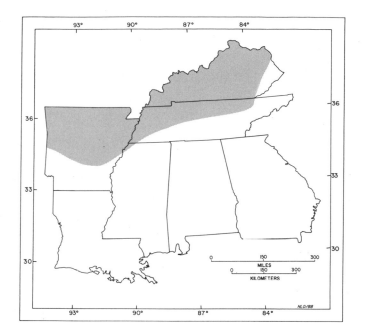

Photo courtesy D. C. Lovell and R. S. Mellott

Peromyscus maniculatus nubiterrae

Deer Mouse

Distribution. This mouse inhabits higher elevations in the Appalachian Mountains. In the south-central region, this subspecies is known to occur in the highlands of the eastern parts of Kentucky and Tennessee, as well as in adjacent northeastern Georgia.

Description. Similar in appearance to *P. leucopus.* Tail long (more than length of body), sharply bicolored, tufted at tip. Eyes and ears appear large. Pelage dark brownish dorsally in adults, grayish in juveniles as in other species of *Peromyscus;* ears edged with white. Total length, 175–195; tail, 80–105; hind foot, 20–23; ear, 17–20; weight, 13–29 g.

Natural History. Coniferous forests, mixed evergreen-deciduous forests, and other woodlands with adequate cover are frequent habitats of this deer mouse, which also lives among rocks and logs adjacent to mossy stream banks. It is one of the common small mammals at higher elevations in Great Smoky Mountains National Park, where it has been taken from about 1,500 to more than 6,000 feet in elevation. Where its range overlaps that of *P. leucopus,* this deer mouse is found in cooler, moister areas rather than open woodlands. It constructs nests of shredded vegetation, feathers, and debris and places them in burrows abandoned by other mammals, in hollow logs and stumps, in crevices, and in and beneath structures made by humans. These mice are agile climbers. They are nocturnal and are active throughout the year.

The food of this mouse consists of a wide variety of seeds, nuts, and fruits, as well as some animal matter, especially insects. The deer mouse frequently stores seeds in hollows of logs and trees for consumption during winter. Reproductively active animals have been taken in all months except January, and breeding may extend throughout the year. Adult females produce several litters annually. Gestation lasts 25 to 27 days. Litters, which are smaller on average than those of *P. m. bairdii,* usually comprise two to four young. Neonates are naked and blind at birth as in most other murids. Their eyes open at about 15 days, and young are weaned at about 30 days. These mice have lived as long as eight years in captivity but rarely live more than a year in the wild. Their major predators are owls, hawks, snakes, weasels, foxes, bobcats, and skunks. Deer mice harbor numerous internal and external parasites.

Selected References. Barbour and Davis (1974); Webster *et al.* (1985).

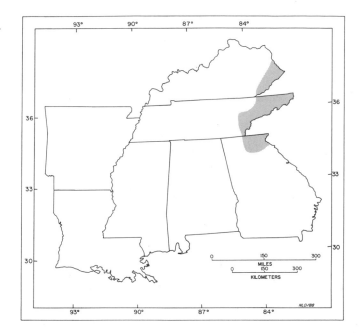

Peromyscus polionotus

Oldfield Mouse

Distribution. This species is restricted to the southeastern United States, ranging from Mississippi to the Atlantic Coast and from North Carolina to parts of Florida. In the south-central states, the oldfield mouse is found in northeastern Mississippi, parts of Alabama, and most of Georgia.

Description. Smallest member of genus in region. Pelage brown to gray fawn in color dorsally, with darker midline; venter cream to white; tail short, sharply bicolored, mostly white except for brown stripe on dorsal surface. Total length, 122–150; tail, 40–60; hind foot, 15–19; ear, 11–15; weight, 8–15 g.

Natural History. The oldfield mouse is found in dry, sandy habitats with herbaceous vegetation, especially fallow fields, but also along roadsides and ditches, as well as adjacent to fields of corn, cotton, peanuts, and melons. One study revealed that it is most abundant in habitats consisting of lespedeza and mixed forbs. It seems to avoid clay and rocky soils. These mice are nocturnal. They are capable diggers and construct extensive burrow systems, the entrances to which are marked by mounds of sand; nest cavities usually are located 18 to 24 inches below ground. When these mice are in their burrows, they usually plug the entrances with soil. Their diet consists mostly of seeds of grasses and herbs, but they consume green plant material and insects occasionally.

Breeding occurs throughout the year, with a peak of activity in December and January. Gestation lasts about 22 days. In a recent laboratory study, litter size ranged from 1 to 8 young, with a mean of 4.1 and a mode of 4; rate of survival of young from large litters during the first three weeks was significantly lower than for those in smaller litters. These mice reach adult size and sexual maturity at about 30 days of age. These are docile little animals, and they rarely bite when handled.

Numbers of oldfield mice seem highest from November to March and lowest in June and July. Whether the reduced numbers of mice in midsummer are due to predation or decreased activity is not known. High mortality, especially of young, has been reported, as is true for other mice and for voles. Owls and snakes may be the major predators on these mice, but small carnivores no doubt feed on them as well. Little is known about parasites living in association with *P. polionotus*.

Selected References. Golley (1962); Stevenson (1976).

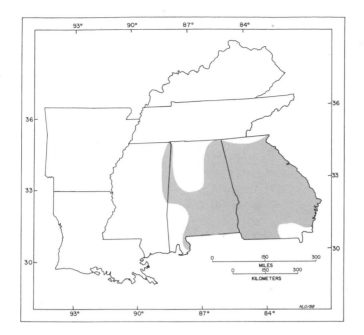

Photo courtesy J. N. Layne

Ochrotomys nuttalli

Golden Mouse

Distribution. The golden mouse ranges across the southeastern part of the United States from Virginia to central Florida and westward to Oklahoma and Texas. It occurs throughout most of the south-central region, being absent only from northern Kentucky and southern Louisiana.

Description. Small, richly colored mouse, about size of *Peromyscus maniculatus.* Dorsum golden brown to orangish brown; venter pale, tinged with pale golden color; pelage dense and soft. Total length, 145–180; tail, 60–85; hind foot, 15–20; ear, 15–18; weight, 15–28 g.

Natural History. Golden mice are found in a variety of habitats, including brushy areas, woodlands, floodplains, borders of fields, and thickets bordering swamps and dense woods. They frequently are found in thickets of greenbrier, honeysuckle, blackberry, and grapevine. They are highly arboreal.

Golden mice generally build globular nests as high as 15 feet or more in trees but occasionally locate the nests on the ground in stumps or under logs and rocks. The nests usually consist of leaves lined with shredded bark and grasses; feathers are used sometimes. These mice frequently construct feeding platforms near their arboreal nests. Their food consists mostly of seeds and invertebrates, which they usually carry to the platforms to be consumed. Golden mice are docile, social animals; up to eight have been found occupying the same nest. Populations vary from 1 to about 20 mice per acre, depending on season and habitat.

Breeding probably occurs year-round, with peaks in spring and late summer. Gestation lasts 25 to 30 days. Litter size ranges from one to four young, averaging slightly less than three with a mode of two. Young are relatively precocial at birth, grow rapidly, and are weaned when 17 to 21 days old. They attain adult size in 8 to 10 weeks. For small rodents, these mice have long life-spans; captive animals have lived as long as 8.5 years, but average longevity in the wild is probably a year or less (6.5 months in one study).

Major ectoparasites of golden mice are mites, fleas, ticks, lice, and botfly larvae. Internal parasites include bacteria, protozoans, cestodes, and nematodes. Little is known about predation on this species, but owls and snakes may take a toll.

Selected Reference. Linzey and Packard (1977).

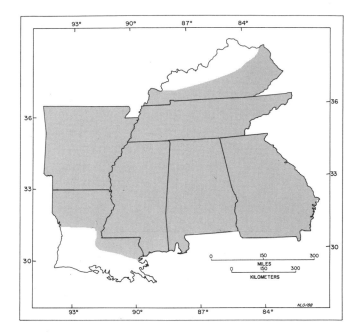

Photo courtesy D. W. Linzey

Sigmodon hispidus

Hispid Cotton Rat

Distribution. This species ranges from northern South America through Central America and Mexico into the United States as far north as Virginia and Nebraska, with some isolated populations in the Southwest. Except in northern and central Tennessee, most of Kentucky, and southernmost Louisiana, this cotton rat is found throughout the south-central region.

Description. Medium-sized rat with long, coarse pelage. Tail sparsely haired; pelage grizzled yellowish brown dorsally, frequently with salt-and-pepper appearance; grayish ventrally, sometimes with buffy wash. Total length, 225–290; tail, 85–120; hind foot, 28–34; ear, 16–18; weight, 50–150 g.

Natural History. This cotton rat is a Neotropical species that has been steadily extending its geographic range northward in recent years. It inhabits a broad variety of places where suitable cover is present, commonly at the edges of woodlands and in grassy areas of all kinds, especially roadsides, edges of fields and pastures, and along railroad grades. Broad, well-marked runways with piles of droppings and cut pieces of vegetation are usual indicators of the presence of these rats. Although primarily herbivores, they also consume invertebrates, small vertebrates, and on occasion bird eggs. They are mostly nocturnal and crepuscular but may be observed foraging during the day. They construct spherical nests of shredded vegetation in burrows or beneath debris, logs, rocks, or densely matted plant materials. Home ranges usually average an acre for males, about half that for females.

Cotton rats are prolific breeders and produce litters of 1 to 15 young after about 27 days of gestation. Neonates are well developed at birth, weigh six to eight grams, and are capable of running about within a few hours. Young grow rapidly; their eyes open within hours of birth, they gain one or two grams of weight per day, and they are weaned at 10 to 15 days. These mice attain sexual maturity when two months old or less.

Cotton rats support numerous internal and external parasites, and they serve as a reservoir for several diseases of humans, including rabies, Chagas' disease, and encephalomyelitis. Owls, hawks, snakes, and small carnivores are their major predators. In some parts of the south-central region, *S. hispidus* is considered a pest to agricultural crops, including sugarcane, cotton, and potatoes, during periods of high population density.

Selected Reference. Cameron and Spencer (1981).

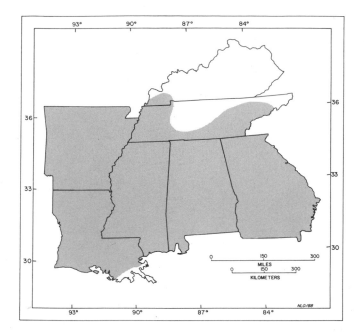

Photo courtesy J. K. Jones, Jr.

Neotoma floridana

Eastern Woodrat

Distribution. The range of the eastern woodrat includes much of the eastern United States, west to eastern Colorado and south to the Gulf Coast. Except in extreme southern Louisiana and parts of eastern Tennessee and northeastern Georgia, this species occurs throughout the south-central region.

Description. Largest native rat in region. Pelage brownish to brownish gray dorsally, grayish white ventrally; tail brownish above and pale below, not sharply bicolored; feet whitish. Total length, 350–435; tail, 135–190; hind foot, 35–42; ear, 25–30; weight, 250–360 g.

Natural History. In upland areas, this rodent is found mostly near rocky outcrops, crevices, caves, and piles of boulders. In lowlands, these woodrats inhabit woodlands and brush bordering streams, roads, and fields. They construct conspicuous dwellings, which they inhabit individually, of sticks, stones, and almost any other item they can carry. Their propensity to take shiny objects to their nests has earned them their reputation as "pack rats." They situate their dwellings among rocks, in fissures, on ledges, at the bases of trees, in hollow logs, and, in lowland areas, sometimes in small trees and tangles of vines. They invade man-made structures readily. They construct one or more spherical nests deep within their dwellings, which also provide shelter for a variety of invertebrates and some small vertebrates. They usually deposit fecal materials in toilet areas nearby. These woodrats are mostly nocturnal. They consume a great variety of plant materials, obtained from the ground and by climbing into trees and brush. They store food for winter use because they do not hibernate. Their home ranges vary considerably with habitat, but frequently average half an acre, those of males the larger.

After a gestation period of about 35 days, one to five young (usually two or three) are born; reproduction continues throughout the year. Young weigh 10 to 15 grams at birth. They begin foraging for themselves when three to four weeks old. They attain adult size in eight to nine months and sexual maturity a few months earlier, but these rats probably do not breed in their first year. Woodrats have a long life expectancy compared with that of other rodents; some may live two or three years under natural conditions. Their major predators are owls, snakes, and most mammalian carnivores.

Selected Reference. Wiley (1980).

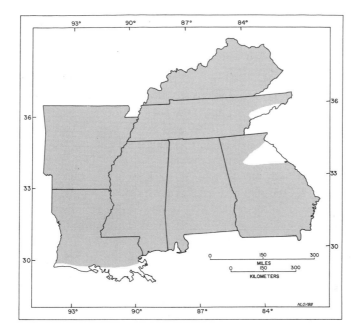

Photo courtesy R. W. Wiley

Clethrionomys gapperi

Southern Red-Backed Vole

Distribution. This species ranges across much of Canada, southward in the western mountains to Arizona and New Mexico, and in the Appalachian Mountains to northern Georgia. In the south-central region, it is confined to extreme eastern parts of Kentucky and Tennessee, and adjacent Georgia.

Description. Medium-sized vole with small eyes and relatively large ears. Broad band of reddish brown fur on dorsum from face to rump; sides of head and body grayish; tail bicolored, dark brown to black above, gray or whitish below; venter usually pale grayish. Total length, 120–155; tail, 33–45; hind foot, 17–20; ear, 12–16; weight, 16–42 g.

Natural History. This vole frequents mesic habitats in forested areas but may live in adjacent wet meadows, as well as rocky places. Available free water apparently is an important habitat requirement because these voles drink large quantities of water. Although these voles live in burrows, they use runways constructed by other animals. They are common in preferred habitats but seldom occur in high densities. Most of their activity is nocturnal, but they may be seen foraging about during the day. They construct nests of grass, leaves, and moss and place them in underground chambers. Common food items include green foliage, seeds, nuts, fruits, and berries, as well as some invertebrates. These voles store food, especially seeds, for consumption in winter; they also raid food caches of other animals. In addition, they eat roots and bark of small trees in the cold months.

As with many other murids in the seven-state region, females of this species are polyestrous and undergo postpartum estrus. Breeding occurs mostly from March to October. The gestation period lasts from 17 to 19 days. Litter size varies from 1 to 10 young, averaging between 4 and 6. Larger litters are produced over a shorter breeding season in montane areas. Neonates weigh about two grams at birth and are hairless, with eyes and ears closed. Eyes and ears open at 12 to 13 days, and young are weaned as early as 17 days of age. Adults undergo two seasonal molts, one in spring to summer pelage and another in autumn to the longer, heavier winter coat.

Ectoparasites of this vole include fleas, lice, ticks, mites, and chiggers. Cestodes, nematodes, and protozoans are known internal parasites. Predators reported for these voles are weasels, coyotes, snakes, owls, and hawks.

Selected References. Merritt (1981); Johnson and Johnson (1982).

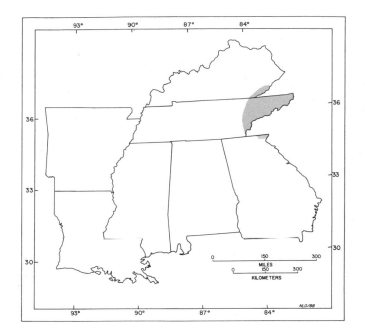

Photo courtesy E. C. Birney

Microtus chrotorrhinus

Rock Vole

Distribution. This species ranges from Labrador and the maritime provinces of Canada to northeastern Minnesota, and southward in the Appalachian Mountains to North Carolina. In the south-central region, the rock vole is known only in the mountains of eastern Tennessee but perhaps also inhabits extreme southeastern Kentucky.

Description. Resembles meadow vole in size. Pelage yellowish brown on dorsum, grayish to grayish white on venter; yellowish orange to dull rufous on face and snout. Younger animals more grayish overall with paler face than adults. Total length, 140–185; tail, 42–60; hind foot, 19–23; ear, 13–17; weight, 30–48 g.

Natural History. Rock voles usually are found in rocky habitats in or near forested areas. In Great Smoky Mountains National Park, they live at elevations from about 2,600 feet to the tops of the highest mountains, although they are most often encountered above 3,000 feet. Surface water or subsurface streams are other important components of the habitat, as are mosses and forbs. These voles make most of their runways, tunnels, and burrows beneath leaf litter, moss-covered rocks, and logs. These animals may be active at any time, but most movement occurs at dusk and after dark. Most of the activities of this vole apparently take place underground or at least under cover, typically in association with *Clethrionomys gapperi*. There is no evidence that these species compete. Main components of the rock vole's diet are stems, leaves, and roots of grasses and forbs, berries, and mushrooms, as well as other fungi; it eats insects on occasion.

Several litters, ranging in size from one to seven young (averaging three), are produced each year. The gestation period is 19 to 21 days. Most breeding apparently occurs from March to October, at least in the southern part of the range of the species. Females born early in the year produce young in the same breeding season.

Several endoparasites, notably cestodes and nematodes, and ectoparasites—fleas, mites, ticks, botfly larvae—are known to infest rock voles. They have been reported as prey for bobcats, rattlesnakes, and copperheads. Other small carnivores, other snakes, and raptorial birds no doubt also consume rock voles on occasion. Relatively little is known about the biology of this species.

Selected References. Kirkland and Jannett (1982); Johnson and Johnson (1982); Tamarin (1985).

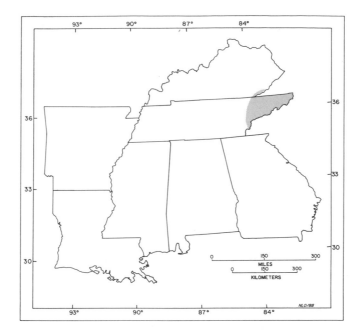

Photo courtesy R. W. Barbour

Microtus ochrogaster

Prairie Vole

Distribution. This vole ranges from the prairie provinces of Canada southward to northeastern New Mexico and adjacent Texas and Oklahoma, and east as far as West Virginia. In the south-central region, this species occurs throughout most of Kentucky, central Tennessee, and northern Arkansas, and in north-central Alabama. In addition, a unique and isolated subspecies formerly inhabited a small area in southwestern Louisiana and adjacent Texas.

Description. Medium-sized, stocky vole with compact body and short, bicolored tail. Pelage long and coarse, grizzled brownish to grayish brown dorsally, buff, ochraceous, or silvery ventrally; eyes small; ears almost concealed in fur. Total length, 125–165; tail, 24–45; hind foot, 17–22; ear, 11–14; weight, 20–70 g.

Natural History. This vole is found where there is substantial grassy cover, such as in meadows and pastures, and at roadsides, railroad grades, and edges of fields. It lives also in some cultivated fields, such as alfalfa, and at the forest edge, but usually not in woodlands. Prairie voles have extensive runway systems below the grass canopy. They may be seen at any time night or day, but much of their activity is during daylight hours. Their diet consists primarily of green vegetation, especially during summer; they may consume roots, seeds, bark, and stems in winter. These voles sometimes cache food in underground chambers. They may cause damage to young trees in orchards by eating the bark.

Prairie voles form pair bonds, and both females and males participate in construction of nests and caring for young. They build nests in dense grass above ground or in shallow burrows. Breeding occurs throughout the year, with peaks in the spring and autumn. The gestation period lasts about 21 days. Litter size varies from one to eight young, averaging three to five; females may produce three, four, or more litters per year. Young weigh about three grams at birth, develop rapidly, and are weaned when about three weeks old. Sexual maturity and breeding begin when animals are four to six weeks of age. As in other species of *Microtus,* the sparse juvenile pelage is replaced by a subadult coat, which is closely followed by adult pelage.

Hawks, owls, snakes, and small mammalian carnivores commonly prey on prairie voles. Ectoparasites of this species include mites, ticks, lice, and fleas.

Selected References. Johnson and Johnson (1982); Tamarin (1985); Stalling (1990).

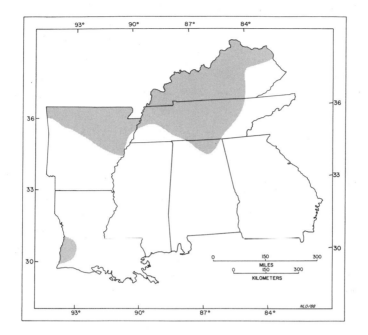

Photo courtesy R. W. Barbour

Microtus pennsylvanicus

Meadow Vole

Distribution. This species has a wider range than any other New World member of the genus *Microtus,* occurring in Alaska, Canada, and the eastern and northern parts of the United States southward on western mountains into northernmost Mexico. In the south-central region, this vole is found in eastern Kentucky and Tennessee and in north-central Georgia.

Description. Large, robust vole; tail relatively long and not sharply bicolored. Dorsum dark brown to chestnut, venter usually silvery gray; pelage soft and dense, not so coarse as that of *M. ochrogaster.* Total length, 150–185; tail, 35–52; hind foot, 18–24; ear, 12–16; weight, 35–60 g.

Natural History. This vole inhabits grasslands, wet meadows, and swampy areas, as well as roadsides and edges of fields. In this region, meadow voles frequently compete with *M. ochrogaster* for available habitats. Generally, *M. pennsylvanicus* prefers moist, low-lying, grassy areas, whereas prairie voles inhabit somewhat drier uplands. Meadow voles may be active at any time but are mostly nocturnal and crepuscular. Their activity is correlated directly with the amount of vegetative cover present. Runways and piles of plant clippings indicate the presence of this species. Its diet includes mostly stems and seeds of green grasses and other herbaceous plants, but it will eat crops, especially alfalfa, and animal matter occasionally. Like some other microtines, this species may girdle trees in orchards. These voles may be cannibalistic, especially of young. They build nests, consisting of finely shredded grass, on the surface of the ground or occasionally in a shallow burrow or beneath trash.

Males are promiscuous breeders. The gestation period is 21 days. Litter size averages between 4 and 6 young, depending on age and environment; 1 to 11 offspring is the recorded range. Females produce several litters during the breeding season, which may extend throughout the year. Neonates are essentially hairless, with eyes and ears closed; these open by 8 days of age, and weaning takes place 12 to 14 days after birth. Populations are subject to dramatic fluctuations. Meadow voles have a high breeding potential, as well as a high rate of loss to predation. Owls, hawks, snakes, weasels, mink, foxes, domestic cats, and other carnivores take these animals in large numbers. A variety of ecto- and endoparasites has been recorded for this species.

Selected References. Reich (1981); Tamarin (1985); Johnson and Johnson (1982).

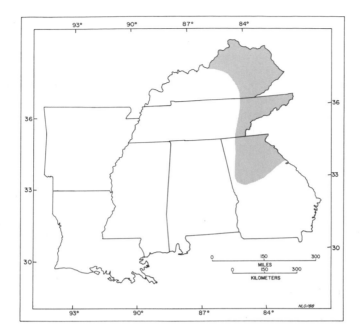

Photo courtesy R. W. Barbour

Microtus pinetorum

Woodland Vole

Distribution. This species ranges from southernmost Canada to northern Florida and from the Atlantic Coast to the central Great Plains. It occurs throughout the south-central states, except in parts of southern Georgia, Alabama, Mississippi, and Louisiana.

Description. Small vole with slender, cylindrical body modified for semi-fossorial life. Tail short, faintly bicolored; eyes and ears small. Fur soft, short, and dense; pelage reddish to brownish chestnut to almost black dorsally, grayish buff to silvery ventrally. Total length, 120–140; tail, 18–25; hind foot, 15–20; ear, 10–13; weight, 20–40 g.

Natural History. This vole lives in a wide range of habitats, including leaf litter of forests and woodlands, and grassy fields with brush and brambles. It is found also beneath mats of honeysuckle, along fencerows and roadways, and in orchards with suitable cover. These are burrowing mammals that spend much time below ground. Apparently they are most active during the day below ground and at night above ground. They construct nests of grasses and leaves in burrows. They eat a wide variety of grasses, stems, roots, seeds, nuts, and bark, which they store in underground chambers. These microtines cause damage to orchards by girdling trees, and they damage crops such as potatoes and peanuts, as well as planted seeds, bulbs, and nursery stock. They consume some animal matter and also are known to be cannibalistic. However, this species normally is quite social; several females with litters may occupy the same nest, and males and females may form monogamous pairs and share their burrow system with offspring.

In the south-central region, breeding occurs throughout the year, with least activity during summer. Young are born after a gestation period of 20 to 24 days. Their eyes and ears are closed at birth but open seven to nine days later. Litter size ranges from one to six young, averaging fewer than three. Large litters are unsuccessful because females have only four mammae (fewer than other microtines), to which the offspring attach firmly when nursing. Young are weaned at 17 to 21 days of age and are fully mature when 10 to 12 weeks old.

Primary predators of woodland voles are hawks, owls, snakes, foxes, and opossums. Numerous endo- and ectoparasites are known to infest these voles.

Selected References. Smolen (1981); Tamarin (1985); Johnson and Johnson (1982).

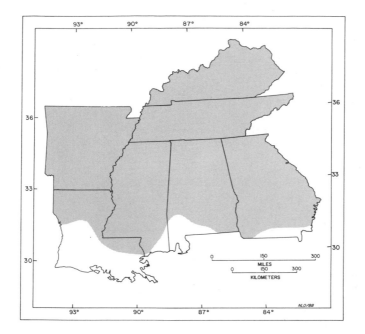

Photo courtesy R. R. Patterson

Neofiber alleni

Round-Tailed Muskrat

Distribution. This species is endemic in parts of peninsular Florida and adjacent southern Georgia.

Description. Resembles a diminutive muskrat; tail round, hind feet slightly webbed. Underfur dense, gray at base to rich brown at tip on back, pale buff on belly; guard hairs dark brown and glossy. Total length, 285–380; tail, 100–160; hind foot, 40–50; ear, 15–22; weight, 200–350 g.

Natural History. This species occupies a variety of marshy habitats but seems to prefer places with shallow water, substrate of sand, and dense aquatic vegetation. It constructs spherical or dome-shaped houses of aquatic grasses and other plant materials and attaches them to emergent vegetation. The houses rest on sphagnum, often at the bases of cypress trees or clumps of brush. Interior chambers, which are lined with fine dry grasses, are about 100 mm in diameter, usually with two exits beneath the water. These houses are utilized by other organisms, especially rice rats. This species frequently constructs a feeding platform consisting of a pad of vegetation near its house. The platforms are elevated slightly above the surface of the water, are 100 to 150 mm in diameter, and contain one or two plunge holes. Populations fluctuate greatly, but frequently range from 25 to 100 round-tailed muskrats per acre in good habitat.

This species is mostly nocturnal, with peaks of activity shortly after dark and just before dawn. Aquatic grasses make up its basic diet, but it also consumes stems, roots, and seeds of other plants. These muskrats breed throughout the year, with a peak in late autumn. Following 26 to 29 days of gestation, litters of 1 to 4 young (averaging 2.2) are born; four to six litters may be produced annually. Neonates are blind and almost naked, with pinnae folded; they weigh 10 to 15 grams. At 14 to 18 days, their eyes are open, all teeth are erupted, and they can care for themselves. Weaning occurs in about 21 days and sexual maturity at 90 to 100 days.

This species harbors numerous endoparasites, of which cestodes, trematodes, and nematodes seem most common. Mites are the most prevalent ectoparasites. Known predators include herons, owls, hawks, snakes, bobcats, and domestic cats. Round-tailed muskrats are not trapped commercially for pelts. They may damage sugarcane.

Selected References. Birkenholz (1972); Perry (1982); Boutin and Birkenholz (1987).

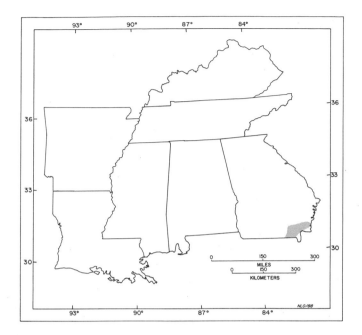

Photo courtesy J. N. Layne

Ondatra zibethicus

Muskrat

Distribution. The muskrat ranges from the Arctic circle southward through the United States, except in Florida and some arid parts of the Southwest, to northernmost Mexico. In the south-central states, this species occurs everywhere in suitable habitat except the extreme southern parts of Alabama and Georgia.

Description. Resembles large vole adapted for aquatic conditions; tail flattened laterally; hind feet webbed. Fur consists of thick underlayer and long, glossy overlayer of guard hairs; pelage generally dark brown but varies from white and silver to tan, brown, and blackish. Total length, 455–550; tail, 200–255; hind foot, 65–78; ear, 20–25; weight, 700–1,500 g.

Natural History. Muskrats live in saline, brackish, and freshwater marshes, ponds, sloughs, lakes, ditches, streams, and rivers. Habitat requirements include a source of permanent water and protected sites for shelter and rearing of young. These mammals either construct conical houses or dig burrows in banks. Water depth, soil texture, and amount of aquatic vegetation influence the selection of sites for houses; soil type and slope of bank determine the complexity and permanence of burrows. Muskrats build their houses above water level, with several underwater entrances. They locate one or more nest chambers lined with fresh plant materials in the center of the dwelling. They also construct small feeding houses. Muskrats are mostly nocturnal, with peaks of activity just after dark and before dawn. *O. zibethicus* feeds mostly on roots and basal parts of aquatic vegetation. This species may consume animal matter, such as crayfish, fish, mollusks, and turtles, during food shortages or when these animals are especially abundant.

Gestation lasts 25 to 30 days. Litter size ranges from four to eight young, averaging between six and seven. As many as five or six litters are produced each year. Young are blind and almost hairless, and have a rounded tail at birth. They are weaned at about four weeks of age and usually begin breeding the following spring. Dominant ectoparasites of the species are mites and ticks; a large number of endoparasites also are known. Raccoons and mink are important predators, but humans are a major cause of mortality in muskrats. In the 1983–1984 season, more than 400,000 pelts were marketed in the south-central region.

Selected References. Willner *et al.* (1980); Perry (1982); Boutin and Birkenholz (1987).

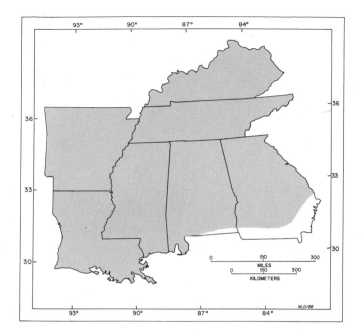

Photo courtesy R. Altig

Synaptomys cooperi

Southern Bog Lemming

Distribution. This bog lemming ranges from southeastern Canada and the northeastern United States west to Kansas and Nebraska and south to parts of Arkansas and Tennessee. In the south-central states, this species is found only in northeastern Arkansas, parts of Kentucky, and eastern Tennessee.

Description. Robust, volelike, with short tail (usually shorter than hind foot). Pelage long, loose, chestnut to grizzled brown on dorsum, silver to pale gray on venter. Eyes and ears small; shallow groove on each upper incisor; lower incisors broad and blunt. Total length, 125–154; tail, 17–24; hind foot, 20–24; ear, 10–14; weight, 30–50 g.

Natural History. These creatures live in numerous habitats, including bogs and various types of mesic grasslands and shrublands, as well as in deciduous and coniferous forests. Frequently, *S. cooperi* occupies habitats that are marginal for other voles. Runways with piles of droppings and cuttings generally indicate the presence of this species; their feces are characteristically bright green in color. These animals are mostly nocturnal but may forage during the day. They eat primarily grasses and sedges, but also mosses, fruits, fungi, bark, and roots. They construct nests of dry leaves and grass, usually placing them in underground chambers, but on saturated substrates locating them above ground under fallen logs or debris.

The estimated gestation period is 21 to 23 days. Litter size ranges from one to eight young, but three is the most common number of offspring. Females are polyestrous, and breeding apparently occurs in all seasons of the year. Neonates are pinkish except for pale gray pigmentation on the dorsum. Their pinnae are folded over and their eyes are closed; claws are present on the toes. Weights of new-born animals range from three to four grams. Young are well furred by 7 days of age, pinnae unfold by the second day, and eyes open at about 10 or 11 days. Lower incisors erupt between six and eight days of age. Young reach nearly adult proportions at about three weeks, when weaning takes place.

Numerous parasites live in association with these rodents. Ectoparasites of this species include mites, lice, ticks, and chiggers; endoparasites include some trematodes and cestodes. Bog lemmings are undoubtedly taken by numerous predators, including coyotes, foxes, and weasels, owls and hawks, and snakes.

Selected Reference. Linzey (1983).

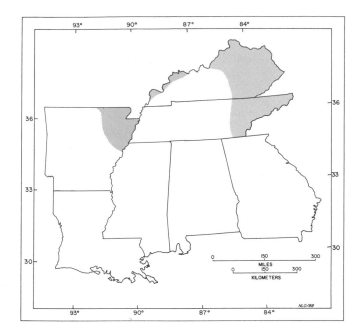

Photo courtesy R. W. Barbour

Zapus hudsonius

Meadow Jumping Mouse

Distribution. This species ranges from coast to coast across southern Alaska and central Canada, southward to the Rocky Mountains, the Great Plains, the Great Lakes states and Ohio River drainage, and the southern end of the Appalachians. In the south-central region, this mouse lives in northern Georgia and adjacent Alabama, most of Tennessee, the northeast-ernmost edge of Mississippi, and most of Kentucky, though there it appar-ently is absent from the Inner Bluegrass area and the Cumberland Plateau.

Description. Hind legs much longer than forelegs; tail long and attenu-ate. Pelage down middle of back dark ochraceous to dark brownish, sides ochraceous to pale orangish; venter white, sometimes suffused with ochra-ceous; tail distinctly bicolored, dark brown above and yellowish white below, not white tipped; ears dark with narrow, pale edges. Total length, 190–240; tail, 108–145; hind foot, 28–32; ear, 12–15; weight, 15–20 g.

Natural History. This species lives in a variety of habitats with adequate herbaceous ground cover, but seems most abundant in weedy-grassy fields and rather thick vegetation near ponds, streams, and marshes. These mice are mostly nocturnal but may forage about at dusk or dawn, and even dur-ing daylight hours. *Z. hudsonius* is a profound hibernator, usually entering hibernation in September and emerging in late April or May. Seeds of grasses and fruits of some woody shrubs are major components of its diet; it also consumes insects and fungi.

Females, which are polyestrous, begin breeding soon after emergence from hibernation and may have as many as three litters per season. Gesta-tion takes from 17 to 21 days. Litter size ranges from 2 to 8 young, with a mean of 4.5. Neonates have minute vibrissae but otherwise are naked; their eyes are closed, and their pinnae are folded over the external ear openings. The pinnae unfold and claws appear during the first week of life. During the third week the young develop hair, and their ears and eyes begin to open. They achieve adult proportions when about 60 days old.

These mice apparently harbor relatively few parasites, but some proto-zoans, trematodes, cestodes, ticks, mites, and fleas live in association with them. Larval botflys and lice also have been reported. Hawks, owls, some snakes, and small mammalian carnivores are the major predators of this species.

Selected Reference. Whitaker (1972).

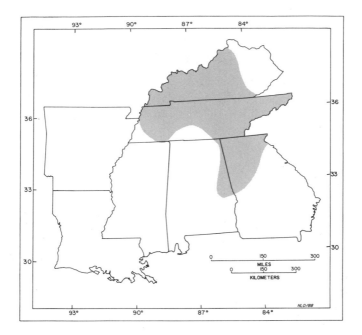

Photo courtesy R. W. Barbour

Napaeozapus insignis

Woodland Jumping Mouse

Distribution. This jumping mouse is found throughout southeastern Canada and the northeastern United States. In the south-central region this species ranges through the higher parts of the Appalachian Highlands of eastern Kentucky and Tennessee, and northern Georgia.

Description. Tail long, hind feet elongated for saltation, front feet small; resembles *Z. hudsonius.* Pelage coarse with stiff guard hairs; dorsal stripe brown to black; sides orange-brown, sometimes with yellow or reddish tint; venter white; tail distinctly bicolored, grayish brown above, white below, usually with white tip. Upper incisors grooved as in *Zapus.* Total length, 205–256; tail, 115–160; hind foot, 28–34; ear, 15–18; weight, 17–26 g.

Natural History. This species seems to prefer mesic mixed and coniferous woodlands, including damp rocky areas within forests and forest-edge vegetation. In areas where both the meadow jumping mouse and woodland jumping mouse occur, the latter is restricted to forested habitats. *N. insignis* is mainly nocturnal but may be active in late morning and early evening, especially in rainy or cloudy weather. These mice hibernate from about mid-September to May. They do not store food in the hibernaculum. Seeds and other plant materials make up most of their diet; they also eat insects, other invertebrates, fungi, fruits, and nuts.

Most reproduction takes place from May through July, but a second peak of breeding may occur in August and September, especially in southern populations. The gestation period is poorly known but probably ranges from about 23 to 29 days. Litter size ranges from 2 to 7 young, with an average of 4.5. Newborn young have loose, rugose, pinkish skin and are hairless except for facial vibrissae. Their eyes and ears are closed. Pigment spots appear on the skin at about 10 days of age. By day 14, the body is covered with fine hair, and the offspring become well furred by day 24. Young attain the general appearance of adults by day 34, except that the pelage is duller in overall appearance, yellowish brown rather than orange-brown on the sides. They molt to adult pelage (there is no subadult coat) between days 63 and 80; adults molt once a year.

Home ranges from half an acre to nine acres have been reported. Densities of two to five mice per acre seem to be the rule, but a far greater range of numbers has been observed. Parasites and predators are much as in *Zapus.*

Selected References. Whitaker and Wrigley (1972); Wrigley (1972).

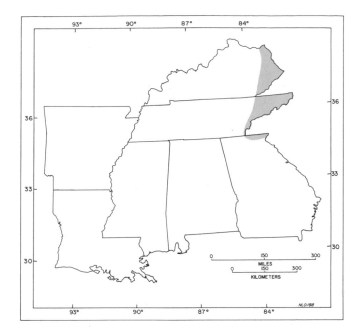

Photo courtesy R. W. Barbour

Erethizon dorsatum

Porcupine

Distribution. The present range of the porcupine includes most of Alaska and Canada, and extends as far south as Pennsylvania in the East and throughout most of the western half of the continental United States to northern Mexico. This species evidently has been extirpated from the south-central region; it apparently once inhabited eastern Kentucky and probably Tennessee and northernmost Georgia.

Description. Dorsum completely covered with long quills. Body short, robust; legs short, bowed, with a pigeon-toed stance; feet heavy, plantigrade, with naked soles; toes clawed, four on front feet, five on hind feet. Face short, muzzle blunt, eyes relatively small; tail short and clublike. Prominent infraorbital foramen on skull. Total length, 650–1,030; tail, 160–250; hind foot, 75–100; ear, 28–40; weight, 5–12 kg or more.

Natural History. Porcupines are not restricted to any specific habitat; they live in open tundra, desert shrubland, and grasslands, and in coniferous, mixed, and deciduous woodlands. Most often they are found in wooded areas. These are usually solitary animals except during the breeding season and in winter, when several animals of both sexes may occupy a den. Porcupines make their dens in caves, crevices, hollow logs, brushpiles, and abandoned buildings. They are vegetarians, in winter eating mostly bark and foliage of woody plants and in summer consuming buds, new leaves, and numerous forbs, grasses, and succulent wetland plants.

The breeding season is from September to the end of November. Gestation takes from 205 to 217 days. A single young (multiple births are rare) is born between April and June. The newborn is precocious; its eyes are open and teeth present. Its quills are soft and well formed at birth but harden within an hour, and the young animal is capable of climbing soon after birth. Offspring generally remain with the female throughout the first summer. Females reach sexual maturity when about 1.5 years old. Porcupines probably live five to seven years under natural conditions.

This species hosts a great number of internal and external parasites. The most efficient predator on porcupines is the fisher; coyotes, mountain lions, bobcats, and wolves occasionally kill them. Humans take the greatest toll on these mammals, through bounty systems, poisoning, indiscriminate shooting and trapping, and highway kills.

Selected References. Woods (1973); Dodge (1982).

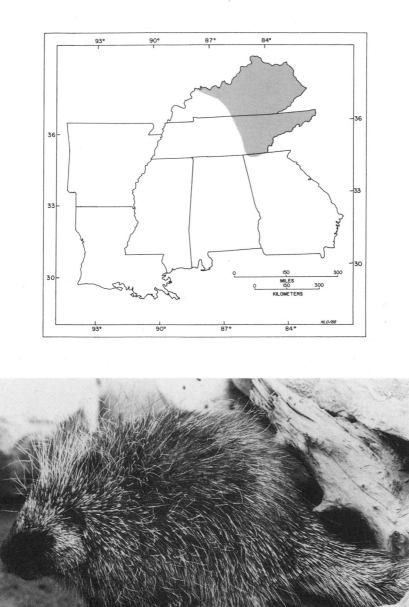

Photo courtesy J. L. Tveten

Order Carnivora

Carnivores

Recent carnivores are grouped into 12 families containing about 100 genera and more than 270 species (among them the aquatic pinnipeds). Members of this order inhabit all major land masses, including Antarctica, where pinnipeds are found along the coasts, and Australia, where, in addition to native pinnipeds, the wild dog (dingo) lives, having been introduced by early humans several thousand years ago. Domestic dogs and cats, as well as the mongoose, have been introduced by man on some oceanic islands. The fossil history of the order dates back to the early Paleocene.

Carnivores generally are flesh-eaters, but some species regularly consume fruits, nuts, and other plant materials; others are true omnivores. Except for the African aardwolf, terrestrial taxa have well-developed canines and an unusual pair of teeth, the carnassials (the fourth upper premolar and the first lower molar), which are specialized for shearing. Carnassials are best developed in the family Felidae and least developed in the families Ursidae and Procyonidae.

Five families of carnivores occur in the south-central states. Of 18 native species (representing 13 genera), 2 species, the gray wolf and the red wolf, have been extirpated from the region. Domestic dogs and cats occur in the feral state as well.

Key to Families of Carnivores

1.   Claws retractile, can be completely concealed in fur; molars 1/1; premolars 2/2 or 3/2 ....Felidae
1'. Claws not retractile, not concealed in fur; molars 1/2 or more; premolars not less than 3/3... 2
2.   Tail conspicuously ringed; molars 2/2 .... Procyonidae
2'. Tail not ringed; molars 1/2 or 2/3 3
3.   Size small to medium (*Lutra* largest); molars 1/2; premolars 4/4 (*Martes*), 4/3 (*Lutra*), or 3/3 ....Mustelidae
3'. Size medium to large (*Vulpes* smallest); molars 2/3; premolars 4/4 . 4
4.   Size large; feet plantigrade; large cheekteeth flattened, slightly cuspidate (lacking conspicuous cutting edges) .... Ursidae
4'. Size medium; feet digitigrade; large cheekteeth not flattened, noticeably cuspidate (with conspicuous cutting edges) ....Canidae

Key to Canids

1.   Total length more than 1,050; condylobasal length of skull more than 160; weight more than 9 kg 2

1'. Total length less than 1,050; condylobasal length of skull less than 155; weight less than 9 kg 5
2.   Total length usually more than 1,400; length of first lower molar more than 25; condylobasal length more than 200 3
2'. Total length less than 1,400; length of first lower molar less than 25; condylobasal length less than 200 4
3.   Premolars relatively broad; second upper molar and inner lobe of first upper molar relatively small; cingulum on outer edge of first upper molar inconspicuous .... *Canis lupus*
3'. Premolars relatively narrow; second upper molar and inner lobe of first upper molar relatively large; cingulum on outer edge of first upper molar usually conspicuous .... *Canis rufus*
4.   Dorsal pelage usually brownish gray; orbits rising gradually above rostrum .... *Canis latrans*
4'. Dorsal pelage variable in color; orbits usually rising abruptly above rostrum .... *Canis familiaris*
5.   Dorsal surface of skull more or less flattened from nasals to orbits; temporal ridges prominent 6
5'. Dorsal surface of skull rising abruptly at orbits; temporal ridges rarely prominent .... *Canis familiaris*
6.   Dorsal pelage reddish; ears tipped with black; condylobasal length usually more than 130; temporal ridges not lyre shaped . *Vulpes vulpes*
6'. Dorsal pelage grizzled grayish; ears lacking black tips; condylobasal length less than 130; temporal ridges lyre shaped
       .... *Urocyon cinereoargenteus*

Key to Procyonids

1.   Tail longer than 300, striped only on upper surface; no face mask; weight less than 2 kg; incisors with secondary lobes
       .... *Bassariscus astutus*
1'. Tail shorter than 300, striped on both upper and lower surfaces; prominent face mask; weight more than 4 kg; incisors without secondary lobes .... *Procyon lotor*

Key to Mustelids

1.   Feet webbed; tail thickened at base and tapering toward tip; premolars 4/3 .... *Lutra canadensis*
1'. Feet not webbed; tail not thickened at base and not tapering toward tip; premolars 4/4 or 3/3 2
2.   Tail approximately as long as hind foot; claws on front foot markedly longer than those on hind foot; braincase triangular in outline
       .... *Taxidea taxus*

2'. Tail considerably longer than hind foot; claws on front foot about same size as or slightly longer than those on hind foot; braincase not markedly triangular in outline 3

3.   Pelage grizzled dark brown to blackish, with pale head, neck, and shoulder; premolars 4/4 .... *Martes pennanti*

3'. Pelage variable in color but not grizzled, lacking pale head, neck, and shoulder; premolars 2/3 or 3/3 4

4.   Pelage black, with white stripes or spots on dorsum; auditory bulla as long as or longer than maxillary toothrow 5

4'. Pelage brown, yellowish brown, or white; auditory bulla shorter than maxillary toothrow 6

5.   Two white dorsal stripes of variable length and width merging with white spot on head and neck; length of skull more than 65 .... *Mephitis mephitis*

5'. Four to six white dorsal stripes, broken into spots posteriorly; length of skull less than 65 .... *Spilogale putorius*

6.   Total length usually more than 475; length of skull more than 55 .... *Mustela vison*

6'. Total length usually less than 450; length of skull less than 55 7

7.   Total length more than 230; tail at least one-third length of body, with distinct black tip; length of skull more than 40 .... *Mustela frenata*

7'. Total length less than 230; tail less than one-third length of body, lacking distinct black tip; length of skull less than 40 .. *Mustela nivalis*

Key to Felids

1.   Tail long, more than 500; weight more than 30 kg; zygomatic breadth more than 115 .... *Felis concolor*

1'. Tail short, less than 200; weight less than 25 kg; zygomatic breadth usually less than 100 2

2.   Tail shorter than hind foot; length of skull more than 130 .. *Lynx rufus*

2'. Tail longer than hind foot; length of skull less than 130 ... **Felis catus*

Canis latrans

Coyote

Distribution. Coyotes range from Alaska across northern Canada to New Brunswick and Nova Scotia, and southward to Costa Rica. They may have been transplanted by humans in some places. *C. latrans* lives throughout the seven-state region, having occupied much of its range there in the past 25 years.

Description. Doglike in appearance, with long legs, narrow muzzle, erect ears, and bushy, black-tipped tail. Pelage grizzled buff or gray overlaid with black-tipped hairs dorsally, whitish, cream, or pale gray with yellowish tint ventrally. Face reddish brown or gray. Melanistic individuals occur in some places. Males slightly larger than females. Total length, 1,000–1,350; tail, 270–420; hind foot, 165–220; ear, 90–120; weight, 5–16 kg.

Natural History. Coyotes inhabit grasslands, brushy areas, forest edges, and both upland and bottomland forests. Eastward expansion of the coyote population probably is correlated with changing agricultural practices involving creation of more open lands. This canid is mainly nocturnal, but it may be observed during daytime, especially along highways and in open fields. Coyotes place their dens in a wide variety of ecological situations, including brush-covered slopes and banks, and in thickets, hollow logs, and crevices. They sometimes take over burrows made by other animals, and they may use the same dens for several years. Insects, rodents, rabbits, birds, and numerous fruits and grasses are frequent food items. Scavenging carrion is common, especially in winter months. In addition, coyotes occasionally consume domestic poultry, livestock, and watermelons.

Coyotes live singly, in pairs, or in small packs or family groups. Most breeding occurs from February to the end of March. Gestation takes about 63 days. Litter size ranges from 2 to 12 young; the average is 6. Neonates weigh 240 to 275 grams and are blind and helpless at birth. They begin to eat solid food at about three weeks of age, are weaned at five to seven weeks, and reach adult size by about nine months.

Coyotes are host to a variety of parasites. Distemper and hepatitis are common diseases; rabies is not. Historically, coyotes have been killed by nearly every means possible devised by humans. This species is an important furbearer; more than 20,000 pelts were taken during the 1983–1984 season in the south-central region.

Selected References. Bekoff (1977, 1978); Voigt and Berg (1987); Novak *et al.* (1987).

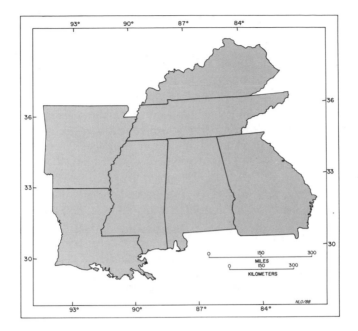

Photo courtesy R. W. Barbour

Canis lupus

Gray Wolf

Distribution. The original range of this species included all of Canada, all of the United States except parts of the Southwest and Southeast, and the plateau of central Mexico. It has been extirpated from much of the southern part of that range. In the south-central region, gray wolves evidently once inhabited Kentucky and most of Tennessee.

Description. Largest wild canid in North America. Fur long and variable in color, from pure white through mottled gray and brown to coal black, but usually grizzled gray, with dark spot above base of tail. Males generally larger than females. Total length, 1,500–2,040; tail, 350–500; hind foot, 220–310; ear, 125–140; weight, 18–80 kg.

Natural History. Wolves originally occupied most habitats within their geographic range. They are highly mobile on land and also are good swimmers. Wolves are social animals, usually functioning in packs of 5 to 8 members, but packs containing up to 36 animals have been reported. Most packs are family groups. Wolves prey on large mammals but may eat almost any species of animal, including domestic livestock. Most studies of wolf predation on wild species have shown that young, old, and otherwise inferior members of prey populations constitute most of the animals killed.

Dens of gray wolves generally are located in well-drained sites, and extensive trail systems radiate from them. In addition to burrows, crevices, hollow logs, brushpiles, and clumps of dense vegetation may be used as denning sites. Gray wolves frequently occupy the same dens for several years. Breeding may occur anytime between January and April. These wolves show mate preferences, but there is no courtship. After a gestation period of about 63 days, an average of 6 young (range 1 to 11) are born, blind and helpless. Their eyes open at 11 to 15 days, deciduous teeth are in place by three weeks of age, and pups are weaned at about five weeks. They reach sexual maturity in about two years but usually do not breed until year three.

Wolves may live 16 years, but 10 years is probably an old age for those in the wild. They harbor numerous internal and external parasites. Diseases afflicting them include rabies, distemper, cancer, and arthritis, but human activities, especially hunting, trapping, and poisoning, are the major causes of mortality. The gray wolf's fur is highly valued.

Selected References. Mech (1974); Paradiso and Nowak (1982); Carbyn (1987).

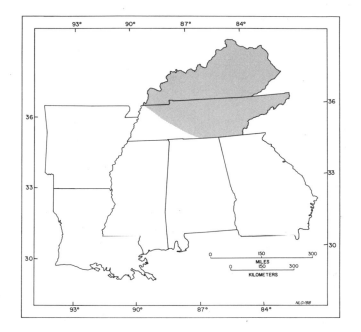

Photo courtesy R. W. Barbour

Canis rufus

Red Wolf

Distribution. The original range of the red wolf included the southeastern United States, west to central Texas and Oklahoma and north to southern Indiana and Virginia. The species was eradicated by trapping and poisoning but persisted until the 1970s in swampland of southern Louisiana. Today the red wolf exists in the south-central region only in captivity and in refuges off the coasts of Georgia and Mississippi.

Description. Generally intermediate in size between gray wolf and coyote. Pelage coarse, tail bushy and tipped with black, muzzle, ears, nape, and outer surfaces of legs tawny; cinnamon-buff and tawny interspersed with gray and black dorsally, back appearing blackish; nose, throat, and belly whitish. Mostly black individuals (white on feet, chin, and throat) reported in some areas. Total length, 1,350–1,650; tail, 345–430; hind foot, 210–250; ear, 120–130; weight, 16–41 kg.

Natural History. Red wolves apparently inhabited pine forests and bottomland hardwood forests, as well as some parts of coastal prairies and marshes. Dens of this species have been found in hollow logs, stumps, culverts, and sand knolls, and banks of canals, ditches, and reservoirs. Entrances to dens generally are screened from view by vines, brushpiles, trees, and shrubs. These wolves are most active at night; during daylight they have been observed resting in weedy fields, tall grass, and clumps of brush. Mated pairs, sometimes with an extra male, usually travel together; packs of 5 to 11 animals may come together temporarily. *C. rufus* apparently is not a major predator of big game; rabbits, rodents, and other small animals are its most frequently taken prey. There are some sketchy reports of red wolf predation on domestic livestock.

Breeding probably occurs from late December to early March; young are born in April and May. Litter size ranges from 2 to 10 young, averaging 6.6. Young reportedly reach sexual maturity and begin breeding sometime after two years of age. Before their extirpation from this region, humans were the greatest threat to red wolves through deliberate killing and habitat modification. These animals are known to be infested with hookworms, heartworms, and numerous other parasites. Also, mange is commonly found on red wolves. There is considerable evidence that hybridization with coyotes contributed to the decimation of populations of *C. rufus*.

Selected References. Paradiso and Nowak (1972, 1982); Carbyn (1987).

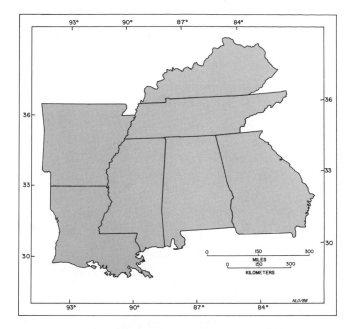

Photo courtesy R. W. Barbour

Vulpes vulpes

Red Fox

Distribution. This species ranges throughout most of Canada and the United States. It does not occur in some areas of the Rocky Mountains and adjacent plains and arid regions of the Southwest. The red fox is found throughout the south-central states except in coastal areas of Georgia and Louisiana.

Description. General appearance that of a small dog. Tail long, bushy, tipped with white; backs of ears, legs, and feet black; reddish yellow to tawny dorsally, whitish or grayish on cheeks, throat, and belly. Total length, 900–1,140; tail, 300–430; hind foot, 135–175; ear, 75–95; weight, 2.7–7.8 kg.

Natural History. Red foxes are found most commonly in oak-pine wooded uplands that are interspersed with farms and pastures. The species lives also in some bottomland woods, especially adjacent to cane fields and other agricultural areas. Although principally nocturnal, these foxes may be seen in broad daylight and even more often at dawn and dusk.

The major part of this species' diet consists of small mammals, such as rabbits, mice, and voles, but red foxes also eat small birds, eggs, insects, and considerable amounts of plant materials, especially certain fruits. On occasion they eat carrion found along roadways. They frequently locate their dens along edges of fields and woodlands, along stream banks and gullies. They also use crevices, burrows made by other animals, and retreats in or under abandoned buildings.

Red foxes are monogamous and may remain mated for life. Breeding occurs in January and February. After a gestation period of 51 to 53 days, 1 to 11 young (usually 4 or 5) are born. At birth the offspring weigh about 10 grams, and their eyes are closed. Both parents provide food for the kits, which first appear outside the den at about three weeks of age. They are weaned when about two months old and disperse at about six months. They reach sexual maturity and begin breeding when 10 to 12 months of age.

High mortality of red foxes results from motor vehicle kills, hunting, and trapping. During the 1983–1984 season, hunters and trappers took more than 21,000 red foxes in the south-central region. Numerous internal and external parasites are reported in *V. vulpes*. These animals seem especially subject to coccidiosis, distemper, and rabies.

Selected References. Samuel and Nelson (1982); Voigt (1987); Novak *et al.* (1987).

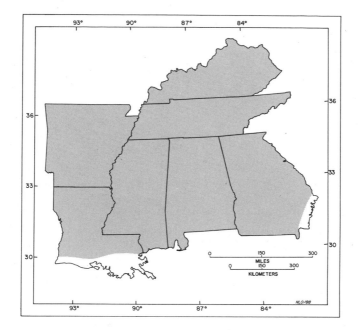

Photo courtesy R. Altig

Urocyon cinereoargenteus

Gray Fox

Distribution. The gray fox ranges from southern Canada to northern Venezuela and Colombia. It does not inhabit parts of the Great Plains or the highlands of the northwestern United States. The species occurs throughout the south-central region except in the southern delta of Louisiana.

Description. Skull unique in having lyrate ridges on braincase. Grizzled dorsum; black-tipped hairs forming longitudinal stripe down back and on dorsum of tail; tail bushy with black tip; parts of neck, sides, and legs cinnamon. Venter buff; white fur on ears, throat, chest, belly, and hind legs; black, white, and rufous facial markings. Males slightly larger than females. Total length, 800–1,025; tail, 280–375; hind foot, 125–150; ear, 60–80; weight, 2.5–7.0 kg.

Natural History. Gray foxes usually inhabit deciduous forests, but they explore old fields and roadsides on occasion. They place their dens in hollow logs, cavities under rocks and brush, abandoned buildings, and burrows constructed by other animals. Unlike other foxes, gray foxes are capable of climbing trees for foraging, resting, and escaping. These animals are primarily nocturnal and crepuscular. They consume a wide variety of plant and animal materials, varying seasonally and geographically. They eat plant parts throughout the year; rodents are important prey in winter, invertebrates in summer. Gray foxes also ingest birds, eggs, and carrion when available, and they occasionally take domestic poultry.

The peak of breeding is in February and March. After a gestation period of 51 to 63 days, 1 to 10 young (usually 3 to 5) are born; their eyes are closed, and they weigh about 10 grams. Both parents provide food for the young until they begin to forage at about three months of age. These foxes reach sexual maturity at about 10 months and probably breed annually thereafter. Average life expectancy in the wild is probably four to five years. Harvest by humans is the leading cause of mortality of gray foxes. Trappers and hunters took nearly 50,000 gray foxes in the south-central region during the 1983–1984 season. Other animals that prey on gray foxes include eagles, coyotes, and bobcats. Infectious diseases are major sources of death, and gray foxes are susceptible to rabies, distemper, leptospirosis, mange, and hepatitis.

Selected References. Fritzell and Haroldson (1982); Samuel and Nelson (1982); Fritzell (1987).

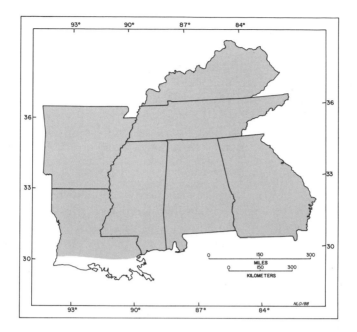

Photo courtesy R. Steibben

Ursus americanus

Black Bear

Distribution. The original range of this bear encompassed all of North America except treeless areas of northern Canada and desert regions of the Southwest. It has been extirpated from many areas of the aboriginal range. Previously, black bears lived throughout the south-central region, excluding extreme southern Louisiana. Remnant populations still live in the Appalachians in Tennessee and in remote enclaves in Georgia, Alabama, Mississippi, Louisiana, and Arkansas.

Description. Compact, heavily structured body, with relatively massive legs and feet. Head moderate size, with tapered nose, small eyes, and small, erect, rounded ears; feet plantigrade, with strong, curved, nonretractible claws; tail short. Fur generally uniform in color except for brownish muzzle. White blaze present occasionally on chest. Black color phase prevalent in south-central region; brown phase may be present. Total length, 1,250–1,800; tail, 80–125; hind foot, 185–280; ear, 130–145; weight, 100–250 kg. Males average 10 percent larger than females.

Natural History. Because of requirements for space, food, water, and cover, bears are mostly inhabitants of woodlands and are limited to secluded forests and swamplands in this region. Black bears bed down in dense thickets, canebrakes, and rock or brush shelters by day. They are normally nocturnal but sometimes are active in daylight. These are excellent climbers, and young often take refuge in trees when threatened.

Other than sows with cubs, black bears tend to be solitary except at mating, which normally takes place from May to July. Young are born in January or February in a den in a hollow tree or underground, after about seven months' gestation. Neonates weigh 170 to 280 grams and are virtually naked, with eyes closed. Litter size ranges from one to four young, two or three being most common. Young usually accompany the female for about 16 months; they reach maturity in about 3 years and full adult size in about 6. Adult females breed again after their young disperse.

Black bears consume a variety of plant and animal materials, according to food availability. Numerous parasites live in association with bears, but none appear of importance in regulation of populations. Malnutrition and hunting are major causes of mortality. In the 1983–1984 season, hunters killed a total of 80 black bears in the south-central states.

Selected References. Eiler *et al.* (1989); Jonkel (1978); Pelton (1982); Kolenosky (1987); Novak *et al.* (1987).

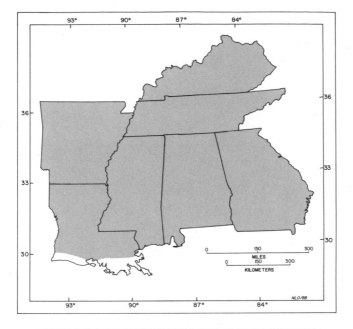

Photo courtesy R. W. Barbour

Bassariscus astutus

Ringtail

Distribution. This species ranges from southern Oregon southward and eastward to the Mississippi River and central Mexico. In the south-central states, ringtails have been reported only in the northern half of Louisiana and the southern part of Arkansas.

Description. Small, slender, somewhat catlike; feet semiplantigrade, with semiretractile claws on each of five toes on each foot; tail about length of body, appears flat but hairs can be erected to form cylinder. Muzzle pointed; ears large, erect, round; eyes large. Eye ring black surrounded by prominent white eye patches. Dorsum pale buff with black-tipped hairs; feet and venter white or buffy white; tail white, with black tip and six to nine usually incomplete black bands ventrally. Total length, 615–810; tail, 310–440; hind foot, 60–78; ear, 45–50; weight, 725–1,100 g. Males slightly larger than females.

Natural History. Ringtails inhabit a wide variety of rocky and wooded habitats, usually within a half mile of standing water. They make dens in caves, crevices, and burrows, as well as rock piles and brushpiles, hollows in trees, and buildings. These animals are active year-round and are nocturnal. They run, leap, and climb with apparent ease. Ringtails are omnivorous; small mammals, fruits, and arthropods make up most of their diet, but they take other invertebrates, reptiles, and birds opportunistically. They eat carrion occasionally.

Mating usually occurs in March or April. Gestation takes about 51 to 54 days. Most young are born in May and June. Litter size ranges from 1 to 5 young, averaging 3 to 4. Neonates are altricial and almost naked, with eyes and ear canals closed; they weight 18 to 30 grams. Their eyes and ears open between 20 and 34 days. Young are fully furred by six weeks of age. They are weaned between 8 and 12 weeks and reach adult size at about 23 weeks; they achieve sexual maturity at about 10 months.

Known predators on *B. astutus* are owls, snakes, and domestic dogs and cats. Bobcats and coyotes are also potential predators. Humans are the greatest threat to these animals; some are killed by vehicles, but many are killed by trappers, often in traps set for other, more valuable furbearers. Ringtails are too uncommon in the seven-state region to be a factor in the fur trade.

Selected References. Kaufmann (1987, 1982).

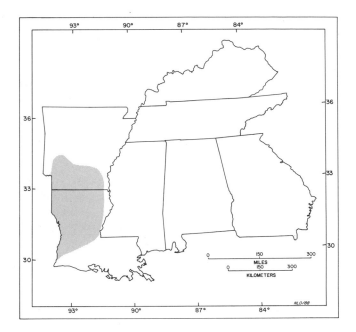

Photo courtesy J. L. Tveten

Procyon lotor

Raccoon

Distribution. The raccoon ranges across North America, from Nova Scotia and British Columbia throughout the United States, except in some portions of the Rocky Mountains and Great Basin, southward to Panama. This species occurs throughout the south-central states, where it probably is the most common wild carnivore.

Description. Body stocky, with broad head, pointed nose, and bushy tail. Feet pentadactyl and plantigrade. Black mask on whitish face; four to seven dark rings on tail, rings poorly defined and infrequently interrupted below. General body color gray to blackish dorsally, paler ventrally. Variable amounts of yellow and brown in fur; cinnamon and albino raccoons not uncommon. Total length, 730–950; tail, 220–260; hind foot, 100–125; ear, 50–65; weight, 5–15 kg or occasionally more.

Natural History. The raccoon is usually most abundant near water, especially in bottomland forests along streams, hardwood swamps, flooded timber near reservoirs, marshes, and wooded areas near urban developments. It also is common in agricultural areas, especially near corn fields. Tree dens may be in any hollow limb or trunk of sufficient size; ground dens are in burrows dug by other animals, especially in areas where hollow trees are scarce. Raccoons also utilize as dens crevices and caves, rock piles and brushpiles, drains, abandoned buildings, and clusters of dense vegetation. This species is omnivorous and opportunistic; hundreds of species of plant and animal foods have been recorded in its diet. Raccoons are typically active from sunset to sunrise, but may forage during the day. Males ordinarily mate with several females during the breeding season, which extends from December to June; the peak of activity is in February and March. Gestation usually takes 63 to 65 days. Litter size ranges from 1 to 8 young (usually 2 to 5). Young leave the den and forage with the mother at 8 to 12 weeks.

Activities of man—hunting, trapping, and hitting animals with vehicles—are the chief causes of mortality in raccoons. Malnutrition in young during the winter is another major cause of death. Except for distemper, diseases and parasites seem to cause relatively few deaths in this species. Raccoons harbor numerous parasites. In the 1983–1984 season, more than a half million raccoon pelts were marketed from the south-central states.

Selected References. Lotze and Anderson (1979); Kaufmann (1982); Sanderson (1987); Novak *et al.* (1987).

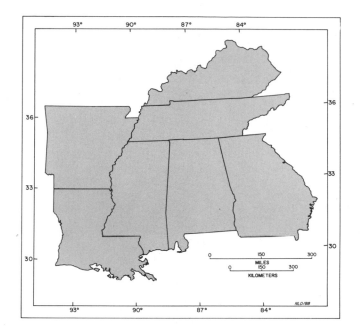

Photo courtesy K. Steibben

Martes pennanti

Fisher

Distribution. The fisher originally ranged from coast to coast across central Canada and the northern United States, extending southward in the mountains of California in the West and the Appalachians in the East. Before extirpation, this species inhabited northeastern Tennessee and most of Kentucky.

Description. Largest member of genus *Martes*. Body long and slender (weasel shaped); tail bushy, about one-third total length; legs short; face pointed, ears rounded; feet with retractable but unsheathed claws. Fur long except on face; pelage generally black, but hoary gold or silver on face, neck, and shoulders owing to tricolored guard hairs. Patches of white occasionally around genital area and in axillae of forelegs. Total length, 800–1,050; tail, 280–400; hind foot, 90–130; ear, 40–46; weight, 1.8–5.4 kg. Males larger, heavier, and more muscular than females.

Natural History. Fishers usually are found in forests with trees of various ages and species. Quantity of overhead cover, availability of denning sites, and food supply govern the preference of habitats. Fishers locate their dens mostly in large trees but also use hollow logs, brushpiles and rock piles, crevices, and burrows of other animals. Dens are of two types, one used for cover and protection and the other for whelping. These animals climb readily. Perhaps because of their smaller size, females seem more arboreal than males. Fishers are active both day and night, with peaks of activity at dawn and dusk. Rabbits, porcupines, and small rodents are their major foods, but they consume invertebrates and other small vertebrates opportunistically.

Fishers are solitary except during the breeding season in March and April. Following delayed implantation, gestation occurs, taking from 30 to 60 days. Litter size varies from 1 to 6 young, averaging 2.8. Young are blind, helpless, and sparsely furred; they weigh about 40 grams, and their eyes open in about 53 days. Nursing lasts three months or more. Males are not involved with care of young, which reach the approximate size of adults at about five months of age; they begin breeding when one year old. Numerous endo- and ectoparasites are associated with fishers but probably do not cause death. Because of its size, strength, and agility, this species has few natural enemies. Trapping and habitat destruction, however, are major threats to this mustelid.

Selected References. Powell (1981); Douglas and Strickland (1987); Strickland *et al.* (1982).

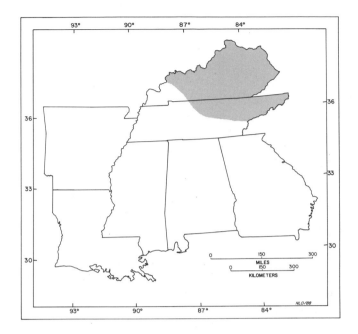

Photo courtesy R. Altig

Mustela frenata

Long-Tailed Weasel

Distribution. This species ranges from southern Canada southward into northern South America, excluding arid areas of the United States and Mexico. In the south-central region, this mustelid is reported everywhere except in southern Louisiana.

Description. Largest of North American weasels. Body long and slender, legs short, tail proportionally long. Dorsum brown in summer; venter whitish, tinged with yellowish or buffy brown; tail uniformly brown except for black tip. Winter pelage is much the same color (slightly paler dorsally) in seven-state region, but longer and denser. Animals in some areas have white or yellow facial markings. Males larger than females. Total length, 285–430; tail, 85–140; hind foot, 30–50; ear, 18–25; weight, 85–250 g.

Natural History. Long-tailed weasels live in forest-edge habitats as well as in brushlands, woodlands, fencerows, and sometimes agricultural and urban areas. They commonly use burrows of other mammals as den sites, but also make dens in brushpiles and rock piles, under stumps and logs, and among tree roots, as well as occasionally under human dwellings. Weasels forage for food during all hours of the day and night. Their major food items are small mammals (mice, rats, voles, rabbits, chipmunks, pocket gophers), but they also eat invertebrates, amphibians, reptiles, and birds. Weasels may kill more prey than they can eat; they cache surplus carcasses in their den areas.

Mating occurs in July and August. This species exhibits delayed implantation, after which gestation occurs, lasting about 27 days. The blind and helpless neonates, born in midspring, weigh about three grams. Litter size varies from 1 to 12 young, averaging 5 to 8. Eyes open at about five weeks of age, and young are weaned at six to eight weeks. They remain with the adult female during their first summer. Females reach sexual maturity and mate when three to four months old; males attain sexual maturity and first breed at about one year. Adult weasels are usually solitary except during the mating season. Home ranges vary from 30 or 40 acres to 180 acres or more.

The parasites and diseases afflicting *M. frenata* are not well known. Other carnivores and birds of prey kill weasels; various snakes also prey on them. Unlike the white winter pelage of northern populations of this species, the fur of long-tailed weasels in this region is not especially valuable.

Selected References. Svendsen (1982); Fagerstone (1987).

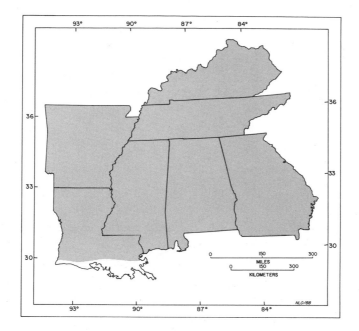

Photo courtesy R. W. Barbour

Mustela nivalis

Least Weasel

Distribution. In North America, this species is found from Alaska and parts of northern Canada southward in the United States to Oklahoma, and as far east as western Pennsylvania and the Appalachians of North Carolina. The least weasel is known only in extreme eastern Tennessee in the south-central region but also may occur in eastern Kentucky and northwestern Georgia.

Description. Smallest carnivore in North America. Summer pelage brown dorsally, white ventrally. At low latitudes and elevations, pelage brown or mottled in winter; at high latitudes and elevations, pelage entirely white after autumnal molt. Winter pelage present from about November to March. Tail is short with no black tip. Total length, 180–215; tail, 25–45; hind foot, 20–28; ear, 10–15; weight, 30–65 g. Males appreciably larger than females.

Natural History. The least weasel has been recorded in a wide variety of habitats, including open woodlands, brushy or grassy areas, fencerows, marshes, and cultivated fields. Least weasels may forage over areas of several acres in search of food. The abundance of other small mammals seems important in determining the local distribution of this species. This diminutive weasel specializes in small prey; voles and mice make up most of its diet, but it takes shrews, moles, birds, and invertebrates on occasion.

This species locates its nests in old burrows of other mammals, as well as in brushpiles and rock piles and under haystacks. These animals may be active night or day. Adults are solitary except during periods of breeding, which may occur at any time of the year. Nestling females are bred by males even before their eyes are open. Delayed implantation is not known for this species. Gestation takes about 35 days; litter size ranges from 1 to 10 young, with 4 to 5 the average. Young are born blind and hairless, weighing about 1.5 grams. Growth and pelage development are rapid; the young reach maturity and disperse at 12 to 14 weeks.

The estimated life expectancy of this species is less than one year. Lack of food may be the leading cause of mortality of this weasel. Least weasels are susceptible to distemper, and they harbor numerous endo- and ecto-parasites. Raptors and other carnivores are known to prey on them. They are too small to be of value in the fur trade.

Selected References. Svendsen (1982); Fagerstone (1987).

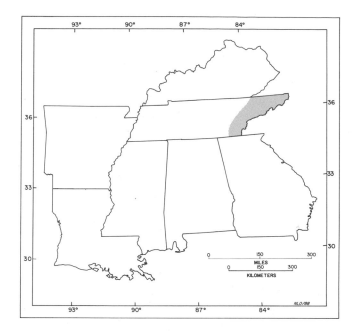

Photo courtesy J. F. Parnell

Mustela vison

Mink

Distribution. The mink is found in all except the extreme northern part of Canada and throughout the continental United States excluding Arizona. Thus *Mustela vison* ranges throughout the south-central region.

Description. Body long and thin, with short, sturdy legs; head flattened, with short, rounded ears and pointed nose. Feet with semiwebbed toes, fully furred except for pads on toes and soles. Pelage soft and lustrous, with thick underfur and long, glossy guard hairs; dorsal color varies from dark brown to nearly black, ventral surface somewhat paler; white patches may occur on chin, chest, and abdomen; tail thickly furred and similar to body in color but progressively darker toward tip. Total length, 510–680; tail, 135–210; hind foot, 50–75; ear, 19–27; weight, 0.7–1.6 kg. Marked sexual dimorphism; males average 10 percent larger than females.

Natural History. The mink is a semiaquatic species that is seldom found far from permanent water. Common den sites are bank burrows of other animals, especially muskrats, but mink also den in beaver lodges, brushpiles and rock piles, and cavities among roots of trees. Mammals (lagomorphs, rodents) are the mink's most common prey, but it consumes invertebrates, fish, and birds as available. Most mink, especially males, are primarily nocturnal. However, both sexes are known to forage at dawn and dusk, and occasionally may be encountered during the day.

Males and females generally associate only for brief periods during the mating season, which occurs from late February to April. Copulation is frequently vigorous and prolonged. Young are born 28 to 30 days after implantation, usually from late April to the end of May. Litter size is one to eight young, averaging four. Neonatal mink are altricial and weigh 8 to 10 grams. Their eyes open and deciduous teeth appear at about three weeks of age. The young grow rapidly, attaining 40 percent of adult body weight and 60 percent of adult body length by seven weeks of age. Young mink are playful, usually vocalizing and attacking one another until the litter disperses in early autumn.

The mink is one of the most valuable North American furbearers. In the 1983–1984 season, more than 65,000 pelts were marketed from the seven-state region. Mink are host to numerous internal parasites as well as mites, fleas, and lice. Diseases in wild populations are not well known.

Selected References. Linscombe *et al.* (1982); Eagle and Whitman (1987); Novak *et al.* (1987).

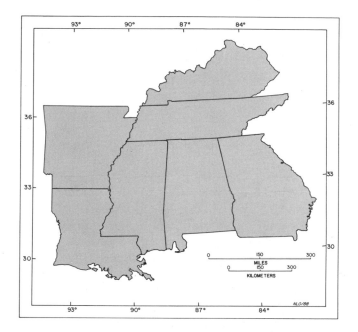

Photo courtesy W. D. Zehr

Taxidea taxus

Badger

Distribution. The range of the badger extends from northern Alberta, Canada, to central Mexico, and from the Pacific Coast to the north-central states. In the south-central region, this species is reported only in northwestern Arkansas.

Description. Body depressed; legs short, stout, with long, recurved foreclaws and short, shovel-like hind claws. Head broad and flattened; neck short and muscular; eyes small; ears small and rounded. Pelage shaggy, longer on sides than back; white medial stripe extending from near nose over head to shoulder and back region; cheeks white with black patch in front of each ear; fur grizzled grayish or brownish dorsally, hairs frosted with long white tips; yellowish-white ventrally; feet black or brown; tail yellowish brown, short, and bushy. Total length, 680–780; tail, 110–135; hind foot, 100–130; ear, 40–58; weight, 5–12 kg.

Natural History. Badgers seem to prefer open country and tend to inhabit areas with loose, sandy soils; they generally avoid rocky soils and heavily wooded sites. Evidence suggests that their range is extending eastward in correlation with the clearing of forests.

These animals are exceptionally well adapted for rapid digging. They are mostly nocturnal, foraging at night and remaining underground during the day, but it is not uncommon to observe them moving about in daytime. Their digging ability is a unique adaptation for capturing prey from underground burrows, including pocket gophers, ground squirrels, and other rodents. They also consume rabbits, bird eggs and nestlings, lizards, snakes, and invertebrates opportunistically, as well as plants, especially corn.

Badgers are promiscuous; most breeding takes place in late July and August. After a period of delayed implantation, parturition occurs in March or April. Litter size varies from one to five young, usually being three. Young are weaned when about 8 weeks old but remain with the female for about a year. These animals may live as long as 15 years but probably seldom achieve that age in nature. They have few natural enemies but frequently are killed by humans—by motor vehicles and agricultural equipment, and through trapping and indiscriminate shooting. Badgers are too geographically restricted in the south-central region to be a factor in the fur trade. They host numerous endo- and ectoparasites, and are susceptible to tularemia and rabies.

Selected References. Lindzey (1982); Long (1973); Messick (1987).

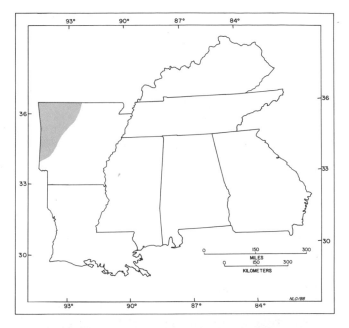

Photo courtesy D. Randall

Spilogale putorius

Eastern Spotted Skunk

Distribution. This species ranges from northeastern Mexico northward through the Great Plains to the Canadian border, and over much of the eastern United States. It is found throughout much of the south-central region but is absent from coastal areas of Georgia and Louisiana, as well as from northern Kentucky and parts of the Mississippi Valley.

Description. Small, slender, not much larger than a squirrel. Pelage black with white spots and four to six broken stripes; tail bushy, tipped with white; claws on forefeet twice length of those on hind feet. Musk pungent. Total length, 470–585; tail, 175–240; hind foot, 40–55; ear, 20–26; weight, 325–650 g.

Natural History. These skunks live in a variety of habitats, including pastures, woodlands, forest edges, croplands, fencelines and hedgerows, and farmyards. They have a preference for rocky outcrops and ledges where natural cavities and crevices provide shelter and den sites. Spotted skunks are mostly nocturnal. They are omnivorous, feeding on small mammals, reptiles, insects and other invertebrates, and some plant materials. *Spilogale* is an agile climber, enabling it to feed on bird eggs and nestlings. It occasionally raids poultry houses to eat eggs and kill domestic fowl.

Breeding occurs from late March to the end of April. Some females produce a second litter in late summer (July–August). Gestation is estimated at 50 to 65 days; there is a short delayed implantation, probably about 10 to 14 days. Females produce a litter of two to nine young, but the usual number is four or five. Young weigh about 10 grams at birth; their eyes and ears are closed. Neonates are almost hairless, but the characteristic color pattern shows in the skin. Their eyes open within 30 days. The young are weaned when about eight weeks old, but they may forage with the female for some time. Females begin breeding when they are about 9 or 10 months of age.

These skunks exhibit a unique defensive behavior; it consists of standing and walking on the forelimbs, with hindquarters and tail in the air. Like striped skunks, spotted skunks carry a wide variety of endo- and ectoparasites; they are particularly susceptible to distemper, rabies, and nasal nematodes. Also, many spotted skunks are killed on roadways. Trapping of this species is relatively limited.

Selected References. Howard and Marsh (1982); Rosatte (1987).

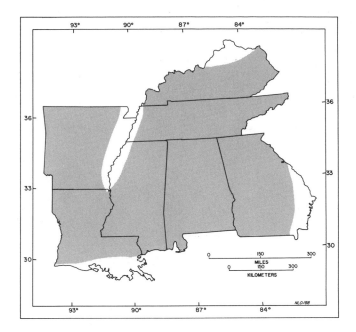

Photo courtesy New York Zoological Society

Mephitis mephitis

Striped Skunk

Distribution. This skunk ranges over most of southern Canada, from British Columbia, Hudson Bay, and Nova Scotia, through the United States to northern Mexico, excluding some arid regions of the Southwest. It is found throughout the south-central states, except in the lower Mississippi Delta in southeastern Louisiana.

Description. About size of domestic cat, but with head relatively small, triangular; ears short, rounded; eyes small. Legs short; long, curved claws on front feet. Fur dense, coarse, and oily; black or brownish black dorsally with narrow white stripe on middle of forehead and on nape that divides (usually) into two white stripes continuing for part or all of body length; black ventrally; tail relatively long and bushy. Coloration highly variable; some animals almost entirely black, others mainly white on back. Total length, 520–770; tail, 170–280; hind foot, 65–85; ear, 25–30; weight, 1.2–5.5 kg. As in most other mustelids, males larger than females.

Natural History. These skunks seem to prefer open habitats or forest edge. They are abundant on agricultural lands wherever there are adequate supplies of food and cover, and they also adapt to life in urban areas, especially beneath houses and garages. Essentially nocturnal, they emerge about dusk to forage, locating food mainly by odor. Small, shallow holes and overturned stones and displaced sticks are usual signs left by foraging animals. Striped skunks are opportunistic omnivorous predators; they feed heavily on insects and other invertebrates but occasionally consume mice and other small mammals, birds and eggs, and fruits and other vegetable matter.

Most breeding apparently occurs from February to April in this region. Males are polygamous and may mate with several females in succession. Parturition usually occurs in May and June. Size of litters ranges from 2 to 10 young, usually 5 to 7. Neonates weigh about 32 to 35 grams. Their eyes and external auditory meatuses are closed at birth; these structures usually open at 22 to 27 days. The unmistakable musk, caused by a sulfur-containing chemical (mercaptan) produced by two anal scent glands, is present at birth. Young are nursed for six to seven weeks; they disperse in August or September. These animals may live as long as 10 years, but few probably live more than 3 years in the wild.

Selected References. Wade-Smith and Verts (1982); Godin (1982); Rosatte (1987).

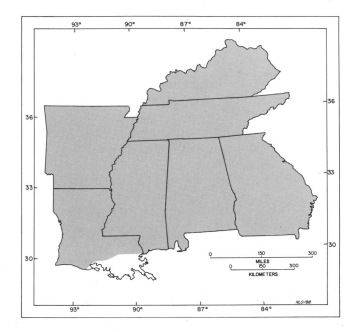

Photo courtesy N. L. Olson

Lutra canadensis

River Otter

Distribution. The original range of this otter encompassed all of North America except the northern parts of Alaska and Canada and the arid Southwest. In the seven-state region, this species occurs presently in favorable habitats associated with major waterways; it is absent from mountainous areas of the Ozarks and southern Appalachians.

Description. Largest mustelid in region. Long bodied; head small, flattened, with broad muzzle; ears and eyes small, tail about one-third of total length, tapered from base to tip; legs short, toes fully webbed. Fur thick and glossy; color ranging from dull brown to dark reddish brown dorsally, pale brown or grayish ventrally; throat and muzzle silvery gray to brownish white. Total length, 890–1,200; tail, 350–520; hind foot, 100–140; ear, 20–30; weight, 4.5–15 kg.

Natural History. Otters spend most of their time in and near rivers, creeks, bayous, and lakes, especially those bordered by timber. These are playful mammals, seemingly taking particular delight in sliding down mud banks into the water. Slides may be used so extensively over time that they become deep troughs. Otters can be seen any time of day, but most activity occurs from dawn to midmorning and in the evening. They do not excavate dens, but use burrows of other animals and natural shelters. Fish constitutes most of the diet; otters also consume crustaceans, amphibians, insects, birds, and small mammals when available.

In the south-central states, breeding takes place in late winter and early spring. Copulation normally occurs in the water. Delayed implantation results in a total gestation of 290 to 380 days; actual gestation of 60 to 63 days following implantation has been reported. Litter size ranges from one to six young (usually two or three).

River otters have few natural predators, although bobcats, dogs, coyotes, and alligators have been reported to kill them. Of internal parasites reported, roundworms may be the most damaging. Taking otters for their fur is the most apparent human impact on populations. In the period 1980–1982, nearly 30,000 otters were harvested in the region. Another cause in the decline of numbers is habitat destruction, owing in part to degradation of water quality because of increased siltation and pesticide residues.

Selected References. Novak *et al.* (1987); Melquist and Dronkert (1987); Toweill and Tabor (1982).

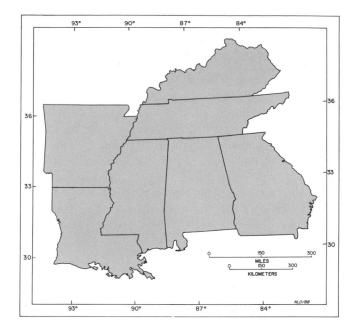

Photo courtesy Michigan Department of Natural Resources

Felis concolor

Mountain Lion

Distribution. The original range of the mountain lion was probably the largest of any terrestrial mammal in the Western Hemisphere, extending from southern Yukon to the tip of Chile. This species has been extirpated from most of the south-central region; it may remain in a few areas of Arkansas and perhaps in Louisiana.

Description. One of largest native North American cats. Adults tawny, gray, red, or shades of brown dorsally, with paler venter; tail long, more than one-third of total length, tipped with black; ears rounded, without tufts, blackish externally. Claws long, sharp, curved, and retractile. Distinctive three-lobed appearance to heel pads on both front and hind feet. Total length, 1,500–2,740; tail, 535–900; hind foot, 220–295; ear, 75–100; weight, 35–100 kg.

Natural History. Mountain lions live primarily in rough, rocky, wooded uplands, large tracts of bottomland forest and swamps, and remote mountainous regions, avoiding humans. They spend most of their time on the ground but readily climb trees and rocks to escape pursuit or to gain an advantageous position when hunting. White-tailed deer are their staple food, but they also eat smaller mammals, taking feral pigs and domestic livestock occasionally. Once a mountain lion has eaten its fill, it may hide the remainder of its kill in a food cache for several days.

Mountain lions are polygamous; home ranges of males generally overlap those of several females. Females usually do not breed with more than one male during an estrous period. The gestation period is 90 to 96 days. Litters consist of one to six young, weighing about 480 grams each. Their eyes and ear canals are closed at birth but open in 5 to 14 days. Kittens remain in or near the den until two to three months old, when they are weaned and begin accompanying the female on hunting trips. Young may remain with the mother for up to two years. Mountain lions first breed when they are about 2.5 years old. Free-ranging animals may live as long as 10 to 12 years. Mountain lions are exceptionally free of ectoparasites but obtain endoparasites from their prey. Causes of mortality of mountain lions include injury from large prey, fighting, and in the case of kittens, killing by other mountain lions. Starvation, disease, and deaths caused by humans also take a toll on this species.

Selected References. Dixon (1982); Currier (1983); Lindzey (1987).

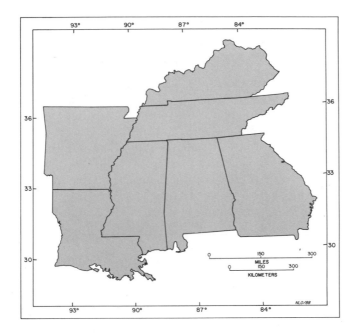

Photo courtesy R. W. Barbour

Lynx rufus

Bobcat

Distribution. This species ranges across southern Canada, throughout most of the United States, and in Mexico as far south as Oaxaca. Bobcats are found throughout most of the seven-state region; they are scarce in Kentucky, however, and are absent from the lower coastal areas of Louisiana.

Description. Dorsum grayish, buffy, or reddish, venter whitish, both usually with black spots; conspicuous black bars on insides of front legs; ears tipped with short tuft of black hairs; facial fur frequently streaked with black; ruff extends along each side of face; tail white below with black band above, tip white. Bobcat tracks show four toes; elevated fifth toe present on forefeet; claws retractile. Total length, 810–1,050; tail, 130–185; hind foot, 160–185; ear, 60–78; weight 5.7–20 kg.

Natural History. Bobcats live in a wide array of habitats, but they seemingly prefer areas with dense understory vegetation, including heavily wooded uplands and bottomland forests, brushy areas, swamps, and partly open farmlands. These cats use trails, roads, and other openings for hunting and as resting sites. As they travel throughout their home ranges, bobcats leave scent marks, using feces, urine, and excretions from anal glands. Mainly nocturnal and crepuscular, bobcats are almost exclusively carnivorous. Rabbits and hares are their most common prey, but they also take rodents and occasionally other terrestrial vertebrates. Although capable of killing deer, bobcats are not a significant cause of deer mortality.

Breeding may occur anytime in southern populations, but peaks from December through April. Gestation ranges from 50 to 70 days, with a mode of 62 days. On rare occasions bobcats produce two litters per year. Litter size varies from one to six young. Kittens commonly weigh 280 to 340 grams at birth, and their eyes are closed for the first few days. Young nurse for about two months and remain with the female until the following spring. Males reach adult proportions at about three and a half years of age, but females reach adult size in two-thirds that time.

Natural deaths of adult bobcats result mostly from starvation, disease, predation, and injuries. This species is of economic importance in the south-central region; about 15,000 pelts were harvested in the 1983–1984 season.

Selected References. McCord and Cardoza (1982); Novak *et al.* (1987); Rolley (1987).

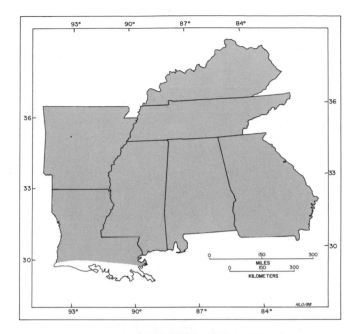

Photo courtesy R. W. Barbour

Order Artiodactyla

Even-Toed Ungulates

Even-toed ungulates are native to all continents except Antarctica and Australia, where they have been introduced. Artiodactyla contains 9 modern families, with 80 Recent genera and 185 Recent species. Two families, Cervidae and Bovidae, and three species—*Cervus elaphus, Odocoileus virginianus,* and *Bos bison*—are or were native to the south-central states. The white-tailed deer is the most common and widespread species in this region at present; native populations of wapiti and bison have been extirpated. Fallow deer (*Cervus dama,* family Cervidae) and feral pigs (*Sus scrofa,* family Suidae) have been introduced into the region. The order first appears in the fossil record in deposits dated from the early Eocene.

Key to Artiodactyls

1. Horns or antlers present; no upper incisors 2
1'. Horns or antlers absent; upper incisors present .... *Sus scrofa
2. Antlers (males only) without bony core, shed annually 3
2'. Horns (both sexes) with bony core, not shed .... *Bos bison*
3. Antlers not palmated at extremities 4
3'. Antlers (main beam) palmated at extremities .... *Cervus dama
4. Upper canine teeth present; tail without white markings
.... *Cervus elaphus*
4'. Upper canine teeth absent; tail white ventrally .. *Odocoileus virginianus*

Cervus elaphus

Wapiti or Elk

Distribution. This species formerly ranged from coast to coast and from northern British Columbia to Mexico in the West and to northern Louisiana and Georgia in the East. Elk were extirpated from the eastern United States in the early 1800s.

Description. Second largest member of deer family in North America, surpassed only by moose. Dorsum grayish brown to dark brown; venter dark brown to black; large white or yellowish rump patch. Typical antlers of adult bulls with long, round beams that sweep up and back, usually bearing six tines; brow and bez tines close together near base of beam and extending out above muzzle. Total length, 2,030–2,970; tail, 120–160; hind foot, 460–660; ear, 150–300; weight, 265–490 kg.

Natural History. Elk browse and graze on a wide variety of plants, depending on local availability of forage. These gregarious animals are known to undertake long migrations between summer and winter ranges, but some populations are nonmigratory. Males and females tend to occupy separate areas most of the year.

Elk are polygamous; bulls maintain harems of cows and calves. Rutting activities begin in August and continue to November. One calf (twins are rare) is born in May or June after a gestation period of eight months or more. At birth, calves weigh about 13 kilograms. They hide for the first 18 to 20 days after birth except when nursing. Cows generally stay apart from other elk until the calves are able to travel. Cows and calves congregate into herds by July. Yearling females may be bred; yearling males are fertile and may contribute to breeding, but bulls more than three years old are the major participants in rutting activities. Cows more than eight years of age may have reduced fertility, but there is no evidence that fertility in bulls declines with age.

This is a popular and much-sought-after game species that seems especially sensitive to human activities. Disease and stress increase with overcrowding of animals, especially on winter feeding grounds. Elk are known to live for more than 20 years, but mean life expectancy is much lower; cows usually live longer than bulls. Other than legal harvesting, major causes of death of this species are malnutrition, diseases, parasites, predation, and accidents.

Selected References. Boyd (1978); Peek (1982).

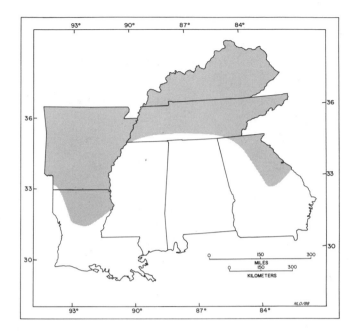

Photo courtesy R. W. Barbour

Odocoileus virginianus

White-Tailed Deer

Distribution. This species ranges from south-central Canada throughout most of the United States and southward into South America. It is recorded in each of the 48 contiguous states but evidently is rare in California, Nevada, and Utah. It is a widespread and common inhabitant of the south-central region.

Description. Long legs with narrow, pointed hooves, conspicuous ears, and naked nose pad. Tail of adult distinctive: long, broad at base, brown dorsally with prominent white fringe, white ventrally, carried erect when animal is disturbed. Dorsum brownish gray to reddish brown, with white band around muzzle and eye; venter white. Total length, 1,340–2,060; tail, 152–330; hind foot, 360–520; ear, 140–229; weight, 25–150 kg.

Natural History. White-tailed deer are browsers and grazers. The tremendous adaptability of this species is reflected in the great diversity of foods it consumes, according to food availability. The breeding season (rut) occurs from October to January, with peak activity in November. Does are in estrus for about 24 hours; if they are not bred, estrus will occur again in approximately 28 days. Bucks may accompany does for several days during the period of heat.

After gestation, which takes 195 to 212 days, fawns (usually one, frequently two, occasionally three) are born in May or June. Fawns weigh 2.5 to 4 kilograms at birth. Most does begin to breed when about a year and a half old (although some breed earlier) and achieve full size at about four years of age. Bucks likewise are about one and a half years old at the time of their first participation in the rut, and reach maximum size at four to five years. Few animals live longer than 10 years. Antlers are present on bucks, and occasionally on does, from April through February, beginning in the second year of life. Skin and hair (velvet) cover these deciduous, bony structures as they grow; the antlers shed the velvet when they reach full size in August and September.

White-tailed deer are the most important game species in the seven-state region. Other than hunting, the main causes of this animal's death are predation, automobile accidents, diseases, parasites, starvation, crippling from gunshot and arrow wounds, getting caught in fences, and poaching.

Selected References. Halls (1978, 1984); Hesselton and Hesselton (1982).

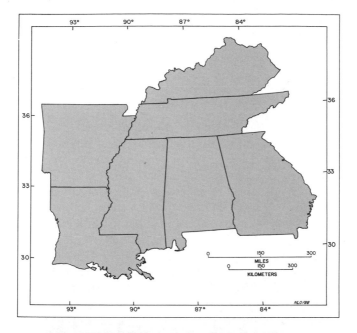

Photo courtesy R. W. Barbour

Bos bison

Bison

Distribution. In North America, bison once were widespread from Alaska and western Canada across the United States and into northern Mexico. The species ranged over most of the south-central region, being unknown only in southern and coastal parts of Georgia and coastal Alabama, Mississippi, and Louisiana. The species no longer occurs in the wild but is common on preserves and ranches.

Description. Largest native terrestrial mammal in North America. Pelage composed of long, coarse guard hairs and thick, woolly undercoat; hair long and shaggy over forehead, neck, shoulders, and forelegs, but short and straight over hindquarters. Legs short and stout; hooves black. Total length, 2,130–3,800; tail, 550–850; hind foot, 500–680; weight, 310–900 kg. Bulls considerably larger and more heavily built than cows.

Natural History. Bison are grazers during all seasons of the year. In the wild they evidently used forested areas primarily for shade, to escape from insects and other disturbances, and for shelter during severe weather. Wild bison undertook annual migrations, apparently seeking suitable grazing and weather conditions. Captive herds can utilize poorer forage and can survive colder weather than cattle.

The breeding season is from July to October. Females tend to be seasonally polyestrous, with a cycle lasting about three weeks. A few heifers conceive as yearlings, but most breed first when they are two years old. Males attain sexual maturity according to a similar time frame. The gestation period is 270 to 300 days, after which usually one calf (rarely twins) is born, weighing 15 to 25 kilograms. Calves are usually reddish tan, becoming the color of adults at about four months. They begin grazing and drinking water when about seven days old but may nurse for seven to eight months. Some animals survive more than 20 years, and a few live as long as 40 years.

An estimated 30 million bison inhabited North America when European man arrived; subsequently, they nearly were extirpated through overhunting. This bovid harbors a variety of endo- and ectoparasites, and its gregarious nature works to perpetuate spread of parasites and diseases among animals of all ages. Bison are mostly diurnal, with several grazing periods interspersed with rest and rumination. An adult cow usually leads the group, but not the same animal on all occasions.

Selected References. Reynolds *et al.* (1982); Meagher (1986).

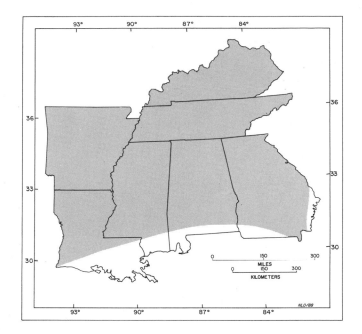

Photo courtesy R. W. Barbour

Introduced Mammals and Species of Possible Occurrence

Ninety-five species of mammals that occur, or once occurred, in the south-central states are treated in the foregoing accounts. In addition to these, eight species (four rodents, two carnivores, and two artiodactyls) introduced from outside North America are present in the region in sufficient numbers in the wild to be mentioned briefly here. All are included in keys in the preceding text. Many other exotic mammals exist in captivity; some of these no doubt escape confinement from time to time, but we have made no effort to document such occurrences. Also, we have not included the mouse opossums, *Marmosa alstoni,* specimens of which were captured in or near New Orleans in 1917 and 1935, and *Marmosa mexicana,* a specimen of which was taken in the same city in 1917 (Lowery, 1974). Both species no doubt were transported to Louisiana on banana boats from eastern Middle America; it is unlikely that either could long survive there.

In a second section of this chapter, we have listed five species of native North American terrestrial mammals that, although unreported in the south-central states, may live there or once may have ranged into the region. Several other unlisted taxa possibly may be found as well.

Introduced Species

Mus musculus (house mouse). Probably originally a native of Asia, this common Eurasian murid was introduced into North America in the seventeenth century by early settlers. It now ranges throughout the south-central states, and in fact over much of the temperate and tropical regions of the New World. It is a common rodent in and around human habitations, but feral populations also exist. There is some recent evidence that *Mus domesticus,* not *M. musculus,* is the proper name for the species introduced into the Americas.

House mice (especially the young) may be confused with members of the native genera *Reithrodontomys* and *Peromyscus.* They differ from the latter

Mus musculus

Photo courtesy R. W. Barbour

in having a nearly naked tail covered with conspicuous scaly annulations, nearly naked ears, a grayish (usually) or dark buffy (rather than whitish) belly, molars with three longitudinal rows of tubercles, and a distinct notch on the occlusal surface of each upper incisor that is best seen in lateral view. The house mouse differs in the same ways from *Reithrodontomys*, and also in that the face of each upper incisor is smooth rather than grooved.

Rattus norvegicus (Norway rat). This rat lives throughout the south-central region in urban environments, in and around human habitations elsewhere, and even in rice and cane fields. It is about the size of the eastern woodrat (*Neotoma floridana*), from which it can be distinguished easily as follows: tail scantily haired and scaly in appearance; ventral color usually grayish (or some color other than white); crowns of molars cuspidate and more or less squared, not elongate and prismatic as in *Neotoma;* well-developed temporal ridges on skull. The Norway rat was introduced into North America from Europe about the time of the American Revolution.

Rattus rattus (black rat). This murid is a denizen of cities and large towns, where it frequently is limited to the upper stories of buildings (and is thus sometimes referred to as the "roof rat"), whereas *R. norvegicus* occupies the ground floors and subterranean parts of structures. This species mainly is confined to the southern parts of the seven-state region.

The black rat differs from the native woodrat in the same ways as described for *R. norvegicus*. It may be distinguished from the latter as follows: tail longer (rather than shorter) than head and body; ears larger; females

Rattus norvegicus

Photo courtesy R. W. Barbour

Myocaster coypus

Photo courtesy R. W. Barbour

usually with five pair of mammae rather than six; temporal ridges on skull bowed outward rather than essentially parallel.

Originally a native of Asia like *R. norvegicus,* the black rat spread throughout Eurasia and first was introduced into North America at East Coast ports in early colonial times. Many subsequent introductions no doubt have occurred at other coastal cities, as is true also in the cases of *Mus* and *R. norvegicus.*

Myocastor coypus (nutria or coypu). A native of southern South America, the nutria was introduced into the United States as a furbearer. It made its first appearance on the West Coast, in California in 1899, and was introduced again later in Washington. The species was established in the south-central states on Avery Island, Louisiana, in the late 1930s. Some nutria escaped in following years, and many were freed by a hurricane in 1940. Through both new introductions and natural dispersal nutria spread rapidly, and the species now is common to abundant in Gulf coastal marshes and along major waterways on the Coastal Plain of the seven-state region.

Adult nutria resemble beavers at first glance, but the long, round tail and less sightly and somewhat more yellowish pelage easily distinguish the two. See also the key to rodent families.

Canis familiaris (domestic dog). Feral dogs inhabit many rural areas in the south-central states and constitute a menace to native wildlife, as do ferral domestic cats. Under certain circumstances, wild dogs will mate with

Cervus dama

Photo after Feldhamer *et al.*, 1988

coyotes, producing a hybrid animal known as a "coydog." Most hybrids apparently are fertile.

Felis catus (domestic cat). Feral domestic cats are a significant destructive force insofar as small native birds and mammals are concerned. Feral cats are common throughout the seven-state region.

Sus scrofa (wild pig). A member of the family Suidae, this species was probably introduced into North America in early colonial times. It is widespread in the south-central states, northward to Tennessee. Common in some wooded areas, *S. scrofa* can be considerably destructive to local habitats, as in Great Smoky Mountains National Park in the past.

Cervus dama (fallow deer). The fallow deer, a native of Europe, has been introduced at several sites in the south-central states over the years. Of recent report, for example, there are herds on Saint Simons and Jekyll islands, Georgia; a herd estimated at about 600 deer on a 170,000-acre management unit (Land Between the Lakes) in western Kentucky; and a free-ranging population of about 1,000 deer in central Alabama (mostly Wilcox and Dallas counties). No doubt other herds exist as well.

Species of Possible Occurrence

Nyctinomops macrotis (big free-tailed bat). This migratory species is found in the warm months to the west of the south-central region, but autumn migrants have been reported in central Iowa, southeastern Kansas, and south-central Texas. It possibly can be found as a migrant in the region, most likely in Arkansas or Louisiana. This species differs from the resident free-tailed bat (*Tadarida brasiliensis*) in being much larger, in having the ears joined at their bases, and in having two pairs (rather than three) of lower incisors.

Spermophilus tridecemlineatus (thirteen-lined ground squirrel). This ground-dwelling sciurid is known in eastern Oklahoma and southwestern Missouri, and probably can be found in extreme northwestern Arkansas. An inhabitant of areas of relatively short grass, it should be looked for along mowed highway rights-of-way and in cemeteries, on golf courses, and the like.

Spermophilus tridecemlineatus

Photo courtesy U.S. Fish and Wildlife Service

Baiomys taylori (northern pygmy mouse). This small mouse occupies grassy habitats in much of southeastern Texas except areas immediately adjacent to the Sabine River. This species has been rapidly expanding its range northward and westward in recent years, and also may be moving to the east. If so, it will be found first in southwestern Louisiana. *B. taylori* resembles a small member of the genus *Peromyscus,* with a short tail and dark grayish dorsal pelage.

Felis onca (jaguar). The jaguar evidently once was common in southern Texas and probably lived also in western Louisiana (see Lowery, 1974). This species has been extirpated in the United States.

Baiomys taylori

Photo courtesy R. W. Manning

Felis pardalis (ocelot). This beautiful small felid once inhabited much of southern Texas and possibly ranged eastward into parts of Louisiana (see Lowery, 1974). In Texas, the species presently is limited to a few favorable areas in the lower Rio Grande valley.

Glossary

This list of terms, modified from Jones *et al.* (1983, 1985) and Jones and Birney (1988), includes those frequently used in descriptions of mammals. Not all of the terms have been used in the foregoing text. Some that appear on one or more of the three figures in the glossary are not otherwise defined. Where a term listed has two or more meanings in the English language, only the one applying to mammalian biology is given.

abdomen. Ventral part of body, lying between thorax (ribcage) and pelvis.

acanthocephalan. Spiny-headed worm of parasitic phylum Acanthocephala.

aestivation. Torpidity in summer.

agouti hair. Hair with alternate pale and dark bands of color.

albinism. Lack of external pigmentation (may be only partial).

allopatric. Occupying disjunct or nonoverlapping geographic areas.

altricial. Pertaining to young that are blind, frequently naked, and entirely dependent on parental care at birth.

alveolus. Socket in jaw bone that receives root(s) of tooth.

angular process. Posterior projection of dentary ventral to condyloid (articular) process; evident but not labeled in Fig. 102.

annulation. Circular or ringlike formation, as in dermal scales on tail of a mammal or in dentine of a tooth.

anterior. Pertaining to or toward front end.

antler. Branched (usually), bony head ornament found on cervids, covered with skin (velvet) during growth, shed annually.

arboreal. Pertaining to activity in trees.

articular condyle. Surface of condyloid (articular) process (Fig. 102), articulating lower jaw with skull.

auditory bulla. Bony capsule enclosing middle ear; when formed by tympanic bone, termed *tympanic bulla* (see Fig. 103).

auditory meatus. Opening leading from external ear to eardrum (see Fig. 102).

axilla. Pertaining to the armpit.

Figure 3. *Lateral views of skull and lower jaw of a coyote, showing cranium and mandibular features (after Beckoff, 1977).*

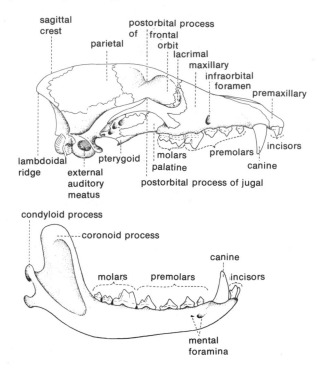

baculum. Sesamoid bone (os penis) present in penis of males of certain mammalian groups.

basal. Pertaining to the base.

baubellum. See *os clitoridis.*

beam. Main trunk of antler.

bez tine. First tine above brow tine of antler.

bifid. Divided into two nearly equal lobes.

bifurcate. Divided into two branches.

bipedal. Moving on two legs.

blastocyst. In embryonic development of mammals, ball of cells produced by repeated division (cleavage) of fertilized egg; stage of implantation in uterine wall.

boreal. Northern, of high latitudes.

braincase. Posterior portion of skull; part that encloses and protects brain.

breech birth. Birth in which posterior part of body emerges first.

brisket. Breast or lower part of chest.

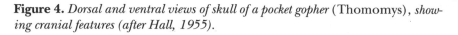

Figure 4. *Dorsal and ventral views of skull of a pocket gopher* (Thomomys), *showing cranial features (after Hall, 1955).*

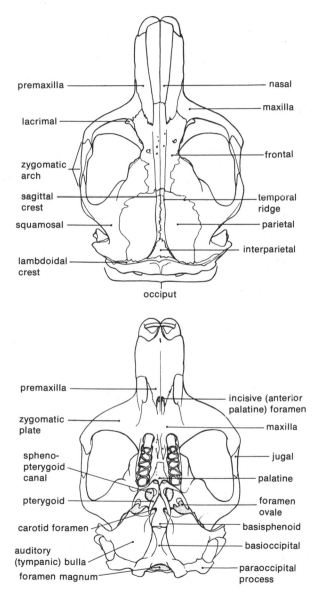

brow tine. First tine above base of antler.

buccal. Pertaining to cheek.

bulla. See *auditory bulla.*

bunodont. Having low-crowned, rectangular, grinding teeth, as in certain omnivores.

calcar. Spur of cartilage or bone that projects medially from ankle of many species of bats and helps support uropatagium.

canine. One of four basic kinds of mammalian teeth; anteriormost tooth in maxilla and counterpart in dentary, frequently elongate, unicuspid, and single rooted; never more than one per quadrant (see Figs. 102, 104). Also a term pertaining to dogs or to Canidae.

carnassials. Pair of large, bladelike teeth (last upper premolar and first lower molar) that occlude with scissorlike action, possessed by most modern members of order Carnivora.

carnivore. Animal that consumes meat as primary component of diet.

carpal. Any one of group of bones in wrist region, distal to radius and ulna, and proximal to metacarpals.

caudal. Pertaining to tail or toward tail (caudad).

cavernicolous. Living in caves or mines.

centimeter (cm). Unit of linear measure in metric system equal to 10 millimeters; 2.54 cm equals one inch.

cestode. Tapeworm of parasitic class Cestoda, phylum Platyhelminthes.

cheekteeth. Collectively, postcanine teeth (premolars and molars).

cingulum. Enamel shelf bordering margin(s) of a tooth (termed *cingulid* for shelf of tooth in lower jaw).

circumboreal. Around the boreal (northern) parts of the world.

claw. Sheath of keratin on digits, usually long, curved, and sharply pointed.

cline. Gradual change in morphological character through a series of interbreeding populations; character gradient.

commensalism. Two species living together, the commensal benefiting and the host not affected.

condyle. Process or knob on the bone.

condylobasal length. See Fig. 104.

coprophagy. Feeding upon feces.

coronoid process. Projection of posterior portion of dentary dorsal to mandibular condyle (see Fig. 102).

cosmopolitan. Common to all the world; not local or limited, but widely distributed.

cranial breadth. Measurement of cranium taken across its broadest point perpendicular to long axis of skull; frequently used for insectivores.

crepuscular. Pertaining to periods of dusk and dawn (twilight); active by twilight.

Figure 5. *Dorsal and ventral views of skull of a river otter, showing cranial features and measurements (after Hall, 1955).*

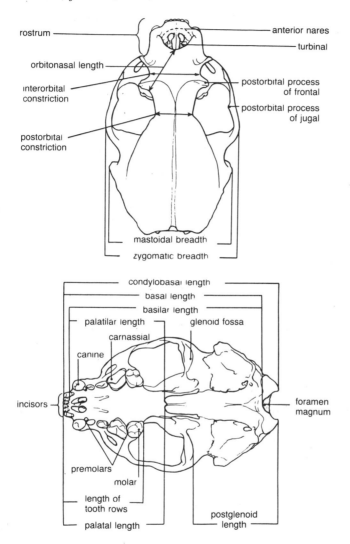

Cretaceous. See *geologic time.*
cursorial. Pertaining to running and locomotion by running.
cusp. Point, projection, or bump on crown of tooth.
cuspidate. Presence of cusp or cusps on tooth.
deciduous dentition. Juvenile or milk teeth, those that appear first in lifetime

of a mammal, consisting (if complete) of incisors, canines, and premolars; generally replaced by adult (permanent) dentition.

delayed implantation. Postponement of embedding of blastocyst (embryo) in uterine epithelium for several days, weeks, or months; typical of some carnivores.

dental formula. Convenient way of designating number and arrangement of mammalian teeth (for example, i 3/3, c 1/1, p 4/4, m 3/3); letters indicate incisors, canines, premolars, and molars, respectively; numbers before slashes indicate number of teeth on one side of upper jaw, whereas those following slashes indicate number on one side of lower jaw.

dentary. One of pair of bones that constitute entire lower jaw (mandible) of mammals.

dentine. Hard, generally acellular material between pulp and enamel of tooth, sometimes exposed on surface of crown.

dentition. Considered collectively, teeth of a mammal.

dewclaw. Vestigial digit on foot.

dewlap. Pendulous fold of skin under neck.

diastema. Space between adjacent teeth; for example, space between incisors and cheekteeth in species lacking canines.

dichromatism. Two distinct color phases.

digit. Finger or toe.

digitigrade. Walking on digits, with wrist and heel bones held off ground.

distal. Away from base or point of attachment, or from any named reference point (as opposed to *proximal*).

distichous. Arranged alternately in two vertical rows on opposite sides of an axis, as in hairs on tail of some rodents.

diurnal. Pertaining to daylight hours; active by day.

dorsal. Pertaining to back or upper surface (dorsum).

echolocation. Use of acoustical images produced from echoes of ultrasound pulses to "see in the dark."

ectoparasite. Parasite living on, and feeding from, external surface of an animal (for example, flea, louse, tick, mite).

enamel. Hard outer layer of tooth consisting of calcareous compounds and small amount of organic matrix.

endemic. Native to particular region.

endoparasite. Parasite living within host (for example, flatworm, tapeworm).

Eocene. See *geologic time.*

epiphysis. Secondary growth center near end of long bone.

estrous cycle. Recurring growth and development of uterine endometrium, culminating in time when female is receptive to male.

estrus. Stage of reproductive receptivity of female to male; "heat."

excrescence. Dermal projection, as on face and ears of bats.

extirpation. Extinction, usually within specified geographic area.

familial name. Name applying to group of animals of family rank, ending in *-idae* (names of subfamilies end in *-inae*).

feces. Excrement.

fecundity. Rate of producing offspring; fertility.

femur. Single bone of upper (proximal) part of each hind (pelvic) limb.

fenestrate. Having openings.

feral. Having reverted to wild state, in reference to domestic animals.

fetal membranes. Tissue layers that surround, or attach to, the growing mammalian embryo (chorion, amnion, allantois).

fetus. Embryo in later stages of development (still in uterus).

fibula. Smaller of two bones in lower part of hind (pelvic) limb.

flank. Side of animal between ribs and hips.

flatworm. See *trematode.*

foramen. Any opening, orifice, or perforation, especially through bone.

foramen magnum. Large opening at posterior of skull through which spinal cord emerges from braincase (see Figs. 102, 104).

fossa. Pit or depression in bone; frequently site of bone articulation or muscle attachment.

fossorial. Pertaining to life under surface of ground.

frontal bone. See Fig. 103.

fusiform. Compact, tapered; pertaining to body form with shortened projections and no abrupt constrictions.

geologic time. Mammals arose in the *Mesozoic* era, which began some 230 million years ago. Periods of the Mesozoic (from oldest to youngest) are the *Triassic; Jurassic,* which began about 180 million years ago; and *Cretaceous,* which began about 135 million years ago. The following *Cenozoic* era, termed the "Age of Mammals," was the time of evolution and radiation of major modern groups. The Cenozoic is divided into two periods, the *Tertiary* (beginning about 65 million years ago and continuing until 2 million years ago) and *Quaternary* (2 million years ago to present). Subdivisions of the Tertiary, termed *epochs,* are (oldest to youngest) the *Paleocene; Eocene,* which began about 58 million years ago; *Oligocene,* which began about 36 million years ago; *Miocene,* which began about 25 million years ago; and *Pliocene,* which began about 12 million years ago. The Quaternary has only two epochs, *Pleistocene* (2 million years ago to 10,000 years ago) and *Holocene,* or *Recent* (10,000 years before the present until now).

gestation period. Period of development of embryo in uterus; period between fertilization and parturition.

gram (g). Unit of weight in metric system; there are 28.5 grams in an ounce.

granivorous. Subsisting on diet of grains, seeds from cereal grasses.

gravid. Pregnant.

greatest length of skull. Measurement encompassing overall length of skull, including teeth that may project anterior to premaxilla; frequently recorded instead of condylobasal length in some kinds of mammals.

guano. Excrement of bats or birds, sometimes sold commercially as fertilizer.

guard hairs. Outer coat of coarse protective hairs found on most mammals.

hallux. First (most medial) digit of hind foot (pes).

hamular process. Hooklike projection, such as hamular process of pterygoid bone.

hectare. Unit of land area in metric system equal to 10,000 square meters or 2.47 acres.

heifer. A bovid that has not produced a calf and is less than three years old.

herbivorous. Consuming plant material as primary component of diet.

hibernaculum. Shelter in which animal hibernates.

hibernation. Torpidity in winter.

Holarctic. Parts of New World and Old World together lying north of tropics.

home range. Area in which an animal lives, containing all necessities of life; generally is not entirely defended and therefore can overlap with home ranges of other animals.

horn. Structure projecting from head of mammal and generally used for offense, defense, or social interaction; horns of members of family Bovidae are formed by permanent hollow keratin sheaths growing over bony cores (see also *pronghorn*).

humerus. Single bone in upper (proximal) portion of each front (pectoral) limb.

hypsodont. Pertaining to a particularly high-crowned tooth; such teeth have shallow roots.

imbricate. Overlapping, as shingles of a roof.

implantation. Process by which blastocyte (embryo) embeds in uterine lining.

incisive foramen. See Fig. 103.

incisor. One of four basic kinds of mammalian teeth, usually chisel shaped; anteriormost of teeth; always rooted in premaxilla in upper jaw (see Figs. 102, 104).

infraorbital canal. Canal through zygomatic process of maxilla, from anterior wall of orbit to side of rostrum (see Fig. 102).

infraorbital foramen. Foramen through zygomatic process of maxilla (see Fig. 102 and above).

inguinal. Pertaining to region of groin.

insectivorous. Preying on insects.

interfemoral membrane. See *uropatagium.*

interorbital. Between the eye sockets.

interparietal. Unpaired bone on dorsal part of braincase between parietals and just anterior to supraoccipital (see Fig. 103).

interspecific. Between or among species (interspecific competition, for example).

intraspecific. Within a species (intraspecific variation, for example).

jugal bone. Bone connecting maxillary and squamosal bones to form mid-part of zygomatic arch (see Fig. 103).

juvenile pelage. Pelage characteristic of young mammals.

karyotype. Morphological description of chromosomes of cell, including size, shape, position of centromere, and number.

keel. Ridge that provides expanded surface for attachment.

keratin. Tough, fibrous protein especially abundant in epidermis and epidermal derivatives.

kilogram (kg). Unit of weight in metric system (frequently shortened to *kilo*) equal to 1,000 grams or 2.2 pounds.

kilometer (km). Unit of linear measure in metric system equal to 1,000 meters or slightly more than six-tenths of a mile.

labial. Pertaining to lips; labial side of a tooth is side nearer lips.

lactating. Secreting milk.

lateral. Located away from midline; at or near sides.

lingual. Pertaining to tongue; lingual side of a tooth is side nearer tongue.

live trap. Any of several kinds of traps designed to catch mammals alive.

loph. Ridge on occlusal surface of tooth formed by elongation and fusion of cusps.

malar process. Projection of maxillary that makes contact with jugal bone and forms base of zygomatic arch.

mammae. Milk-producing glands unique to mammals; their growth and activity governed by hormones of ovary, uterus, and pituitary; developed in both sexes but degenerate in males.

mandible. Lower jaw; in mammals composed of single pair of bones, the dentaries.

manus. Forefoot or hand.

marsupium. External pouch formed by fold of skin in abdominal wall and supported by epipubic bones; found in most marsupials and some monotremes; encloses mammary glands and serves as incubation chamber.

masticate. To chew.

mastoid. Bone bounded by squamosal, exoccipital, and tympanic bones.

mastoid process. Exposed portion of petromastoid bone; situated anterior to auditory bulla.

maturational molt. Molt from juvenile or subadult pelage to adult pelage.

maxilla. Either of pair of relatively large bones that form major portion of side and ventral part of rostrum; contributes to hard palate, forms anterior root of zygomatic arch, and bears all upper teeth except incisors; also termed *maxillary* (see Figs. 102, 103).

maxillary toothrow. That part of toothrow in cranium seated in maxilla; length includes all postincisor teeth and generally is taken parallel to long axis of skull (measurement shown in Fig. 104 is of total upper toothrow).

medial. Pertaining to middle, as of a bone or other structure.

melanism. Unusual darkening of coloration owing to deposition of abnormally large amounts of melanins in integument.

mesic. Pertaining to habitats or areas with available water or moisture; moderately moist or humid.

Mesozoic. See *geologic time.*

metabolic water. Water formed biochemically as end product of fat and carbohydrate metabolism in body of animal.

metacarpals. Bones of forefoot (hand) exclusive of phalanges.

metatarsals. Bones of hind foot exclusive of phalanges.

meter (m). Unit of linear measure in metric system equal to 100 centimeters or 39.37 inches.

milk dentition. See *deciduous dentition.*

millimeter (mm). Unit of linear measure in metric system; 25.4 mm equals one inch.

Miocene. See *geologic time.*

mist net. Net of fine mesh used to capture birds and bats, usually 2 meters high and 6–30 meters long.

molar. One of four basic kinds of mammalian teeth; any cheektooth situated posterior to premolars and having no deciduous precursor; normally not exceeding three per quadrant (see Figs. 102, 104).

molariform. Pertaining to teeth the form of which is molarlike.

molt. Process by which hair is shed and replaced.

monestrous. Having a single estrous cycle per year.

monotypic. Containing only one immediately subordinate taxon; for example, a genus that contains only one species.

musk gland. One of several kinds of glands in mammals with secretions that have a musky odor.

muzzle. Projecting snout.

nail. Flat, keratinized, translucent epidermal growth protecting upper portions of tips of digits in some mammals; modified claw.

nape. Back of neck.

nares. Openings of nose.

natal. Pertaining to birth.

nematode. Roundworm of parasitic or free-living phylum Nematoda.

neonate. Newborn.

nictitating membrane. Thin membrane at inner angle of eye in some species (such as cats), which can be drawn over surface of eyeball; "third" eyelid.

nocturnal. Pertaining to night (hours without daylight); active by night.

nomadic. Wandering.

nominal species. Named species (sometimes implies species in name only).

occipital bone. Bone surrounding foramen magnum and bearing occipital condyles (see occiput in Fig. 103); formed from four embryonic elements, a ventral basioccipital, a dorsal supraoccipital, and two lateral exoccipitals.

occiput. General term for posterior portion of skull (see Fig. 103).

occlusal. Pertaining to contact surfaces of upper (cranial) and lower (mandibular) teeth.

Oligocene. See *geologic time.*

omnivorous. Having diet of both animal and vegetable food.

orbit. Bony socket in skull in which eyeball is situated (see Fig. 102).

ordinal name. Name applying to an order of organisms.

os clitoridis. Small sesamoid bone present in clitoris of females of some mammalian species; homologous to baculum in males.

ossify. To become bony or hardened and bonelike.

palate. Bony plate formed by palatine bones and palatal branches of maxillae and premaxillae (see Fig. 103).

Paleocene. See *geologic time.*

palmate. Having webbing between digits or having flattened tines on antler.

papilla. Any blunt, rounded, or nipple-shaped projection.

parapatric. Occupying locally contiguous, but not overlapping, geographic areas.

parietal. Either of pair of bones contributing to roof of cranium posterior to frontals and anterior to occipital (see Figs. 102, 103).

parturition. Process by which fetus of therian mammals separates from uterine wall of mother and is born; birth.

patagium. Web of skin; in bats, the wing membrane.

patronym. Scientific name based on name of person or persons.

pectoral. Pertaining to chest.

pectoral girdle. Shoulder girdle, composed in most mammals of clavicle and scapula or scapula alone.

pelage. Collectively, the hairs on a mammal.

pelvic girdle. Hip girdle, composed of ischium, ilium, and pubis.

penicillate. Ending in tuft of fine hairs.

phalangeal epiphyses. Growth centers just proximal to articular surfaces of phalanges; fusion of epiphyses to shafts of pelanges used to determine age in bats.

phalanges. Bones of fingers and toes, distal to metacarpals and metatarsals.

pigment. Minute granules that impart color to an organism; such granules are usually metabolic wastes and may be shades of black, brown, red, or yellow.

pinna. Externally projecting part of ear.

placenta. Composite structure formed by maternal and fetal tissues across which gases, nutrients, and wastes are exchanged.

placental scar. Scar that remains on uterine wall after deciduate placenta detaches at parturition.

plantar pad. Cutaneous pad or tubercle on sole of foot.

plantigrade. Having foot structure in which phalanges and metatarsals or metacarpals touch ground; having basic structure of ambulatory (walking) locomotion.

Pleistocene. See *geologic time.*

Pliocene. See *geologic time.*

plumbeous. The color of lead; dark gray.

pollex. Thumb; first (most medial) digit on hand (manus).

polyestrous. Having more than one estrous cycle each year.

polygamous. Breeding with two or more members of opposite sex.

polygynous. Breeding with several females.

postauricular. Behind the ear.

posterior. Pertaining to or toward rear end.

postorbital process. Projection of frontal bone that marks posterior margin of orbit (see Figs. 102, 104).

postpartum estrus. Receptivity of female to male directly after giving birth.

precocial. Pertaining to young born at relatively advanced stage, capable of moving about shortly after birth and usually of some feeding without parental assistance.

prehensile. Adapted for grasping by curling or wrapping around.

premaxilla. One of paired bones at anterior end of rostrum (see Figs. 102, 103); also termed *premaxillary.*

premolar. One of four basic kinds of mammalian teeth; situated anterior to molars and posterior to canines; only cheekteeth usually present in both permanent and milk dentitions; normally not exceeding four per quadrant (see Figs. 102, 104).

progeny. Offspring.

pronghorn. Modified horn (in both sexes of Antilocapridae) that grows over permanent bony cores and is shed annually; slightly curved, with one anterolateral prong in males and some females.

proximal. Toward or near point of reference or attachment (as opposed to *distal*).

pterygoid. Either of paired bones in ventral wall of braincase, posterior to palatines (see Figs. 102, 103).

pubic symphysis. Midventral plane of contact between two halves of pelvic girdle.

quadrupedal. Using all four limbs for locomotion.

rabies. Viral disease of central nervous system, transmitted by infected canids, skunks, bats, and some other mammals to one another and also to humans, usually in saliva transmitted through biting.

race. Informal term for subspecies.

radius. Medial of two bones in lower part of front (pectoral) limb.

ramus. Horizontal portion of dentary, that part in which teeth are rooted.

range. Geographic area inhabited by a particular taxon.

Recent. See *geologic time.*

recurved. Curved downward and backward.

reentrant angle. Inward infolding of enamel layer on side, front, or back of cheektooth.

refugium. Geographic area to which species retreats in time of stress, such as glacial episode.

retractile. Capable of being drawn back or in (as retractile claws of felids).

riparian. Referring to floodplains or valleys of watercourses.

root. Portion of tooth that lies below gum line and fills alveolus.

rooted tooth. Tooth with definitive growth; not evergrowing.

rootless tooth. Tooth that is evergrowing, having continuously open root canal.

rostrum. Facial region of skull anterior to plane drawn through anterior margin of orbits (see Fig. 104).

roundworm. See *nematode.*

rugose. Wrinkled.

rumen. First "stomach" of ruminant mammals; modification of esophagus.

ruminant. Any of the Artiodactyla (including all those occurring in the south-central states) that possesses a rumen; cud chewing.

runway. Worn or otherwise detectable pathway caused by repeated use.

rutting season. Season of sexual activity when mating occurs; particularly applied to deer and other artiodactyls.

sagittal crest. Medial dorsal ridge on braincase, often formed by coalescence of temporal ridges.

saltatory. Adapted for leaping, usually with elongate and unusually well developed hind legs.

saxicolous. Living among rocks.

scansorial. Pertaining to arboreal animals that climb by means of sharp, curved claws.

scapula. Shoulder blade.

scent glands. Sweat or sebaceous glands, or combination of these two, modified for production of odiferous secretions.

scrotum. Pouch of skin outside abdominal cavity containing testes; permanently present in some species, seasonally present in some, and lacking in others.

scute. Thin plate or scale.

sebaceous glands. Epidermal glands that secrete fatty substance and usually open into hair follicle.

septum. Dividing wall, such as one formed by membrane or thin bone.

sexual dimorphism. Difference in sexual or secondary sexual (such as size) features between males and females of same species.

snap trap. Kill trap that usually consists of wooden base and wire bail, spring, and trigger mechanism; designed primarily to catch rodents and insectivores.

species. Group of naturally or potentially interbreeding populations reproductively isolated (or mostly so) from other such groups.

spiny-headed worm. See *acanthocephalan.*

squamosal. Either of pair of bones contributing to side of cranium (see Fig. 103) and forming posterior part of zygomatic arch.

subspecies. Relatively uniform and genetically distinctive population of a species that represents a separately or recently evolved lineage, with its own evolutionary tendencies, definite geographic range, and actual or potential zone of intergradation (interbreeding) with another such group or groups.

supercillary. Pertaining to eyebrow.

supraorbital process. Projection of frontal bone on superior rim of orbit, as in hares and rabbits.

sweat gland. Tubular epidermal gland that extends into dermis and secretes sweat or perspiration and also various scents.

sympatric. Occupying overlapping geographic areas.

symphysis. Relatively immovable articulation between bones.

tapeworm. See *cestode.*

tarsal. Any one of group of bones in ankle region, distal to fibula and proximal to metatarsals.

taxon. Any group (in this case, of mammals) distinctive from other groups at same taxonomic level.

teat. Protuberance of mammary gland in which numerous small ducts empty into common collecting structure that in turn opens to exterior through one or a few pores.

temperate. As a climatic term, pertaining to middle latitudes, those between boreal and tropical regions.

temporal ridges. Pair of ridges atop braincase of many mammals; usually originating on frontal bones near postorbital processes and converging posteriorly to form middorsal sagittal crest (see Fig. 103).

territory. Portion of home range that animal defends against other members of same (and sometimes different) species.

tibia. Larger of two bones in lower part of hind (pelvic) limb.

tine. Spike on an antler.

torpor. Dormancy; state in which body temperature approximates that of surroundings, rate of respiration and heartbeat ordinarily much slower than in active animal.

tragus. Fleshy projection from lower medial margin of ear of most microchiropteran bats.

trematode. Flatworm of parasitic class Trematoda in phylum Platyhelminthes.

trifid. Divided into three nearly equal lobes.

trifurcate. Having three branches.

tubercle. Rough prominence on a bone.

tularemia. Bacterial disease contracted by man through bite of tick harbored principally by hares and rabbits, but also by rodents and birds; also may be transmitted by direct contact with infected animal.

tympanic bulla. See *auditory bulla* and Fig. 103.

tympanum. Eardrum; thin, membranous structure that receives external vibrations from air and transmits them to middle ear ossicles.

type specimen. Specimen (holotype) on which a species or subspecies name is based.

ulna. Outermost of two bones in lower part of front (pectoral) limb.

underfur. Short hairs of mammal that serve primarily as insulation.

ungulates. Hoofed mammals of extant orders Perissodactyla and Artiodactyla; term has no formal taxonomic status but refers to broad group of herbivorous mammals.

unguligrade. Having foot structure in which only unguis (hoof) is in contact with ground.

unicuspid. Single-cusped tooth in shrews posterior to large, anteriormost tooth (an incisor) and anterior to fourth premolar in both upper and lower jaw.

uropatagium. Web of skin between hind legs of bats, frequently enclosing tail; interfemoral membrane.

vacuity. Space or void.

valvular. Capable of being closed, like a valve.

ventral. Pertaining to under or lower surface (venter).

vernacular name. Common (as opposed to scientific) name.

vernal. Pertaining to spring.

vibrissae. Long, stiff hairs that serve primarily as tactile receptors.

volant. Able to fly.

vomer. Unpaired bone that forms septum between nasal passages.

vulva. External genitalia of female.

wool. Underhair with angora growth, serving primarily as insulation.

xeric. Pertaining to dry habitats or areas.

zygomatic arch. Arch of bone enclosing orbit and temporal fossa, formed by jugal bone and parts of maxilla (malar process) and squamosal.

zygomatic breadth. See Fig. 104.

zygomatic plate. Bony plate, part of zygomatic process of maxilla, forming anterior face of zygomatic arch (see Fig. 103).

References

Allen, J. M. 1952. Gray and fox squirrel management in Indiana. Indiana Dept. Conserv., Pittman-Robertson Bull., 1:1–112.

Anderson, S., and J. K. Jones, Jr. 1984. Orders and families of Recent mammals of the world. John Wiley and Sons, New York, 686 pp.

Armstrong, D. M., and J. K. Jones, Jr. 1974. Notiosorex crawfordi. Mamm. Species, 17:1–5.

Armstrong, D. M., J. R. Choate, and J. K. Jones, Jr. 1986. Distributional patterns of mammals in the plains states. Occas. Papers Mus., Texas Tech Univ., 105:1–27.

Baker, V. R. 1983. Late-Pleistocene fluvial systems. Pp. 115–129, in Late-Quaternary environments of the United States: the late Pleistocene (H. E. Wright, Jr., and S. C. Porter, eds.). Univ. Minnesota Press, Minneapolis, 1:xiv + 1–407.

Barbour, R. W., and W. H. Davis. 1969. Bats of America. Univ. Press Kentucky, Lexington, 186 pp.

———. 1974. Mammals of Kentucky. Univ. Press Kentucky, Lexington, 322 pp.

Bekoff, M. 1977. Canis latrans. Mamm. Species, 79:1–9.

——— (ed.). 1978. Coyotes: biology, behavior, and management. Academic Press, New York, 384 pp.

Beneski, J. T., Jr., and D. W. Stinson. 1987. Sorex palustris. Mamm. Species, 296:1–6.

Birkenholz, D. E. 1972. Neofiber alleni. Mamm. Species, 15:1–4.

Bittner, S. L., and O. J. Rongstad. 1982. Snowshoe hare and allies. Pp. 146–163, in Wild mammals of North America . . . (J. A. Chapman and G. A. Feldhamer, eds.). Johns Hopkins Univ. Press, Baltimore, 1,147 pp.

Bohlin, R. G., and E. G. Zimmerman. 1982. Genic differentiation of two chromosome races of the Geomys bursarius complex. J. Mamm., 63:218–228.

Boutin, S., and D. E. Birkenholz. 1987. Muskrat and round-tailed muskrat. Pp. 314–325, in Wild furbearer management and conservation in

North America (M. Novak, J. A. Baker, M. E. Obbard, and B. Mallock, eds.). Ontario Ministry Nat. Res., Toronto, 1,150 pp.

Boyd, R. J. 1978. American elk. Pp. 10–29, *in* Big game of North America . . . (J. L. Schmidt and D. L. Gilbert, eds.). Stackpole Books, Harrisburg, 494 pp.

Brady, N. C. 1984. The nature and properties of soils. Ninth ed. Macmillan Publ. Co., New York, 750 pp.

Braun, E. L. 1950. Deciduous forests of eastern North America. Blakiston Co., Philadelphia, 596 pp.

Caire, W., J. D. Tyler, B. P. Glass, and M. A. Mares. 1990. Mammals of Oklahoma. Univ. Oklahoma Press, Norman, 567 pp.

Cameron, G. N., and S. R. Spencer. 1981. Sigmodon hispidus. Mamm. Species, 158:1–9.

Carbyn, L. N. 1987. Gray wolf and red wolf. Pp. 358–376, *in* Wild furbearer management and conservation in North America (M. Novak, J. A. Baker, M. E. Obbard, and B. Mallock, eds.). Ontario Ministry Nat. Res., Toronto, 1,150 pp.

Chapman, J. A. 1975. Sylvilagus transitionalis. Mamm. Species, 55:1–4.

Chapman, J. A., and G. A. Feldhamer. 1981. Sylvilagus aquaticus. Mamm. Species, 151:1–4.

Chapman, J. A., and G. R. Wilner. 1981. Sylvilagus palustris. Mamm. Species, 153:1–3.

Chapman, J. A., J. G. Hockman, and M. M. Ojeda C. 1980. Sylvilagus floridanus. Mamm. Species, 136:1–8.

Choate, L. L., and J. K. Jones, Jr. 1989. Notes on reproduction in the hispid pocket mouse, Chaetodipus hispidus, in Texas. Texas J. Sci., 41:432–433.

Christensen, N. L. 1988. Vegetation of the Southeastern Coastal Plain. Pp. 317–363, *in* North American terrestrial vegetation (M. G. Barbour and W. D. Billings, eds.). Cambridge Univ. Press, New York, 434 pp.

Currier, M. J. P. 1983. Felis concolor. Mamm. Species, 200:1–7.

Davis, F. W., and J. R. Choate. 1993. Morphologic variation and age structure in a population of the eastern mole, *Scalopus aquaticus.* J. Mamm., 74:1014–1025.

DeBlase, A. F., and R. E. Martin. 1980. A manual of mammalogy . . . Second ed. Wm. C. Brown Co. Publ., Dubuque, 436 pp.

Diersing, V. E. 1980. Systematics and evolution of the pygmy shrews (subgenus *Microsorex*) of North America. J. Mamm., 61:76–101.

Dixon, K. R. 1982. Mountain lion. Pp. 711–727, *in* Wild mammals of North America . . . (J. A. Chapman and G. A. Feldhamer, eds.). Johns Hopkins Univ. Press, Baltimore, 1,147 pp.

Dodge, W. E. 1982. Porcupine. Pp. 355–366, *in* Wild mammals of North

America . . . (J. A. Chapman and G. A. Feldhamer, eds.). Johns Hopkins Univ. Press, Baltimore, 1,147 pp.

Dolan, P. G., and D. C. Carter. 1977. Glaucomys volans. Mamm. Species, 78: 1–6.

Douglas, C. W., and M. A. Strickland. 1987. Fisher. Pp. 510–529, *in* Wild furbearer management and conservation in North America (M. Novak, J. A. Baker, M. E. Obbard, and B. Mallock, eds.). Ontario Ministry Nat. Res., Toronto, 1,150 pp.

Dunaway, P. B. 1968. Life history and populational aspects of the eastern harvest mouse. Amer. Midland Nat., 79:48–67.

Eagle, T. C., and J. S. Whitman. 1987. Mink. Pp. 614–624, *in* Wild furbearer management and conservation in North America (M. Novak, J. A. Baker, M. E. Obbard, and B. Mallock, eds.). Ontario Ministry Nat. Res., Toronto, 1,150 pp.

Eiler, J. H., W. G. Wathen, and M. R. Pelton. 1989. Reproduction in black bears in the southern Appalachian Mountains. J. Wildl. Mgmt., 53: 353–360.

Fagerstone, K. A. 1987. Black-footed ferret, long-tailed weasel, short-tailed weasel, and least weasel. Pp. 547–573, *in* Wild furbearer management and conservation in North America (M. Novak, J. A. Baker, M. E. Obbard, and B. Mallock, eds.). Ontario Ministry Nat. Res., Toronto, 1,150 pp.

Fenneman, N. M. 1939. Physiography of eastern United States. McGraw-Hill Book Co., New York, 691 pp.

Fenton, M. B., and R. M. R. Barclay. 1980. Myotis lucifugus. Mamm. Species, 142:1–8.

Fitch, J. H., and K. A. Shump, Jr. 1979. Myotis keenii. Mamm. Species, 121: 1–3.

Fleharty, E. D., and K. W. Navo. 1983. Irrigated cornfields as habitat for small mammals in the sandsage prairie region of western Kansas. J. Mamm., 64:367–379.

Flyger, V., and J. E. Gates. 1982a. Fox and gray squirrels. Pp. 209–229, *in* Wild mammals of North America . . . (J. A. Chapman and G. A. Feldhamer, eds.). Johns Hopkins Univ. Press, Baltimore, 1,147 pp.

———. 1982b. Pine squirrels. Pp. 230–238, *in* Wild mammals of North America . . . (J. A. Chapman and G. A. Feldhamer, eds.). Johns Hopkins Univ. Press, Baltimore, 1,147 pp.

Forsyth, D. J. 1976. A field study of growth and development of nestling masked shrews (*Sorex cinereus*). J. Mamm., 57:708–721.

French, T. W. 1980a. Sorex longirostris. Mamm. Species, 143:1–3.

———. 1980b. Natural history of the southeastern shrew, Sorex longirostris Bachman. Amer. Midland Nat., 104:13–31.

————. 1982. Ectoparasites of the southeastern shrew, *Sorex longirostris*, and the masked shrew, *S. cinereus*, in Virgo County, Indiana USA. J. Med. Ent., 19:628–630.

Fritzell, E. K. 1987. Gray fox and island gray fox. Pp. 408–420, *in* Wild furbearer management and conservation in North America (M. Novak, J. A. Baker, M. E. Obbard, and B. Mallock, eds.). Ontario Ministry Nat. Res., Toronto, 1,150 pp.

Fritzell, E. K., and K. J. Haroldson. 1982. Urocyon cinereoargenteus. Mamm. Species, 189:1–8.

Fujita, M. S., and T. H. Kunz. 1984. Pipistrellus subflavus. Mamm. Species, 228:1–6.

Gardner, A. L. 1973. The systematics of the genus Didelphis (Marsupialia: Didelphidae) in North and Middle America. Spec. Publ. Mus., Texas Tech Univ., 4:1–81.

————. 1982. Virginia opossum. Pp. 3–36, *in* Wild mammals of North America . . . (J. A. Chapman and G. A. Feldhamer, eds.). Johns Hopkins Univ. Press, Baltimore, 1,147 pp.

George, S. B., J. R. Choate, and H. H. Genoways. 1981. Distribution and taxonomic status of *Blarina hylophaga* Elliot (Insectivora: Soricidae). Ann. Carnegie Mus., 50:493–513.

————. 1986. Blarina brevicauda. Mamm. Species, 261:1–9.

George, S. B., H. H. Genoways, J. R. Choate, and R. J. Baker. 1982. Karyotypic relationships within the short-tailed shrews, genus *Blarina*. J. Mamm., 63:639–645.

Godin, A. J. 1982. Striped and hooded skunks. Pp. 674–687, *in* Wild mammals of North America . . . (J. A. Chapman and G. A. Feldhamer, eds.). Johns Hopkins Univ. Press, Baltimore, 1,147 pp.

Goehring, H. H. 1972. Twenty-year study of *Eptesicus fuscus* in Minnesota. J. Mamm., 53:201–207.

Golley, F. B. 1962. Mammals of Georgia, a study of their distribution and functional role in the ecosystem. Univ. Georgia Press, Athens, 218 pp.

Gottschang, J. L. 1981. A guide to the mammals of Ohio. Ohio State Univ. Press, Columbus, 176 pp.

Greller, A. M. 1988. Deciduous forest. Pp. 287–316, *in* North American terrestrial vegetation (M. G. Barbour and W. D. Billings, eds.). Cambridge Univ. Press, New York, 434 pp.

Grizzell, R. A. 1955. A study of the southern woodchuck, Marmota monax monax. Amer Midland Nat., 53:257–293.

Hall, E. R. 1955. Handbook of mammals of Kansas. Misc. Publ. Mus. Nat. Hist., Univ. Kansas, 7:1–303.

————. 1981. The mammals of North America. Second ed. John Wiley and Sons, New York, 1:1–600 + *90* and 2:601–1181 + *90*.

Hallett, J. G. 1978. Parascalops breweri. Mamm. Species, 98:1–4.

Halls, L. K. 1978. White-tailed deer. Pp. 42–65, *in* Big game of North America . . . (J. L. Schmidt and D. L. Gilbert, eds.). Stackpole Books, Harrisburg, 494 pp.

——— (ed.). 1984. White-tailed deer: ecology and management. Stackpole Books, Harrisburg, and Wildlife Management Inst., Washington, 870 pp.

Hamilton, W. J., Jr., and J. O. Whitaker, Jr. 1979. Mammals of the eastern United States. Second ed. Cornell Univ. Press, Ithaca, New York. 346 pp.

Hansen, R. M., and J. T. Flinders. 1969. Food habits of North American hares. Sci. Ser. Range Sci. Dept., Colorado State Univ., 1:1–18.

Harvey, M. J. 1986. Arkansas bats: a valuable resource. Arkansas Game and Fish Comm., Little Rock, 48 pp.

Heaney, L. R., and R. M. Timm. 1983. Relationships of pocket gophers of the genus *Geomys* from the central and northern Great Plains. Misc. Publ. Mus. Nat. Hist., Univ. Kansas, 74:1–59.

Hesselton, W. T., and R. M. Hesselton. 1982. White-tailed deer. Pp. 878–901, *in* Wild mammals of North America . . . (J. A. Chapman and G. A. Feldhamer, eds.). Johns Hopkins Univ. Press, Baltimore, 1,147 pp.

Hill, E. P. 1972. The cottontail rabbit in Alabama. Bull. Agric. Exp. Sta., Auburn Univ., 440:1–103.

———. 1982. Beaver. Pp. 256–281, *in* Wild mammals of North America . . . (J. A. Chapman and G. A. Feldhamer, eds.). Johns Hopkins Univ. Press, Baltimore, 1,147 pp.

Hoffmeister, D. F. 1986. Mammals of Arizona. Univ. Arizona Press, Tucson, 602 pp.

———. 1989. Mammals of Illinois. Univ. Illinois Press, Urbana, 348 pp.

Howard, W. E., and R. E. Marsh. 1982. Spotted and hog-nosed skunks (*Spilogale putorius* and allies). Pp. 664–673, *in* Wild mammals of North America . . . (J. A. Chapman and G. A. Feldhamer, eds.). Johns Hopkins Univ. Press, Baltimore, 1,147 pp.

Howell, A. H. 1921. A biological survey of Alabama . . . N. Amer. Fauna, 45: 1–88.

Humphrey, S. R. 1974. Zoogeography of the nine-banded armadillo (*Dasypus novemcinctus*) in the United States. BioScience, 24:457–462.

Jackson, H. H. T. 1928. A taxonomic review of the American long-tailed shrews (genera Sorex and Microsorex). N. Amer. Fauna, 51:1–238.

Jenkins, S. H., and P. E. Busher. 1979. Castor canadensis. Mamm. Species, 120:1–8.

Johnson, M. L., and S. Johnson. 1982. Voles. Pp. 326–354, *in* Wild mammals of North America . . . (J. A. Chapman and G. A. Feldhamer, eds.). Johns Hopkins Univ. Press, Baltimore, 1,147 pp.

Jones, C. 1977. Plecotus rafinesquii. Mamm. Species, 69:1–4.

Jones, C., and C. H. Carter. 1989. Annotated checklist of the Recent mammals of Mississippi. Occas. Papers Mus., Texas Tech Univ., 128:1–9.

Jones, C., and R. W. Manning. 1989. Myotis austroriparius. Mamm. Species, 332:1–3.

Jones, C. A., J. R. Choate, and H. H. Genoways. 1984. Phylogeny and paleobiogeography of short-tailed shrews (genus *Blarina*). Pp. 56–148, *in* Contributions in Quaternary vertebrate paleontology . . . (H. H. Genoways and M. R. Dawson, eds.). Spec. Publ. Carnegie Mus. Nat. Hist., 8:1–538.

Jones, J. K., Jr., and E. C. Birney. 1988. Handbook of mammals of the north-central states. Univ. Minnesota Press, Minneapolis, 346 pp.

Jones, J. K., Jr., D. M. Armstrong, and J. R. Choate. 1985. Guide to mammals of the plains states. Univ. Nebraska Press, Lincoln, 371 pp.

Jones, J. K., Jr., D. M. Armstrong, R. S. Hoffmann, and C. Jones. 1983. Mammals of the northern Great Plains. Univ. Nebraska Press, Lincoln, 379 pp.

Jones, J. K., Jr., R. S. Hoffmann, D. W. Rice, C. Jones, R. J. Baker, and M. D. Engstrom. 1992. Revised checklist of North American mammals north of Mexico, 1991. Occas. Papers Mus., Texas Tech Univ., 146:1–23.

Jonkel, C. 1978. Black, brown (grizzly), and polar bears. Pp. 226–248, *in* Big game of North America . . . (J. L. Schmidt and D. L. Gilbert, eds.). Stackpole Books, Harrisburg, 494 pp.

Kaufmann, J. H. 1982. Raccoon and allies. Pp. 567–585, *in* Wild mammals of North America . . . (J. A. Chapman and G. A. Feldhamer, eds.). Johns Hopkins Univ. Press, Baltimore, 1,147 pp.

———. 1987. Ringtail and coati. Pp. 499–508, *in* Wild furbearer management and conservation in North America (M. Novak, J. A. Baker, M. E. Obbard, and B. Mallock, eds.). Ontario Ministry Nat. Res., Toronto, 1,150 pp.

Keith, L. B., and L. A. Windberg. 1978. A demographic analysis of the snowshoe hare cycle. Wildl. Monogr., 58:1–70.

Kellogg, R. 1939. Annotated list of Tennessee mammals. Proc. U.S. Nat. Mus., 86:245–303.

Kennedy, M. L., and M. J. Harvey. 1979. Tennessee mammals: capsule descriptions of twenty-four selected species. Processed by Ecol. Res. Center, Memphis State Univ., 93 pp.

Kennedy, M. L., K. N. Randolph, and T. L. Best. 1974. A review of Mississippi mammals. Stud. Nat. Sci., Eastern New Mexico Univ., 2(1):1–36.

Kirkland, G. L., Jr. 1981. Sorex dispar and Sorex gaspensis. Mamm. Species, 155:1–4.

Kirkland, G. L., Jr., and F. J. Jannett, Jr. 1982. Microtus chrotorrhinus. Mamm. Species, 180:1–5.

Kirkland, G. L., Jr., and H. M. Van Deusen. 1979. The shrews of the *Sorex dispar* group: *Sorex dispar* Batchelder and *Sorex gaspensis* Anthony and Goodwin. Amer. Mus. Novitates, 2675:1–21.

Kolenosky, G. B. 1987. Black bear. Pp. 442–454, *in* Wild furbearer management and conservation in North America (M. Novak, J. A. Baker, M. E. Obbard, and B. Mallock, eds.). Ontario Ministry Nat. Res., Toronto, 1,150 pp.

Küchler, A. W. 1964. Manual to accompany the map potential natural vegetation of the coterminous United States. Spec. Publ. Amer. Geogr. Soc., 36:1–40 + *116* + map.

Kunz, T. H. 1974. Reproduction, growth, and mortality of the vespertilionid bat, *Eptesicus fuscus*. J. Mamm. 55:1–13.

———. 1982. Lasionycteris noctivagans. Mamm. Species, 172:1–5.

Kunz, T. H., and R. A. Martin. 1982. Plecotus townsendii. Mamm. Species, 175:1–6.

Kurta, A., and R. H. Baker. 1990. Eptesicus fuscus. Mamm. Species 356:1–10.

Lackey, J. A., D. G. Huckaby, and B. G. Ormiston. 1985. Peromyscus leucopus. Mamm. Species, 247:1–10.

LaVal, R. K. 1970. Intraspecific relationships of bats of the species *Myotis austroriparius*. J. Mamm., 51:542–552.

Layne, J. N. 1954. The biology of the red squirrel, *Tamiasciurus hudsonicus loquax* (Bangs) in central New York. Ecol. Monogr., 24:227–267.

———. 1959. Growth and development of the eastern harvest mouse, Reithrodontomys humulis. Bull. Florida State Mus., 4:61–82.

Lee, D. S., and J. B. Funderburg. 1982. Marmots. Pp. 176–191, *in* Wild mammals of North America . . . (J. A. Chapman and G. A. Feldhamer, eds.). Johns Hopkins Univ. Press, Baltimore, 1,147 pp.

Lindstedt, S. L., and J. H. Jones. 1980. Desert shrew. Nat. Hist., 89:47–53.

Lindzey, F. G. 1982. Badger. Pp. 653–663, *in* Wild mammals of North America . . . (J. A. Chapman and G. A. Feldhamer, eds.). Johns Hopkins Univ. Press, Baltimore, 1,147 pp.

———. 1987. Mountain lion. Pp. 656–668, *in* Wild furbearer management and conservation in North America (M. Novak, J. A. Baker, M. E. Obbard, and B. Mallock, eds.). Ontario Ministry Nat. Res., Toronto, 1,150 pp.

Linscombe, G., N. Kinler, and R. J. Aulerich. 1982. Mink. Pp. 629–643, *in*

Wild mammals of North America . . . (J. A. Chapman and G. A. Feld-hamer, eds.). Johns Hopkins Univ. Press, Baltimore, 1,147 pp.

Linzey, A. V. 1983. Synaptomys cooperi. Mamm. Species, 210:1–5.

Linzey, A. V., and D. W. Linzey. 1971. Mammals of Great Smoky Mountains National Park. Univ. Tennessee Press, Knoxville, 114 pp.

Linzey, D. W., and A. V. Linzey. 1979. Growth and development of the southern flying squirrel (*Glaucomys volans volans*). J. Mamm., 60: 615–620.

Linzey, D. W., and R. L. Packard. 1977. Ochrotomys nuttalli. Mamm. Species, 75:1–6.

Long, C. A. 1973. Taxidea taxus. Mamm. Species, 26:1–4.

————. 1974. Microsorex hoyi and Microsorex thompsoni. Mamm. Species, 33:1–4.

Lotze, J-H., and S. Anderson. 1979. Procyon lotor. Mamm. Species, 119: 1–8.

Lowery, G. H., Jr. 1974. The mammals of Louisiana and its adjacent waters. Louisiana State Univ. Press, Baton Rouge, 565 pp.

Marshall, L. G. 1984. Monotremes and marsupials. Pp. 59–115, *in* Orders and families of Recent mammals of the world (S. Anderson and J. K. Jones, Jr., eds.). John Wiley and Sons, New York, 686 pp.

Marshall, L. G., J. A. Case, and M. O. Woodburne. 1990. Phylogenetic relationships of the families of marsupials. Pp. 433–505, *in* Current mammalogy (H. H. Genoways, ed.), Plenum Press, New York, 2:1–577.

McBee, K., and R. J. Baker. 1982. Dasypus novemcinctus. Mamm. Species, 162:1–9.

McCord, C. M., and J. E. Cardoza. 1982. Bobcat and lynx. Pp. 728–766, *in* Wild mammals of North America . . . (J. A. Chapman and G. A. Feld-hamer, eds.). Johns Hopkins Univ. Press, Baltimore, 1,147 pp.

McManus, J. J. 1974. Didelphis virginiana. Mamm. Species, 40:1–6.

Meagher, M. 1986. Bison bison. Mamm. Species, 266:1–8.

Mech, L. D. 1974. Canis lupus. Mamm. Species, 37:1–6.

Melquist, W. E., and A. E. Dronkert. 1987. River otter. Pp. 626–641, *in* Wild furbearer management and conservation in North America (M. Novak, J. A. Baker, M. E. Obbard, and B. Mallock, eds.). Ontario Ministry Nat. Res., Toronto, 1,150 pp.

Merritt, J. F. 1981. Clethrionomys gapperi. Mamm. Species, 146:1–9.

Messick, J. P. 1987. North American badger. Pp. 586–597, *in* Wild furbearer management and conservation in North America (M. Novak, J. A. Baker, M. E. Obbard, and B. Mallock, eds.). Ontario Ministry Nat. Res., Toronto, 1,150 pp.

Mohr, C. E. 1933. Pennsylvania bats of the genus Myotis. Proc. Pennsylvania Acad. Sci., 7:39–43.

————. 1936. Notes on the least bat, *Myotis subulatus leibii*. Proc. Pennsylvania Acad. Sci., 10:62–65.

Moncrief, N. D., J. R. Choate, and H. H. Genoways. 1982. Morphometric and geographic relationships of short-tailed shrews (genus *Blarina*) in Kansas, Iowa, and Missouri. Ann. Carnegie Mus., 51:157–180.

Moore, J. C. 1957. The natural history of the fox squirrel, *Sciurus niger shermani*. Bull. Amer. Mus. Nat. Hist., 113:1–71.

Mumford, R. E., and J. O. Whitaker, Jr. 1982. Mammals of Indiana. Indiana Univ. Press, Bloomington, 537 pp.

Murray, G. E. 1961. Geology of the Atlantic and Gulf Coastal Province of North America. Harper, New York, 692 pp.

Novak, M. 1987. Beaver. Pp. 282–312, *in* Wild furbearer management and conservation in North America (M. Novak, J. A. Baker, M. E. Obbard, and B. Mallock, eds.). Ontario Ministry Nat. Res., Toronto, 1,150 pp.

Novak, M., M. E. Obbard, J. G. Jones, R. Newman, A. Booth, A. J. Satterthwaite, and G. Linscombe. 1987. Furbearer harvests in North America, 1600–1984. Ontario Ministry Nat. Res., Toronto, 270 pp.

Nowak, R. M., and J. L. Paradiso. 1983. Walker's mammals of the world. Fourth ed. Johns Hopkins Univ. Press, Baltimore, 1:1–568 and 2:569–1362.

Owen, J. G. 1984. Sorex fumeus. Mamm. Species, 215:1–8.

Packard, R. L. 1956. The tree squirrels of Kansas. Misc. Publ. Mus. Nat. Hist., Univ. Kansas, 11:1–67.

Paradiso, J. L., and R. M. Nowak. 1972. Canis rufus. Mamm. Species, 22:1–4.

————. 1982. Wolves. Pp. 460–474, *in* Wild mammals of North America . . . (J. A. Chapman and G. A. Feldhamer, eds.). Johns Hopkins Univ. Press, Baltimore, 1,147 pp.

Paulson, D. D. 1988. Chaetodipus hispidus. Mamm. Species, 320:1–4.

Peek, J. M. 1982. Elk. Pp. 851–861, *in* Wild mammals of North America . . . (J. A. Chapman and G. A. Feldhamer, eds.). Johns Hopkins Univ. Press, Baltimore, 1,147 pp.

Pelton, M. R. 1982. Black bear. Pp. 504–514, *in* Wild mammals of North America . . . (J. A. Chapman and G. A. Feldhamer, eds.). Johns Hopkins Univ. Press, Baltimore, 1,147 pp.

Pembleton, E. F., and S. L. Williams. 1978. Geomys pinetis. Mamm. Species, 86:1–3.

Perry, H. R., Jr. 1982. Muskrats. Pp. 282–325, *in* Wild mammals of North America . . . (J. A. Chapman and G. A. Feldhamer, eds.). Johns Hopkins Univ. Press, Baltimore, 1,147 pp.

Petersen, K. E., and T. L. Yates. 1980. Condylura cristata. Mamm. Species, 129:1–4.

Pitts, R. M., J. R. Choate, and M. J. Smolen. 1992. Winter breeding by *Geomys breviceps*. Texas J. Sci., 44:370–371.

Powell, R. A. 1981. Martes pennanti. Mamm. Species, 156:1–6.

Purdue, J. R., and B. W. Styles. 1987. Changes in the mammalian fauna of Illinois and Missouri during the late Pleistocene and Holocene. Pp. 144–174, *in* Late Quaternary mammalian biogeography and environments of the Great Plains and prairies (R. W. Graham, H. A. Semken, Jr., and M. A. Graham, eds.). Illinois State Mus. Sci. Papers, 22:1–491.

Ray, C. E. 1967. Pleistocene mammals from Ladds, Bartow County, Georgia. Bull. Georgia Acad. Sci., 25:120–150.

Raymond, M. A. V., and J. N. Layne. 1988. Aspects of reproduction in the southern flying squirrel in Florida. Acta Theriol., 33:505–518.

Reich, L. M. 1981. Microtus pennsylvanicus. Mamm. Species, 159:1–8.

Reynolds, H. W., R. D. Glaholt, and W. W. L. Hawley. 1982. Bison. Pp. 972–1007, *in* Wild mammals of North America . . . (J. A. Chapman and G. A. Feldhamer, eds.). Johns Hopkins Univ. Press, Baltimore, 1,147 pp.

Rolley, R. E. 1987. Bobcat. Pp. 670–681, *in* Wild furbearer management and conservation in North America (M. Novak, J. A. Baker, M. E. Obbard, and B. Mallock, eds.). Ontario Ministry Nat. Res., Toronto, 1,150 pp.

Rosatte, R. C. 1987. Striped, spotted, hooded, and hog-nosed skunk. Pp. 598–613, *in* Wild furbearer management and conservation in North America (M. Novak, J. A. Baker, M. E. Obbard, and B. Mallock, eds.). Ontario Ministry Nat. Res., Toronto, 1,150 pp.

Samuel, D. E., and B. B. Nelson. 1982. Foxes. Pp. 475–490, *in* Wild mammals of North America . . . (J. A. Chapman and G. A. Feldhamer, eds.). Johns Hopkins Univ. Press, Baltimore, 1,147 pp.

Sanderson, G. C. 1987. Racoon. Pp. 486–499, *in* Wild furbearer management and conservation in North America (M. Novak, J. A. Baker, M. E. Obbard, and B. Mallock, eds.). Ontario Ministry Nat. Res., Toronto, 1,150 pp.

Sawyer, S. L., and R. L. Rose. 1985. Homing in and ecology of the southern flying squirrel Glaucomys volans in southeastern Virginia. Amer. Midland Nat., 113:238–244.

Schmidly, D. J. 1974. Peromyscus attwateri. Mamm. Species, 48:1–3.

———. 1983. Texas mammals east of the Balcones Fault Zone. Texas A & M Univ. Press, College Station, 400 pp.

Schwartz, C. W., and E. R. Schwartz. 1981. The wild mammals of Missouri. Second ed. Univ. Missouri Press and Missouri Dept. Conserv., Columbia, 356 pp.

Sealander, J. A., and G. D. Heidt. 1990. Arkansas mammals, their natural history, classification, and distribution. Univ. Arkansas Press, Fayetteville, 308 pp.

Seidensticker, J., M. A. O'Connell, and A. J. T. Johnsingh. 1987. Virginia opossum. Pp. 246–261, *in* Wild furbearer management and conservation in North America (M. Novak, J. A. Baker, M. E. Obbard, and B. Mallock, eds.). Ontario Ministry Nat. Res., Toronto, 1,150 pp.

Shump, K. A., Jr., and A. U. Shump. 1982*a*. Lasiurus borealis. Mamm. Species, 183:1–6.

———. 1982*b*. Lasiurus cinereus. Mamm. Species, 185:1–5.

Smith, C. C. 1968. The adaptive nature of social organization in the genus of tree squirrels *Tamiasciurus*. Ecol. Monogr., 38:31–63.

———. 1970. The coevolution of pine squirrels (*Tamiasciurus*) and conifers. Ecol. Monogr., 40:349–371.

———. 1978. Structure and function of the vocalizations of tree squirrels (*Tamiasciurus*). J. Mamm., 59:793–808.

Smith, W. P. 1991. Odocoileus virginianus. Mamm. Species, 388:1–13.

Smolen, M. J. 1981. Microtus pinetorum. Mamm. Species, 147:1–7.

Snyder, D. P. 1982. Tamias striatus. Mamm. Species, 168:1–8.

Spencer, S. R., and G. N. Cameron. 1982. Reithrodontomys fulvescens. Mamm. Species, 174:1–7.

Stalling, D. T. 1990. Microtus ochrogaster. Mamm. Species, 355:1–9.

Stevenson, H. M. 1976. Vertebrates of Florida, identification and distribution. Univ. Presses Florida, Gainesville, 607 pp.

Strickland, M. A., C. W. Douglas, M. Novak, and N. P. Hunzinger. 1982. Fisher. Pp. 586–598, *in* Wild mammals of North America . . . (J. A. Chapman and G. A. Feldhamer, eds.). Johns Hopkins Univ. Press, Baltimore, 1,147 pp.

Sulentich, J. M., L. R. Williams, and G. N. Cameron. 1991. Geomys breviceps. Mamm. Species, 383:1–4.

Suttkus, R. D., and C. Jones. 1991. Observations on winter and spring reproduction in *Peromyscus leucopus* (Rodentia: Muridae) in southern Louisiana. Texas J. Sci., 43:179–189.

Svendsen, G. E. 1982. Weasels. Pp. 613–628, *in* Wild mammals of North America . . . (J. A. Chapman and G. A. Feldhamer, eds.), Johns Hopkins Univ. Press, Baltimore, 1,147 pp.

Tamarin, R. H. (ed.). 1985. Biology of New World *Microtus*. Spec. Publ. Amer. Soc. Mamm., 8:1–893.

Thomson, C. E. 1982. Myotis sodalis. Mamm. Species, 163:1–5.

Tiemeier, O. W., M. F. Hansen, M. H. Bartell, E. T. Lyon, B. M. El-Rawi, K. J. McMahan, and E. H. Herrick. 1965. The black-tailed jackrabbit in Kansas. Tech. Bull. Kansas Agric. Exp. Sta., 140:1–75.

Tims, T. A., J. K. Frey, T. A. Spradling, and D. W. Moore. 1989. A new locality for the pygmy shrew (*Sorex hoyi winnemana*) in Tennessee. J. Tennessee Acad. Sci., 64–240.

Toweill, D. E., and J. E. Tabor. 1982. River otter. Pp. 688–703, *in* Wild mammals of North America . . . (J. A. Chapman and G. A. Feldhamer, eds.). Johns Hopkins Univ. Press, Baltimore, 1,147 pp.

Tuttle, M. D. 1975. Population ecology of the gray bat (*Myotis grisescens*): factors influencing early growth and development. Occas. Papers Mus. Nat. Hist., Univ. Kansas, 36:1–24.

———. 1976*a*. Population ecology of the gray bat (*Myotis grisescens*): philopatry, timing and patterns of movement, weight loss during migration, and seasonal adaptive strategies. Occas. Papers Mus. Nat. Hist., Univ. Kansas, 54:1–38.

———. 1976*b*. Population ecology of the gray bat (*Myotis grisescens*): factors influencing growth and survival of newly volant young. Ecology, 57: 587–595.

———. 1979. Status, causes of decline, and management of endangered gray bats. J. Wildl. Mgmt., 43:1–17.

Tuttle, M. D., and D. E. Stevenson. 1977. An analysis of migration as a mortality factor in the gray bat based on public recoveries of banded bats. Amer. Midland Nat., 97:235–240.

Udvardy, M. D. F. 1969. Dynamic zoogeography with special reference to land animals. Van Nostrand, Reinhold Co., New York, 445 pp.

Uhlig, H. G. 1955. The gray squirrel, its life history, ecology and population characteristics in West Virginia. West Virginia Conserv. Com., P.-R. Proj. Rept., 31-R:1–175.

van Zyll de Jong, C. C. 1983. Handbook of Canadian mammals. 1. Marsupials and insectivores. Natl. Mus. Canada, Ottawa, 210 pp.

———. 1985. Handbook of Canadian mammals. 2. Bats. Natl. Mus. Canada, Ottawa, 212 pp.

Vaughan, T. A. 1986. Mammalogy. Third ed. Saunders Coll. Publ., Holt, Rinehart and Winston, Philadelphia, 576 pp.

Voigt, D. R. 1987. Red fox. Pp. 378–392, *in* Wild furbearer management and conservation in North America (M. Novak, J. A. Baker, M. E. Obbard, and B. Mallock, eds.). Ontario Ministry Nat. Res., Toronto, 1,150 pp.

Voigt, D. R., and W. E. Berg. 1987. Coyote. Pp. 344–357, *in* Wild furbearer management and conservation in North America (M. Novak, J. A. Baker, M. E. Obbard, and B. Mallock, eds.). Ontario Ministry Nat. Res., Toronto, 1,150 pp.

Wade-Smith, J., and B. J. Verts. 1982. Mephitis mephitis. Mamm. Species, 173:1–7.

Watkins, L. C. 1972. Nycticeius humeralis. Mamm. Species, 23:1–4.

Watkins, L. C., and K. A. Shump, Jr. 1981. Behavior of the evening bat Nyc-ticeius humeralis at a nursery roost. Amer. Midland Nat., 105: 258–268.

Watts, W. A. 1983. Vegetational history of the eastern United States 25,000 to 10,000 years ago. Pp. 294–310, *in* Late-Quaternary environments of the United States: the late Pleistocene (H. E. Wright, Jr., and S. C. Porter, eds.). Univ. Minnesota Press, Minneapolis, 1:1–407.

Webster, W. D., and J. K. Jones, Jr. 1982. Reithrodontomys megalotis. Mamm. Species, 167:1–5.

Webster, W. D., J. K. Jones, Jr., and R. J. Baker. 1980. Lasiurus intermedius. Mamm. Species, 132:1–3.

Webster, W. D., J. F. Parnell, and W. C. Biggs, Jr. 1985. Mammals of the Carolinas, Virginia, and Maryland. Univ. North Carolina Press, Chapel Hill, 255 pp.

Weigl, P. D., M. A. Steele, L. J. Sherman, J. C. Ha, and T. L. Sharpe. 1989. The ecology of the fox squirrel (*Sciurus niger*) in North Carolina: implications for survival in the Southeast. Bull. Tall Timbers Res. Sta., 24: 1–93.

Wells-Gosling, N., and L. R. Heaney. 1984. Glaucomys sabrinus. Mamm. Species, 229:1–8.

Wendland, W. M., A. Benn, and H. A. Semken, Jr. 1987. Evaluation of climatic changes on the North American Great Plains determined from faunal evidence. Pp. 460–472, *in* Late Quaternary mammalian biogeography and environments of the Great Plains and prairies (R. W. Graham, H. A. Semken, Jr., and M. A. Graham, eds.). Illinois State Mus. Sci. Papers, 22:1–491.

Whitaker, J. O., Jr. 1972. Zapus hudsonius. Mamm. Species 11:1–7.

———. 1974. Cryptotis parva. Mamm. Species, 43:1–8.

Whitaker, J. O., Jr., and R. E. Wrigley. 1972. Napaeozapus insignis. Mamm. Species, 14:1–6.

Wiley, R. W. 1980. Neotoma floridana. Mamm. Species, 139:1–7.

Wilkins, K. T. 1986. Reithrodontomys montanus. Mamm. Species, 257:1–5.

———. 1987. Lassiurus seminolus. Mamm. Species, 280:1–5.

———. 1989. Tadarida brasiliensis. Mamm. Species, 331:1–10.

Willner, G. R., G. A. Feldhamer, E. E. Zucker, and J. A. Chapman. 1980. Ondatra zibethicus. Mamm. Species, 141:1–8.

Wolfe, J. L. 1971. Mississippi land mammals: distribution, identification, ecological notes. Mississippi Mus. Nat. Hist., Jackson, 44 pp.

———. 1982. Oryzomys palustris. Mamm. Species, 176:1–5.

Wolfe, J. L., and A. V. Linzey. 1977. Peromyscus gossypinus. Mamm. Species, 70:1–5.

Woods, C. A. 1973. Erethizon dorsatum. Mamm. Species, 29:1–6.

Wrigley, R. E. 1972. Systematics and biology of the woodland jumping mouse, Napaeozapus insignis. Illinois Biol. Monogr., 47:1–117.

Yates, T. L., and D. J. Schmidly. 1978. Scalopus aquaticus. Mamm. Species, 105:1–4.

Zimmerman, J. W. 1990. Burrow characteristics of the nine-banded armadillo, *Dasypus novemcinctus.* Southwestern Nat., 35:226–227.

Index to Scientific and Vernacular Names